A COURSE
IN
CATEGORICAL
DATA ANALYSIS

CHAPMAN & HALL/CRC
Texts in Statistical Science Series

Series Editors
C. Chatfield, *University of Bath, UK*
J. Zidek, *University of British Columbia, Canada*

Randomization, Bootstrap and
Monte Carlo Methods in Biology,
Second Edition
B.F.J. Manly

Readings in Decision Analysis
S. French

Statistical Analysis of Reliability Data
M.J. Crowder, A.C. Kimber,
T.J. Sweeting and R.L. Smith

Statistical Methods for SPC and TQM
D. Bissell

Statistical Methods in Agriculture and
Experimental Biology, Second Edition
R. Mead, R.N. Curnow and A.M. Hasted

Statistical Process Control — Theory and
Practice, Third Edition
G.B. Wetherill and D.W. Brown

Statistical Theory, Fourth Edition
B.W. Lindgren

Statistics for Accountants, Fourth Edition
S. Letchford

Statistics for Technology —
A Course in Applied Statistics,
Third Edition
C. Chatfield

Statistics in Engineering —
A Practical Approach
A.V. Metcalfe

Statistics in Research and Development,
Second Edition
R. Caulcutt

The Theory of Linear Models
B. Jørgensen

A COURSE
IN
CATEGORICAL
DATA ANALYSIS

Thomas Leonard

Professor
Department of Mathematics and Statistics
and
Chair of Statistics
University of Edinburgh
United Kingdom

with contributions by

Orestis Papasouliotis

CHAPMAN & HALL/CRC

Boca Raton   London   New York   Washington, D.C.

Library of Congress Cataloging-in-Publication Data

Leonard, Thomas, 1948–
    A course in categorical data analysis / by Thomas Leonard with contributions by
Orestis Papasouliotis
        p.   cm. — (Texts in statistical science series ; 46)
    Includes bibliographical references and index.
    ISBN 0-8493-0323-0 (alk paper)
    1. Multivariate analysis. I. Papasouliotis, Orestis. II. Title. III. Texts in statistical
science ; 46.
    QA278.L465 1999
    519.5′35—dc21   99-047135
                                                                                                CIP

No claim to original U.S. Government works
International Standard Book Number 0-8493-0323-0
Library of Congress Card Number 99-047135
Printed in the United States of America   1   2   3   4   5   6   7   8   9   0
Printed on acid-free paper

To Helen, James, and Sarah-Jane, my father Cecil, and his great-grandchildren, Edward and Charlotte

Contents

Preface

Categorical data provide an important type of numerical statistical data, which contrasts with measurement data. Categorical data comprise the numbers, or counts, of individuals, objects, or entities in different categories. Sometimes, the dependent variables are counts, and the explanatory variables are counts, indicators, or measurements. Categorical data occur frequently in many disciplines, including medicine (numbers of patients), economics (e.g., numbers of sales or purchases), sociology and psychology (numbers of people), geology (e.g., numbers of transitions between two different types of geological layer), wildlife studies and geography (e.g., numbers of eagles sighted, or numbers of trees growing, in different areas), education (e.g., numbers of students) and biology (e.g., observations on squirrel monkeys, see Leonard, 1977a).

While measurement data can be analysed using such techniques as t-tests, linear regression, and the analysis of variance, it is inappropriate to use these methodologies for categorical data, owing to the properties of the variances of the observed frequencies, and the nonlinear nature of the correct techniques. A different methodology is therefore needed when the observed data are counts, rather than measurements.

Our subject matter provides an excellent topic for a broad range of students. A course primarily based on Chapters 5 through 8 would be appropriate for final-year undergraduates, or master's degree students. Students should possess previous expertise in elementary statistics, including basic probability theory and discrete and continuous random variables, and the normal distribution. They should be familiar with algebraic symbols, natural logarithmic and exponential transformations, mathematical equations, and elementary computing. They should also be prepared to think for themselves.

The current volume attempts to accommodate the need for a textbook, with specific directions for students, given the myriad possible methodologies that have been developed for categorical data. The choices of direction are based upon my experiences when teaching, researching, and consulting in this area over a number of years. For example, the Mantel-Haenszel test (Mantel and Haenszel, 1959) is omitted, simply because students will be more likely to appreciate a "three-directional approach" to the analysis of three-way contingency tables. Measures of association are included because they provide a logical foundation for log-linear models, and because they are justified by a beautiful theorem due to Antony Edwards (1963). Quantities that are not functions of the cross-product ratio receive less attention. Like Birnbaum's 1962 justification of likelihood methods, Edwards' theorem has an elegantly simple proof. Birnbaum's and Edwards' theorems together justify many of the choices of technique described in this text.

Our quite specific choice of subject matter is also based upon my philosophy that the primary objectives of a statistical analysis should include "to extract or infer real-life conclusions from the data, in relation to their scientific, medical, or social background, and to seek the discovery of fresh knowledge". While a mathematical model, such as a log-linear model, may well be very useful when achieving this objective, the primary goal should not be to find a model that closely fits the data, but rather to use different models to focus on possibly meaningful conclusions. The conclusions should also be considered in relation to the background of the data, and the way the data were collected. Furthermore, while a significance test may be useful, statistical significance is not the only criterion that should be considered when evaluating possible practical conclusions. Indeed, "Aitken's Inductive Synthesis" entails much broader perception and contemplation when trying to pursue the notion of scientific truth.

Given the nature of the subject matter, course instructors using this text may well decide to evaluate their students by practical projects. When teaching Statistics 421 at the University of Wisconsin-Madison, I based one project on Goodman's full-rank interaction analysis (see Chapter 5), and another on logistic regression (see Chapter 8). The students obtained many valuable conclusions which influenced the university, the local community, and scientific knowledge. This has continued while teaching a course to fourth-year undergraduates at the University of Edinburgh, although many students have now shown an interest in medical applications.

Students can complete this course without full knowledge of a statistical software package. However, an Splus license is needed to take advantage of special software. For example, the simple functions prog1 and prog2, written by John S.J. Hsu and Orestis Papasouliotis, are available on the World Wide Web. These cover many important aspects of contingency table analysis.

Chapter 1 contains a brief review of the standard probability distributions needed for the analysis of categorical data, together with their interrelationships, and methodology for estimating their parameters from numerical data. While some new statistical software is introduced, permitting precise confidence intervals and tests for binomial probabilities and Poisson means, much of this material will already be familiar to the qualified reader. However, Sections 1.8-1.11 describe more sampling schemes, with practical applications to overdispersed and correlated data. These advanced sections may be omitted on a first reading, and instructors may wish to refer to these as special topics toward the end of their course.

Chapter 2 considers the analysis of two-by-two contingency tables. This is one of the simplest, but most frequently occurring type of categorical data. The methodology selected will revolve around the concept of using the cross-product ratio as a measure of the association between the row and the column variable. Hence, the log-measure of association test (readily computable on a standard calculator, or using prog1) and Fisher's exact test (significance probability from Splus) will be preferred to the chi-squared goodness-of-fit test. Students learn more about "Aitken's Inductive Synthesis", i.e., how to think intuitively when analysing their data, and how to judge the shades of objectivity or subjectivity of their conclusions. The latter depends upon the way the data were collected. Aspects of experimental design will be considered, and new approximate power calculations are recommended for choosing appropriate sample sizes.

In Chapter 3, I unveil Simpson's paradox, an essential ingredient of valid statistical thinking, which appears, at first sight, to defy common sense. This is associated with the problem of "lurking variables" which can invalidate apparent common sense. By understanding this paradox and the resolution I describe, students will be better able to appreciate three-way contingency tables, the need for valid experimental design, and the subjectivity of conclusions when such safeguards are not available.

In a similar spirit, Chapter 4, co-authored by Orestis Papasouliotis and myself, discusses our experiences when analysing the Madison drug and alcohol abuse data. Here, it was difficult to collect a truly random sample of patients, as the interviewers were subjected to various practical constraints. We were nevertheless able to use the methodology of Chapter 2 to develop a two-item questionnaire for screening drug or alcohol abuse. In this chapter we also introduce students to the medical criteria of sensitivity, specificity, and positive and negative predictive values, which are most useful for interpreting two-by-two contingency tables.

In Chapters 5 and 6, I consider larger, r by s, contingency tables, and present Goodman's full-rank interaction analysis as a central paradigm for drawing conclusions from many contingency tables of this type. While a mathematical presentation is included in Chapter 5, nonmathematical students may simply wish to refer to the numerical examples together with the simple computer program, prog1. Goodman's interaction analysis has an excellent track record among students attending my courses and helps them to obtain numerous insightful conclusions from their data.

Chapter 7 develops conditional independence models, which set some of the interaction terms equal to zero. These models are most useful for specially structured tables, or tables with missing cell counts, and for more standard tables they can provide models which too closely fit the data. With this caution in mind, students are encouraged to use prog2 to fit the table iteratively, while preserving row and column totals, following the Deming-Stephan procedure.

Chapter 8 describes logistic regression. This is nowadays the standardly acceptable regression procedure for binary or binomial data, and was pioneered by David R. Cox (1970) and others. The standard methods of analysis are presented in relation to Splus, and a new residual analysis (previously developed while I was teaching Statistics 421 at Wisconsin) is introduced. While some mathematical developments using vectors and matrices are introduced, nonmathematical students may just follow the Splus commands. A general paradigm is thus described, yielding a wide variety of opportunities for further analysis.

In Chapter 9, regression models for Poisson data are described, and we also extend the special section in Chapter 1 for the p-parameter exponential family of distributions. When random sampling is not possible at the design stage, the observed data may experience overdispersion. In this case, standard sampling distributions, such as the binomial, Poisson, and multinomial, will not adequately describe the variability in the data. Among a variety of available procedures for handling overdispersion in generalised linear models, I select the exponential family method, simply because it can be taught as a modest extension of the procedures discussed in Chapters 7 and 8. It is therefore slightly more appealing when compared with generalised linear models, utilising the beta-binomial distribution, or other mixtures of the binomial distribution, as discussed in Chapter 1. Matched pairs logistic regression is also described in this chapter, and applied to the Edinburgh Cataract Study.

In Chapter 10, logistic discrimination analysis is described, as a way of building a logistic regression model. Some final comments on the analysis of three-way contingency tables are made. The content of the book is tailored for a single-semester course.

Much of the modern development of categorical data analysis evolves from the splendid volume by Yvonne Bishop, Stephen Fienberg, and Paul Holland (1975). This contains a much larger compendium of methods than presented here, together with most of the original source references. As the current text is intended to provide a coursebook for students, little attempt is made to reference all recent developments in the area. However, Agresti (1990, 1996) describes a wide-ranging collection of useful procedures. Students interested in multi-level modelling are referred to the text by Longford (1996). Random effects models (e.g., Leonard, 1972; 1975; 1977a and b; 1984; Leonard and Novick, 1986; Lee and Nelder, 1996; Hsu and Leonard, 1997) should be studied with caution, owing to the specialised consequences of the particular assumptions employed.

There are currently two main philosophies of statistics, paralleling my undergraduate and postgraduate training at Imperial College and University College London. The first can be described as the Fisherian, or frequentist philosophy, and follows the teachings of Ronald Fisher, George Box, and David Cox. The second is the Bayesian philosophy, which follows the writings of the Reverend Thomas Bayes, Pierre, Marquis de Laplace, and Dennis Lindley. While I like to extract the best out of both philosophies, the current text is written entirely from a Fisherian viewpoint. For a recent volume on Bayesian methods, as employed more generally, see Leonard and Hsu (1999). For a selective review of Bayesian categorical data analysis, see Leonard and Hsu (1994). The Fisherian significance testing approach presented in the current volume is approximately consistent with the Bayesian paradigm.

I gratefully acknowledge John S.J. Hsu, for his permission to reproduce the information in Table 1.2 and Section 9.3 from his personal research papers, and for his help and advice. Ian Main has provided very helpful advice on applications in geophysics, Drs. Paul and Sarah-Jane Leonard have clarified the differences between standard statistical and medical interpretation, and Bob Wardrop has advised on discrimination cases. My thanks also to Calbert Phillips, Ruth Clayton, Colin Aitken, Ella Mae Matsumura, Scott Binnie, Kubulay Gok, Stacey Cooper, Connie Wang, Kelly McKerrow, Darren Baillie, Ingrid Hansen, Mark Schimke, Jon Lien, and Linda Robb for providing interesting data sets. Scott Binnie also provided substantial help during the Edinburgh Cataracts Study. Helen Goode has provided substantial advice and encouragement.

The book contains numerous valuable contributions by my Wisconsin and Edinburgh colleague, Orestis Papasouliotis. Jean-Marc Bernard has made valuable comments regarding measures of association. I also acknowledge valuable comments from many students attending my courses at the Universities of Wisconsin-Madison and Edinburgh. The facilities of the University of Edinburgh Statistical Laboratory have been employed in the provision of a number of the data analyses.

I am indebted to Catriona Fisher for her kind and generous support, and for preparing the manuscript. Jessica Gaines has kindly provided substantial technical advice. Thanks are also due to Mimi Williams for her excellent copyediting, and Mark Bounds and Stephanie Harding for their encouragement on behalf of the publishers.

While developing my knowledge of categorical data analysis, I have been particularly influenced by the ideas and writings of Irving Jack Good, Stephen Fienberg, Patricia Altham, Leo Goodman, and Dennis Lindley. The Madison Drug and Alcohol Abuse Study was completed in collaboration with Dr. Richard Brown and Mrs. Laura Saunders of the Department of Family Medicine, University of Wisconsin-Madison and received financial support from the U.S. National Institutes of Health. Finally, I am indebted to Irwin Guttman for his many insightful comments while reading the manuscript.

Special Software

Related Software (informally available for licensed Splus users on World Wide Web, gratis from The University of Edinburgh Statistical Laboratory, authored by Orestis Papasouliotis). The following special functions are available at our Internet home address.

theta.zero	Confidence points for binomial probabilities
a.p	Significance probabilities for binomial hypothesis testing
gamma.theta.zero	Confidence points for Poisson means
gamma.a.p	Significance probabilities for Poisson hypothesis testing
fisher.exact	Input for Fisher's exact test for 2×2 contingency tables
prog1	Goodman's full-rank interaction analysis for $r \times s$ contingency tables.
prog2	Fitting quasi-independence models to $r \times s$ contingency tables
resid.logistic	Residual analysis for logistic regression

Readers wishing to study Splus are advised to read first the Splus statistical guide by Venables and Ripley (1994). However, initially, just use our special functions for prog1 and prog2 for contingency table analysis.

Installation of Splus Functions

- In Netscape, you need to access the address

  http://www.maths.ed.ac.uk/~statlab/analysis

- Click on the highlighted text.
- Save it, using the File/Save As option, in the directory of your choice, for example,

  h:/home

- Before the first execution of any of the functions, you have to run the following command in Splus:

  source("h:home/filename.s")

  where the choice of filename is left open to the user.

CHAPTER 1

Sampling Distributions

1.1 Experimental design for a population proportion

Consider a population containing N individuals, and let M denote the unknown number of individuals in the population possessing a particular characteristic. This characteristic might, for example, represent the presence of a particular genotype, which we will refer to as the "genotype Z". Then $\theta = M/N$ is the unknown *population proportion*. Alternatively, let θ denote the proportion of the population who would answer "Yes" to question Q, e.g., "Do you like this brand of cheese?" during a sample survey. However, in the genotype example, θ is also referred to as a *genotype frequency*. We assume that it is too expensive to take a census of the entire population. Hence, θ is typically unknown.

To estimate θ, or infer likely values for θ, we recommend taking a sample of size n from the population, and observing the number x of individuals in the sample possessing the designated characteristic, e.g., the genotype Z. Then the *sample proportion* $y = x/n$ can be considered as a possible estimate for the unknown population proportion. For example, in Wisconsin, with population N equal to about 5 million, a sample of $n = 5500$ white males in Milwaukee, who have happened to attend blood-testing clinics for a variety of reasons, is employed to estimate the genotype frequencies for Wisconsin. Sometimes, this sample is supplemented by data for about 2000 primary-care patients attending University Hospitals in Madison.

If, say, $x = 83$ and $n = 5500$, then $y = 83/5500 = 0.0151 = 1.51\%$ would be taken by many people as a sensible estimate of the corresponding genotype frequency. Note that "little x", the value observed from the data, can be regarded as a numerical realization of "capital X", where X is a random variable. While X is an entity, which possesses different values with different probabilities, x is a specific value, but which can vary on different realisations of the experiment.

The probability distribution of X depends critically upon the experimental design, and how the data were collected. If a single individual is chosen at random from the population, then this individual has unknown probability θ of "success", i.e., of possessing the designated characteristic. Properties S1 and S2 will extend this result to a sample of n individuals.

Random Sampling with and without Replacement: Properties S1 and S2 relate to random sampling with and without replacement. In a legal case in Wisconsin, it was once required to select a random sample of $n = 120$ nursing homes out of a population of about $N = 600$ nursing homes, without using a random number generator on a computer. This was achieved by an attorney, an accountant, and a statistician, by assigning one of the numbers 1 through 600 to each nursing home, writing each number on a piece of paper, crushing the pieces of paper into balls of equal size, and placing them in a hat. The attorney was then blindfolded, and required to draw 120 pieces of paper from the hat, with appropriate shuffling of the hat, between each draw. This was random sampling *without* replacement, as none of the numbers was replaced in the hat. If, instead, each number had been replaced before the shuffling for the next draw, then the random sampling would have been *with* replacement.

Property S1: If the n individuals in the sample are chosen at random, *without* replacement, from the N individuals in the population, then X possesses a *hypergeometric distribution with parameters n, M, and N* and probability mass function

$$f(x) = p(X = x) = {}^{M}C_{x}^{N-M}C_{n-x}/{}^{N}C_{n},$$

for $x = \max(0, n + M - N)..., \min(n, M)$, where, for any integers n and N, with $n \leq N$,

$$^{N}C_{n} = N!/n!(N - n)!$$

denotes the number of ways of choosing n people out of N, in no particular order. Furthermore, the mean and variance of X are

$$\mu = E(X) = n\theta,$$

and

$$\sigma^2 = var(X) = k(n, N)n\theta(1 - \theta),$$

with $\theta = M/N$, and

$$k(n, N) = (N - n)/(N - 1) .$$

If X possesses the above distribution, then this will be represented by the shorthand notation,

$$X \sim H(n, M, N),$$

where $\sim$ denotes "is distributed as", H denotes "hypergeometric", and n, M, and N are the three parameters.

Property S2: If the individuals in the sample are chosen at random, *with* replacement, from the N individuals in the population, then X possesses a *binomial distribution with probability θ and sample size n*, and probability mass function

$$f(x) = p(X = x) = {}^{n}C_{x}\theta^{x}(1 - \theta)^{n-x} \qquad (x = 0, 1, ..., n).$$

Furthermore, the mean and variance of X are

$$\mu = E(X) = n\theta,$$

and

$$\sigma^2 = var(X) = n\theta(1 - \theta).$$

If X possesses the above distribution, then this will be represented by the short-hand notation

$$X \sim B(\theta, n),$$

where B denotes *binomial* and θ denotes the probability of success for any particular individual. For example, in a study of educational awareness of $N = 600$ Nigerian pastors, a random sample of $n = 120$ pastors was chosen. Let $Y = X/n$ denote the sample proportion of pastors who were regarded as *educationally aware*. Here Y is expressed as a random variable. For illustrative purposes, assume that it is known that $\theta = 0.99$. Since $E(X) = n\theta$, we have that $E(Y) = \theta = 0.99$. Also, since $var(Y) = var(X)/n^2$, property S1 tells us that, under random sampling *without* replacement,

$$\begin{aligned} var(Y) &= k(n, N)n^{-1}\theta(1 - \theta) \\ &= (480/599) \times 0.0000825 \\ &= 0.0000661. \end{aligned}$$

Therefore, the standard deviation of Y is 0.00813. However, property S2 tells us that, under random sampling *with* replacement,

$$\begin{aligned} var(Y) &= n^{-1}\theta(1 - \theta) \\ &= 0.0000825, \end{aligned}$$

so that the standard deviation of Y is 0.00908. Indeed, the sample proportion Y will always possess a smaller standard deviation, when the random sampling is *without*, rather than *with* replacement, so that its numerical realization will possess a tendency to be closer to the true population proportion θ.

This key property can be quantified by the *population size adjustment factor* $k(n, N) = (N - n)/(N - 1)$. In our example, $k(n, N) = 480/599 = 0.801$, so that the standard deviation of Y is multiplied by a factor equal to $\sqrt{0.801} = 0.895$. Consequently, random sampling *without*, rather than *with*, replacement is more efficient. This result is reasonable in intuitive terms, since random sampling with replacement can lead to duplications in the sample; e.g., the same individual can be interviewed or tested more than once.

Property S3: Under random sampling *with* replacement, the probability of at least one duplication in the sample is

$$\rho = 1 - (^N P_n / N^n),$$

where for any integers n and N, satisfying $n \leq N$,

$$^N P_n = N!/(N - n)!$$

denotes the number of ways of choosing n people out of N, in some pre-specified order.

For example, when $N = 600$ and $n = 120$, $\rho = 1 - 2.82 \times 10^{-6}$, so that duplications are virtually certain. Also, when $N = 365$ and $n = 23$, $\rho = 0.507$. This confirms that, if there are $n = 23$ people at a party and each is equally likely to possess any one out of $N = 365$ birthdays, then the probability that at least two have the same birthday is greater than 50%.

Now, in many situations, the population size N will far exceed the sample size, even when the sample size n is itself substantial. In this case ρ will approach zero, giving negligible probability of a duplication in the sample. Furthermore, the population size adjustment factor $k(n, N)$ approaches unity, and we have the following property;

Property S4: Under random sampling without replacement, let X possess the hypergeometric distribution

$$X \sim H(n, M, N).$$

Then, as N get large, with n and $\theta = M/N$ fixed, the distribution of X approaches the binomial distribution

$$X \sim B(\theta, n),$$

so that this distribution can be used as an approximation to the hypergeometric distribution. For example, this approximation is very good when $N \geq 20n$ and $0.05 < \theta < 0.95$.

Owing to property S4 we make the following recommendations for consideration at the experimental design stage:

Recommendation E1: Always try to random-sample *without* replacement. However, if $N \geq 20n$, nevertheless analyse your results using the binomial distribution (as a simple approximation to the more complicated hypergeometric distribution); i.e., perform your analysis as if you had instead random-sampled *with* replacement.

Recommendation E2: Seek to protect against unlucky random sampling (e.g., all members of your sample just happening, by chance, to be Newcastle United, or Chicago Bears, supporters) by trying to *replicate* your experiment, i.e., repeating your random sampling under similar conditions, and checking to see if you obtain similar results. Replicate your experiment as often as practical constraints permit.

Suppose then that we take a random sample, *without* replacement, of size $n = 5500$ from a population of size $N = 5$ million. As N is much larger than n, the particular value of N now becomes irrelevant to an analysis, since, with the binomial approximation, our sample proportion Y has mean θ and variance $n^{-1}\theta(1-\theta)$, depending upon θ, but not further upon N. Consider a hypothetical situation, where θ, a genotype frequency, is known to be $\theta = 0.02$. Then the standard deviation of Y is 0.00189. This is a fraction $0.00189/0.02 = 9.44\%$ of the mean or true population proportion (the ratio CV of the standard deviation to the mean is known as the *coefficient of variation*).

It is quite surprising that such a large sample size yields such a high coefficient of variation. Other sample sizes can be considered from the following properties:

Property S5: When considering the sample proportion $Y = X/n$, where

$$X \sim B(\theta, n),$$

the sample size n is related to the coefficient of variation CV by the formula

$$n = (\theta^{-1} - 1)/CV^2. \qquad (*)$$

Property S6: If X is not exactly binomially distributed, but in exact terms, $X \sim H(n, M, N)$, we should choose $n = Nn^*/[N + n^* - 1]$ when n^* is equal to the expression in (*), with θ replaced by M/N.

For example, under binomial sampling, suppose that a geneticist judges, before the investigation is performed, that θ is likely to be in the region of $\theta = 0.02$. Imagine, also, that the geneticist requires excellent accuracy, with $CV = 1\%$. Then property S5 lets us recommend a sample size of

$$
\begin{aligned}
n &= (50 - 1)/0.01^2 \\
&= 490,000.
\end{aligned}
$$

Alternatively, consider an opinion poll for an election between two candidates, where θ is anticipated to lie in some region close to 0.5. When θ is exactly 0.5, property S5 reduces to the recommendation of $n = 1/CV^2$, corresponding to $CV = 1/\sqrt{n}$. For example, values of $n = 900, 2500$, and $10,000$ correspond to values of CV equal to 3.33%, 2%, and 1%. It would therefore appear to be impossible to predict adequately the result of a close election without a sample size exceeding 10,000, even if appropriate random sampling (of people, not telephones!) has occurred, together with full response.

Recommendation E3: The sample size, n, should be selected, according to the formula in property S5, with θ representing a subjective evaluation of the population proportion, and where CV is a designated value for the coefficient of variation.

Quite surprisingly, random samples for the evaluation of genotype frequencies appear to have seldom been collected. For example, in Wisconsin, the sample of size $n = 5500$ for estimating genotype frequencies was collected in quite biased fashion, in relation to the population. In such circumstances, there is no particular justification for a binomial (or hypergeometric) distribution for X, and hence a statement that the sample proportion $Y = X/n$ is an unbiased estimator for an unknown population proportion θ is no longer valid in any objective sense.

Recommendation E4: When random sampling has not occurred, the problem of bias cannot typically be reduced by increasing the sample size.

For example, during the U.S. presidential elections of 1936, a sample of more than 2 million people were asked whether they had voted for Franklin Roosevelt or Alf Landon, and the majority in the sample had voted for Landon. However, the sample was biased toward the Republicans since only people with cars or telephones were questioned. Hence, the newspaper announcements to the effect that Landon had won by a landslide proved to be incorrect. Similar mistakes were repeated in the 1948 Truman-Dewey election, and frequently thereafter.

More generally, a large number of data sets are not based upon random sampling. In such cases, a binomial assumption can only be justified subjectively, and all conclusions are at best subjective. There are degrees of subjectivity based upon how representative a (nonrandom) sample has been collected. So, statisticians need to be pragmatic, and make subjective judgements, either when random sampling has not occurred, or when there is a large nonresponse rate. (This is part of A.C. Aitken's Inductive Synthesis; see Aitken, 1944, p. 3.) Remember that our actual goal is to discover fresh knowledge from the data; it is still possible to obtain strong subjective indications of fresh knowledge, without random sampling. We will frequently make binomial assumptions, subjectively, since the more general p-parameter exponential family of distributions (see Section 1.10), and other alternatives, are more complicated to analyse.

The reader might be alarmed by the large sample sizes needed to estimate population proportions under random sampling. However, as this text progresses, we will find that lower sample sizes are needed for hypothesis testing (rather than estimation) and for discerning interesting features in the data. For example, when comparing treatments for nosebleed, the author once recommended a sample size of 10 for each treatment, since the success rates were projected to be quite different. Nevertheless, samples of this size should be treated with extreme caution, particularly when the randomness of the sampling is open to doubt.

1.2 Further properties of the binomial distribution

Suppose that you ask $n = 20$ people question Q, e.g., whether or not they prefer Bristol Cream Sherry to Bristol Milk Sherry, and let X denote the number of positive responses in your sample. Your sample was not, however, chosen at random from a population. You may then refer to the following property, to judge the reasonability of a binomial assumption for θ.

Property B1: (n Independent Bernoulli Trials). Let $Z_1, ..., Z_n$ denote n independent binary responses, where

$$p(Z_i = 1) = \theta$$

and

$$p(Z_i = 0) = 1 - \theta$$

Then, $X = Z_1 + Z_2 + \cdots + Z_n \sim B(\theta, n)$. [Here each $Z_i \sim B(\theta, 1), E(Z_i) = \theta$, and $var(Z_i) = \theta(1 - \theta)$.]

Property B1 tells us that, if before collecting your data and based upon all information currently available you judge that (a) the n people in the sample will respond independently, and (b) as far as you know, each person has the same probability θ of giving a positive response, then you may assume that $X \sim B(\theta, n)$. Note that θ is no longer necessarily a population proportion, but rather a common probability of a positive response for each individual. Any subjectivity in your appraisal of conditions (a) and (b) can create related subjectivity in your ultimate conclusions. If you instead judge that the different people in the sample might possess different probabilities of preferring Bristol Cream Sherry, for example, because of specific knowledge relating to their social background, then a binomial distribution would be inappropriate. In this case, you could instead try a binary regression model which incorporates your extra information (see Section 8.1). Also, if you were to ask the same person the same question at n different times, and anticipate the same probability θ of a positive response each time, then a binomial distribution for X, the total number of positive responses from the same individual, will be inappropriate unless you can rule out serial correlation. An example of this occurs when there are correlations between binary responses observed at successive time points. The independence property also needs to be checked out more generally. It is not, for example, enough to be able to regard n individuals as "permutable" (meaning that there is a symmetry of information about the individuals). You need to be able to assume that once a value is specified for the response probability θ for any particular individual, or group of individuals, this value would be unaffected by knowledge of the actual responses from any other individual or group of individuals.

Property B2: If X_1 and X_2 are independent, with

$$X_i \sim B(\theta, n_i) \qquad (i = 1, 2),$$

then

$$X_1 + X_2 \sim B(\theta, n_1 + n_2).$$

Property B2 tells you that if you pool two independent samples, of sizes n_1 and n_2, with binomial assumptions for the numbers of positive responses in each sample, then you can assume a binomial distribution for the combined number of positive responses, as long as you have the same θ for each sample. You cannot, however, do this if you have different θ, e.g., if you are combining samples of males and females, with males and females assumed to possess different probabilities of preferring Bristol Cream Sherry. This is a typical implication of the following property.

Property B3: If X_1 and X_2 are independent, with

$$X_i \sim B(\theta_i, n_i) \qquad (i = 1, ..., 2),$$

where $\theta_1 \neq \theta_2$, then $X_1 + X_2$ does not possess a binomial distribution.

1.3 Statistical procedures for the binomial distribution

1.3.1 Estimation

If $X \sim B(\theta, n)$, then $Y = X/n$ is an unbiased estimator of θ with standard deviation $\sqrt{\theta(1-\theta)/n}$. Hence, if x is the observed value of X, $y = x/n$ is an unbiased estimate of θ, with estimated standard error $s_e = \sqrt{y(1-y)/n}$. Suppose, for example, that on $n = 100$ spins of an American roulette wheel (with two zeroes), a zero occurs $x = 5$ times. Then $y = 0.05$ is an unbiased estimate of the long run proportion θ of zeroes, with estimated standard error 0.0218.

1.3.2 The likelihood curve

Under the likelihood approach, all information about θ, given the observed x, and assuming that the binomial assumption is precisely true, is summarised in the likelihood curve

$$\ell(\theta|x) = p(X = x|\theta) = (^nC_x)\,\theta^x(1-\theta)^{n-x} \qquad (0 < \theta < 1). \qquad (1.1)$$

This curve is plotted for several values of n and x in Figure 1.1.

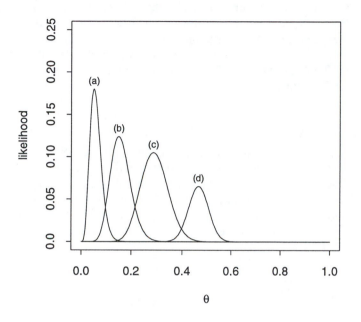

Figure 1.1 *Likelihood curves for binomial probabilities (a) $x = 5$, $n = 100$; (b)*
$x = 12$, $n = 80$; (c) $x = 20$, $n = 70$; (d) $x = 70$, $n = 150$.

Each curve takes the shape of a "beta" curve in θ. Observe that the
maximum of the curve occurs at $\theta = \hat{\theta} = x/n$, which is identical to the
unbiased estimate y. This maximum likelihood estimate is the value of θ
"most likely to have given rise to the value x of X actually observed". The
relative plausibility of other candidates for θ may be judged by comparing
heights of the likelihood curve. For example, when $x = 5$ and $n = 100$,
$\theta_1 = 1/19$ and $\theta_2 = 1/38$ have respective heights of 0.180 and 0.075, so
that θ_1 is preferred to θ_2. It is important to remember that areas under the
likelihood curve are not open to statistical interpretation without further
assumption. The likelihood is not a probability density in θ.

1.3.3 Approximate confidence intervals

The distribution of $Z = (Y - \theta)/S_e$ approaches the standard normal distribution, as n gets large, with θ fixed, and with $S_e = \sqrt{Y(1 - Y)/n}$.
Consequently, an approximate 95% equal-tailed confidence interval for θ is

$$(y - 1.960s_e, y + 1.960s_e),$$

where $s_e = \sqrt{y(1-y)/n}$ denotes the numerical realization of the random variable S_e. The justification of this interval depends upon our normal approximation to the distribution of Z, which is only likely to be at all adequate if $n \geq 100$. For a 99% interval, replace 1.960, the 97.5th percentile of the standard normal distribution by 2.576, the 99.5th percentile. When $x = 5$, and $n = 100$, our approximate 95% and 99% intervals are, respectively, $(0.05 \pm 0.0428) = (0.0072, 0.0928)$ and (0.05 ± 0.0561) which we report as $(0, 0.1061)$.

1.3.4 More precise confidence intervals

As the lower bound of the 99% is negative, the accuracy of the preceding interval is open to question. Exact versions of these intervals are, however, available using our function theta.zero on Splus. This is based upon a method described by Leonard and Hsu (1994), but the theory is too complicated to include in this text. If our home Internet address is accessed (see our section on Special Software), then the command

$$\text{theta.zero } (100, 5, 0.025)$$

creates the response

$$\text{theta value} = 0.01933,$$

and replacing 0.025 by 0.975 gives a theta value of 0.1061. Consequently, our "exact" 95% equal-tailed confidence interval when $x = 5$, and $n = 100$ is $(0.0193, 0.1061)$, a bit different from the approximate interval. The frequency coverage of our confidence intervals, e.g., by computer simulation, will be as close to 95% as permitted by the discrete nature of the binomial probabilities (Leonard and Hsu, 1999, pp. 142-143). Applying theta.zero with values of 0.005 and 0.995 replacing 0.025 suggests the "exact" 99% confidence interval $(0.0132, 0.1280)$. More generally, the values of 100 and 5, appearing in the theta.zero function, should be replaced by whichever values for n and x are currently under consideration.

1.3.5 Hypothesis testing (approximate significance probabilities)

Suppose next that we observe $x = 10$ zeroes during $n = 100$ spins, and that we wish to investigate the null hypothesis

$$H_0 : \theta = \theta_0,$$

where $\theta_0 = 1/19 = 0.05263$, the appropriate value for θ if the roulette wheel is fair. Then we might consider the two significance probabilities

$$\begin{aligned} \alpha_p &= p(X \geq x | H_0), \\ &= 0.03801, \end{aligned}$$

and

$$\alpha_p^* = p(X > x|H_0),$$
$$= 0.01626.$$

where, under H_0, $X \sim B(\theta_0, n)$, so that $y = x/n = 0.10$ and $s_e = $ st.dev. $(X/n) = \sqrt{\theta_0(1 - \theta_0)/n} = 0.0223$. For $n \geq 100$, the approximation

$$\widehat{\alpha}_p \sim \alpha_p^* \sim 1 - \Phi\left(\frac{y - \theta_0}{s_e}\right)$$
$$= 1 - \Phi\left(\frac{0.10 - 0.05263}{0.0223}\right)$$
$$= 1 - \Phi(2.124),$$

where Φ denotes the standard normal distribution function, yields an approximate significance probability of 0.01695.

1.3.6 Hypothesis testing (more precise significance probabilities)

A special function gives a sensible compromise between the exact values of α_p and α_p^* (see our Special Splus functions). The command

$$a.p(100, 10, 0.05263)$$

creates the response

$$\text{significance probability} = 0.02513,$$

which provides our compromise between α_p and α_p^*.

If we are testing H_0 against the two-sided alternative $H_1 : \theta \neq \theta_0$, we regard possible values of X as extreme: if they are either too large or too small when compared with $n\theta_0$, the hypothesised expectation of X. One possible significance probability is

$$\alpha_p = 2\min\{p(X \geq x|H_0), p(X \leq x|H_0)\}.$$

We, however, instead recommend the refinement which doubles the minimum of the one-sided significance probabilities, achieved from the commands $a.p(n, x, \theta_0)$, and $a.p(n, n - x, 1 - \theta_0)$. Continuing our example, with $\theta_0 = 1/19$, the command

$$a.p(100, 90, 0.94627)$$

creates the response

$$\text{significance probability} = 0.97145.$$

Consequently, our recommended two-sided compromise significance probability is

$$\widehat{\alpha}_p \;=\; 2\min(0.02513, 0.97145)$$
$$=\; 0.05026.$$

1.4 The Poisson distribution

Definition 1.1: A random variable X, concentrated on the nonnegative integers $\{0, 1, 2, ...\}$, possesses a *Poisson distribution* with mean and variance both equal to μ, if it has probability mass function

$$f(x) = p(X = x) = e^{-\mu}\mu^x/x! \qquad (x = 0, 1, 2, ...)$$

In this case we write $X \sim P(\mu)$.

The Poisson distribution is sometimes characterized by the theory of stochastic processes. Consider electrons hitting a screen, and suppose that the arrival time of each electron hitting the screen during a fixed time period $T = (0, t^*)$ is recorded. This is an example of a *point process*. For any time interval $(t_1, t_2) \subseteq T$, let $N^*(t_1, t_2)$ denote the number of arrivals at the screen during this interval. Other examples of point processes include the arrivals of cars at pedestrian crossings, the arrivals of customers at a supermarket queue, and claims on a particular type of policy at an insurance company.

Let $\lambda(t)$ denote the "intensity function" of the point process, a nonnegative integrable function defined for all $t \in T$. An intensity function $\lambda(t)$ satisfies the property that, for any $(t_1, t_2) \subseteq T$, the expectation of the number $N^*(t_1, t_2)$ of arrivals in this interval is

$$\mu(t_1, t_2) \;=\; \int_{t_1}^{t_2} \lambda(t)dt$$
$$=\; \text{area under the intensity function between } t_1 \text{ and } t_2.$$

For example, if $\lambda(t) = \lambda$ is constant for $t \in T$, then the expectation of $N^*(t_1, t_2)$ is

$$\mu(t_1, t_2) \;=\; \lambda(t_2 - t_1)$$
$$=\; \text{product of rate of process and width of interval.}$$

Definition 1.2: A point process is a *nonhomogeneous Poisson process* with intensity function $\lambda(t)$, for $t \in T$, if $\lambda(t)$ is not constant for all $t \in T$, and

A. For any small interval of width w, contained in T, the probability of exactly one arrival is approximately $w\lambda(t^*)$ where t^* is lower than the end point of the interval. Moreover, the probability of no arrivals in this interval is approximately $1 - w\lambda(t^*)$, and the probability of more than one arrival is negligible.

B. (Markov, Lack of Memory Property). Arrivals in any small interval $(t^*, t^* + w)$ occur independently of arrivals in $(0, t^*)$, whenever the function $\lambda(t)$ is completely specified.

This definition produces point processes with multiple arrivals possible at any particular time point. It is always essential to check the reasonability of the lack of memory property (B). Note that if $\lambda(t) = \lambda$ is instead constant for all $t \in T$, requirements (A) and (B) instead define a homogeneous Poisson process, with rate λ.

Property P1: For a nonhomogeneous Poisson process with intensity function $\lambda(t), t \in T$,

$$N^*(t_1, t_2) \sim P(\mu(t_1, t_2)),$$

for any interval $(t_1, t_2) \in T$. Furthermore, $N^*(t_1, t_2)$ and $N^*(t_1^*, t_2^*)$ are independent, for any nonoverlapping intervals (t_1, t_2) and (t_1^*, t_2^*) in T.

Property P1 tells us that the conditions of Definition 1.2 characterize situations in which we can take the number of arrivals in any particular time interval to be Poisson distributed. This is just one important justification of the Poisson distribution. The property also holds for a homogeneous process with constant rate λ, and $\mu(t_1, t_2) = (t_2 - t_1)\lambda$. It follows, in general, that the probability of no arrival in the interval (t_1, t_2) is

$$P\{N^*(t_1, t_2) = 0\} = \exp\{-\mu(t_1, t_2)\}.$$

Consider cars arriving at a pedestrian crossing in a homogeneous Poisson process of rate $\lambda = 0.5$/minute. It follows that $N^*(0, 2)$, or indeed the number of arrivals in any 2-minute period, has a Poisson distribution with mean $2\lambda = 1$. Consequently, the variance and standard deviation of $N^*(0, 2)$ are both equal to 1 and $N^*(0, 2)$ has probability mass function

$$p(N^*(0, 2) = j) = e^{-1}/j! \qquad (j = 0, 1, 2, ...).$$

Similarly, $N^*(5, 10)$ has a Poisson distribution with mean 2.5, and is independent of $N^*(0, 2)$.

Property P2: If $X \sim P(\mu)$, then the probability mass function $f(x)$ of X satisfies the initial condition,

$$f(0) = e^{-\mu}$$

and the recurrence relations,

$$f(x + 1) = \mu f(x)/(x + 1) \qquad (x = 0, 1, 2, ...).$$

- As a further example, Steinijans (1976) considers the years recorded for the 38 major freezes on Lake Konstanz between A.D. 875 and 1974. With

t denoting time in centuries after A.D. 875, he estimates that the freezes occur in a nonhomogeneous Poisson process, with rate function

$$\lambda(t) = \beta_0 \exp\left\{-\frac{1}{2}\beta_1(t - \beta_2)^2\right\},$$

where $\beta_0 = 5.29954$, $\beta_1 = 0.11234$, and $\beta_2 = 6.15880$. Then $N^*(t_1, t_2)$ has a Poisson distribution with mean

$$\mu(t_1, t_2) = \text{area under } \lambda(t) \text{ between } t_1 \text{ and } t_2$$
$$= \beta_0(2\pi/\beta_1)^{\frac{1}{2}}[\Phi\{\beta_1^{\frac{1}{2}}(t_2 - \beta_2)\} - \Phi\{\beta_1^{\frac{1}{2}}(t_1 - \beta_2)\}],$$

where Φ denotes the cumulative distribution function of the standard normal distribution. The values $t_1 = 6.15$ and $t_2 = 6.25$ correspond to the years 1490 and 1500. We find that

$$\mu(6.15, 6.25) = 39.633[\Phi(0.03057) - \Phi(-0.00295)]$$
$$= 0.530,$$

and this describes both the expectation and variance of the number of freezes during this decade. The corresponding probability mass function can be calculated using the recursive formula of Property P1, giving

$$f(0) = 0.5886, \quad f(1) = 0.3120, \quad f(2) = 0.0827, \quad \text{and} \quad f(3) = 0.0146.$$

Property P3: (The Poisson approximation to the binomial). If $X \sim B(\theta, n)$ where θ is small, n is large, and $n\theta \geq 1$ is moderate, then, approximately, $X \sim P(n\theta)$.

Property P3 provides a different characterization of the binomial distribution. Suppose, for example, that there are $n = 10^6$ possible coincidences that might occur to you on a particular day, and that each might occur with probability $\theta = 10^{-6}$, with all occurrences independent. Let X denote the number of coincidences occurring during this day. Then, $X \sim B(10^{-6}, 10^6)$, with a quite complicated probability mass function. Also, $E(X) = 1$, and $var(X) = 1 - 10^{-6}$. However, $n\theta = 1$, so that $X \sim P(1)$ approximately. For example, the probability that at least one coincidence occurs is $1 - p(X = 0) \simeq 1 - e^{-1} = 63.21\%$.

Property P4: If $X_1 \sim P(\mu_1)$ and $X_2 \sim P(\mu_2)$ are independent, then

(a) $N = X_1 + X_2 \sim P(\mu_1 + \mu_2)$
(b) The conditional distribution of X_1, given that $N = n$, is $B(\theta, n)$ where $\theta = \mu_1/(\mu_1 + \mu_2)$.

As an example, suppose that the number of X_1 of car accidents in Cornwall during a specified time period is estimated to be distributed as $X_1 \sim P(23.2)$, and the number of car accidents in Devonshire during the same period is estimated to be $X_2 \sim P(34.7)$, with X_1 and X_2 independent. Then $N = X_1 + X_2 \sim P(57.9)$. However, imagine that you are now informed that a total $N = n = 49$ of car accidents was actually observed during this period in Cornwall and Devonshire combined. Then this changes your distribution for X_1 to $B(\theta, n)$ where $\theta = 23.2/57.9 = 0.4007$. For example, the conditional mean of X_1, given that $N = n = 49$, is $n\theta = 49 \times 0.4007 = 19.63$, which is less than the unconditional mean of 23.2.

1.5 Statistical procedures for the Poisson distribution

Let $X \sim P(\mu)$, where μ is unknown. As $E(X) = \mu$, and the standard deviation of X is $\sqrt{\mu}$, X is an unbiased estimator of μ, with standard error $\sqrt{\mu}$. If $X = x$ is observed, then x is an unbiased estimate of μ, with estimated standard error $\sqrt{x}$. The likelihood curve of μ, given that $X = x$, is the "gamma" curve

$$\ell(\mu|x) = e^{-\mu}\mu^x/x! \qquad (0 < \mu < \infty).$$

This curve is plotted for several different values of x in Figure 1.2.

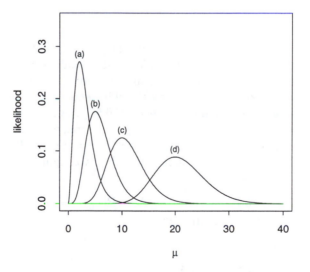

Figure 1.2 *Likelihood curves for Poisson means (a)* $x = 2$, *(b)* $x = 5$, *(c)* $x = 10$, *(d)* $x = 20$.

The maximum of each curve always occurs at the value $\mu = \hat{\mu} = x$, the maximum likelihood estimate of x. For large μ, the distribution of X is approximately normal, with mean and variance both equal to μ. Consequently, the distribution of

$$Z = (X - \mu)/\sqrt{X}$$

approaches a standard normal distribution as μ gets large. This result can be used to justify approximate confidence intervals for μ. An approximate equal-tailed 95% confidence interval of μ is

$$(x - 1.960\sqrt{x},\ x + 1.960\sqrt{x}).$$

For example, when $x = 100$, this interval is (80.4, 119.6). A 99% interval, obtained by replacing 1.960 by 2.576, is (74.2, 125.8). Just as in the binomial case, more precise intervals may be obtained by using a special function on Splus. Our commands,

$$\text{gamma.theta.zero (1,100, 0.025)}$$

and

$$\text{gamma.theta.zero (1,100, 0.975)},$$

give the responses

$$\text{theta.zero} = 81.815$$

and

$$\text{theta.zero} = 121.078,$$

so that our "exact" 95% confidence limits for μ are (81.82, 121.08). The first entry in the above commands should be set equal to unity whenever we have a single unreplicated Poisson frequency, and the second entry gives the value x of this frequency. Changing the third entry to 0.005, and then to 0.995, yields the 99% confidence interval (76.56, 128.20).

Suppose now that it is hypothesised that μ, the expected number of murders in Scotland in 1998, is $\mu_0 = 25$. However, $x = 35$ murders are then observed in 1998. Reference can be made to the two significance probabilities

$$\begin{aligned} \alpha_p &= p(X \geq x | X \sim P(\mu_0)) \\ &= 0.0338, \end{aligned}$$

and

$$\begin{aligned} \alpha_p^* &= p(X > x | X \sim P(\mu_0)) \\ &= 0.0225. \end{aligned}$$

However, our command gamma.a.p$(1, 35, 25)$ creates the compromise significance probability= 0.02765 and avoids the need for the normal approximation

$$\alpha_p \sim \alpha_p^* \sim 1 - \Phi\left(\frac{x - \mu_0}{x^{\frac{1}{2}}}\right) = 1 - \Phi(1.69) = 0.04551.$$

When testing $H_0 : \mu = \mu_0$ against $\mu \neq \mu_0$, you should double the smaller of two responses. Consider a.p$(1, x, \mu_0)$, and one minus the response from gamma.a.p$(1, x + 1, \mu_0)$. In our example, gamma.a.p$(1, 36, 25)$ gives output; significance probability $= 0.01813$. Hence, our two-sided compromise significance probability is

$$2 \min(0.02765, 0.98187) = 0.05530.$$

1.6 The multinomial distribution

Consider a situation where I have n dogs and k kennels $K_1, ..., K_k$. I assign each dog to a kennel at random, and according to probabilities $\xi_1, ..., \xi_k$, summing to unity. Here ξ_i denotes the probability that any particular dog is assigned to the ith kennel K_i for $i = 1, ..., k$. Each dog is assigned to a kennel, independently of the other dogs.

Let $X_1, ..., X_k$ denote the numbers of dogs assigned to kennels $K_1, ..., K_k$, respectively. Then by Property S2 of Section 1.2, $X_i \sim B(\xi_i, n)$ for $i = 1, ..., k$. Hence, estimation and inference procedures and hypothesis testing procedures, given $X_i = x_i$, for an unknown ξ_i, may be based upon the methodology for θ, given $X = x$, as described in Section 1.3, in the single binomial case. Since $X_i \sim B(\xi_i, n)$, the mean and variance of X_i are

$$E(X_i) = n\xi_i,$$

and

$$var(X_i) = n\xi_i(1 - \xi_i).$$

The binomial random variables $X_1, ..., X_k$ are not independent, as $X_1 + \cdots + X_k = n$. Their joint probability mass function is

$$p(X_1 = x_1, ..., X_k = x_k)$$
$$= M^*(n, x_1, ..., x_k)\xi_1^{x_1}\xi_2^{x_2}...\xi_k^{x_k},$$

with

$$M^*(n, x_1, ..., x_k) = n!/x_1!x_2!...x_k!.$$

where each x_i may assume one of the integer values from zero to n, but subject to the overall constraint $x_1 + \cdots + x_k = n$. Furthermore, the collection of cell probabilities $\{\xi_1, ..., \xi_k\}$ falls in the k-dimensional unit simplex $S_U^{(k)}$, which is the set consisting of all possible choices of k real numbers, that are nonnegative and sum to unity.

The above expression for $M^*(n, x_1, ..., x_k)$ is a *multinomial coefficient*. This describes the number of ways in which my n dogs can be assigned to the k kennels, such that $x_1, ..., x_k$ dogs appear in the respective kennels, in no particular order within each kennel. The remaining contribution to the above probability mass function describes the probability that x_1 prespecified dogs get assigned to the first kennel, x_2 prespecified dogs get assigned to the second kennel, and so on, i.e., x_i prespecified dogs get assigned to the ith kennel, for $i = 1, ..., k$.

As a further simple example, note that, according to the Mendelian theory of inheritance, pea plants should yield peas which are either round or wrinkled, and either yellow or green according to the probabilities in the following table.

	Round	Wrinkled
Yellow	9/16	3/16
Green	3/16	1/16

You choose three plants at random from a population of pea plants. What is the probability that two of the plants yield peas which are round and yellow, and one yields peas which are wrinkled and green? According to Mendel's theory, and our joint probability mass function, with $n = 3$ and $k = 4$, our answer is

$$\{3!/2!0!0!1!\} \left(\frac{9}{16}\right)^2 \left(\frac{3}{16}\right)^0 \left(\frac{3}{16}\right)^0 \left(\frac{1}{16}\right)^1$$

$$= \quad 243/4096 = 0.0593.$$

In our pea example, $E(X_1) = 1.688$, $var(X_1) = 0.738$, where $X_1 \sim B(9/16, 3)$ denotes the number of plants with round and yellow peas. Since $X_1 + X_4 \sim B(\xi_1 + \xi_4, n) \sim B(5/8, 3)$, where $X_1 + X_4$ denotes the number of plants with peas which are either round and yellow, or wrinkled and green, $E(X_1 + X_4) = 1.875$, and $var(X_1 + X_4) = 0.703$.

In general n is referred to as the *sample size* of our multinomial distribution, and $\xi_1, ..., \xi_k$ as the *cell probabilities*. Then, we write

$$X_1, ..., X_k \sim M(\xi_1, ..., \xi_k; n),$$

where M denotes multinomial, whenever $X_1, ..., X_k$ possess the joint probability mass function described above. In our pea plant example,

$$X_1, X_2, X_3, X_4 \sim M\left(\frac{9}{16}, \frac{3}{16}, \frac{3}{16}, \frac{1}{16}; 3\right)$$

provides a full notational representation of the appropriate joint distribution.

1.7 Sir Ronald Fisher's conditioning result

The following theorem demonstrates that multinomial frequencies can be interpreted as Poisson frequencies, but conditioned on their sum:

Theorem 1.1: *Let $X_1, ..., X_k$ denote independent Poisson variates, with respective means $\mu_1, ..., \mu_k$. Then, conditional on*

$$Y = X_1 + \cdots + X_k = n,$$

we have

$$X_1, ..., X_k \sim M(\xi_1, ..., \xi_k; n),$$

where

$$\xi_i = \mu_i / \sum_{\ell=1}^{k} \mu_\ell \qquad (i = 1, ..., k).$$

Furthermore $Y \sim P(\mu + \cdots + \mu_k)$.

As an example, you judge that the numbers of goals X_1, X_2, and X_3, scored by Spurs (Tottenham Hotspur), Liverpool, and Glasgow Rangers, respectively, next Saturday, will be independently Poisson distributed with respective means $\mu_1 = 1.5, \mu_2 = 2.5$, and $\mu_3 = 3.5$ (totalling $\mu_1 + \mu_2 + \mu_3 = 7.5$). Saturday arrives, and you are informed that the total numbers of goals scored by the three teams is $X_1 + X_2 + X_3 = 12$. Then, in the absence of further information, your new distribution is

$$X_1, X_2, X_3 \sim M\left(\frac{1}{5}, \frac{1}{3}, \frac{7}{15}; 12\right).$$

Given that $X_1 + X_2 + X_3 = 12$, we have $X_3 \sim B(7/15, 12)$, so that the number of goals scored by Rangers now has conditional mean 5.6 and conditional variance 2.99, when compared with the previous mean and variance of 3.5. Consider also, the following relationship between the Poisson and binomial distributions:

Corollary 1.1: *Let X_1 and X_2 denote independent Poisson variates, with respective means μ_1 and μ_2. Then, conditional on $X_1 + X_2 = n$,*

$$X_1 \sim B(\theta, n),$$

where

$$\theta = \mu_1 / (\mu_1 + \mu_2)$$

and

$$X_2 \sim B(1 - \theta, n).$$

In the football example, suppose that on match day you only learn that $X_1 + X_2 = 3$. Then your new distribution for X_1, the number of goals scored by Spurs, is

$$X_1 \sim B(0.375, 3),$$

so that X_1 has mean 1.125 and variance 0.703.

1.8 More general sampling models

The Poisson, binomial, and multinomial sampling models do not always adequately represent real practical data. Suppose, for example, that we observe the blood counts $x_1, x_2, ..., x_{100}$ in $n = 100$ cells, and that the sample mean $\bar{x}$ and variance s^2 of the counts satisfy

$$\bar{x} = 15.35$$

and

$$s^2 = \sum (x_i - \bar{x})^2 / (n - 1) = 30.72.$$

Then, it would be inappropriate to take, say, the observations to represent a random sample from a Poisson distribution, with mean μ estimated by $\hat{\mu} = \bar{x} = 15.35$. This would automatically estimate the variance of the observations to also be 15.35, far less that the value 36.72 suggested by the data. Another possibility is to use a *Poisson mixture model* for the underlying random variables $X_1, ..., X_n$. Take these random variables to be independent, and all with the same distribution as a random variable X. Conditional on the realization u of some strictly positive random variable U, X has a Poisson distribution with mean u. Then, the unconditional probability mass function of X is

$$f(x) = E[U^x e^{-U} / x!] \qquad (x = 0, 1, 2, ...),$$

where the expectation is taken with respect to the probability distribution of U. The following special cases are particularly important:

(a) U possesses a discrete distribution with probability mass function :

$$p(U = u_k) = q_k \qquad (k = 1, ...\ell).$$

where $\sum_{k=1}^{\ell} q_k = 1$. In this case, the probability mass function of X assumes the flexible form

$$f(x) = \sum_{k=1}^{\ell} q_k u_k^x e^{-u_k} / x! \qquad (x = 0, 1, 2, ...).$$

The mean and variance of X need no longer be equal, and satisfy

$$E(X) = \sum_{k=1}^{\ell} q_k u_k,$$

and

$$Var(X) = \sum_{k=1}^{\ell} q_k (u_k + u_k^2) - (\sum_{k=1}^{\ell} q_k u_k)^2.$$

Moreover, the q_k and u_k, and indeed the number of terms ℓ in the mixture, may be estimated from the data $x_1, ..., x_n$, by maximization of the log-likelihood function

$$L(\mathbf{q}, \mathbf{u}, \ell | x_1, ..., x_n)$$

$$= \sum_{i=1}^{n} \log \sum_{k=1}^{\ell} q_k u_k^{x_i} e^{-u_k} - \sum_{i=1}^{n} \log x_i! .$$

Titterington, Smith, and Makov (1985) describe numerical techniques for performing this maximization. A numerical example is described in Section 1.9, in the binomial situation.

(b) U possesses a Gamma $G(\alpha, \beta)$ distribution with positive parameters α and β, and mean $\xi = \alpha/\beta$. In this case the probability distribution function of U is, for $0 < u < \infty$,

$$G(u) = p(U \leq u)$$
$$= \text{area to the left of } u \text{ under the density curve } g,$$

where the density g is defined by

$$g(u) = \beta^{\alpha} u^{\alpha-1} e^{-\beta u} / \Gamma(\alpha) \qquad (0 < u < \infty),$$

and $\Gamma(\alpha)$ is a standard mathematical function known as the *Gamma function*.

In this case, the mean of X is always less than the variance of X. The mean and variance satisfy

$$E(X) = \xi < \tau\xi = Var(X),$$

where $\tau = (\beta+1)/\beta$ is known as the *overdispersion factor*. In our numerical example, ξ and τ may be estimated by $\widehat{\xi} = \bar{x} = 15.35$ and $\widehat{\tau} = s^2/\bar{x} = 2.00$, respectively. Consequently, α and β may be estimated by $\widehat{\alpha} = \widehat{\xi}/(\widehat{\tau} - 1) = 15.35$, and $\widehat{\beta} = 1/(\widehat{\tau} - 1) = 1$. Under these assumptions, the unconditional distribution of X follows a *Pascal* distribution, with probability mass function

$$f(x) = \frac{\Gamma(\alpha + x)}{\Gamma(x + 1)\Gamma(\alpha)} \beta^{\alpha}/(1 + \beta)^{\alpha+x} \qquad (x = 0, 1, 2, ...).$$

In practice, this probability mass function , with α and β replaced by their numerical estimates, should be compared for fit with a relative frequency histogram of the observations. If the fit is poor, then a discrete mixing distribution of the form described in (a) might be more flexible.

In practice, a large number n of replicated observations will be needed to identify the extra parameters accurately in any probability distribution generalizing the Poisson. For many categorical data problems, sufficient replications are simply unavailable. For this reason, many scientists refer to straightforward Poisson assumptions to avoid the extra complications. However, for unreplicated data, we are frequently left with the conceptual difficulty that a straightforward Poisson assumption might at best possess a subjective justification, given the available information. If an "overdispersion factor" were really appropriate, then this would reduce the apparent statistical significance of many results based upon straightforward Poisson assumptions. Similar conceptual problems can affect binomial and multinomial assumptions, when these are not justified by appropriate random sampling.

1.9 Generalising the binomial distribution

Consider the data in Table 1.1, which provides a subset of a larger table reported by Pearson (1904). The occupations have been rearranged in order, according to the values of the observed proportions x_i/n_i.

Table 1.1 *Numbers of sons following their father's occupation*

Occupation (i)	x_i	n_i	x_i/n_i
1	0	26	0.000
2	6	88	0.068
3	11	106	0.104
4	7	54	0.130
5	6	44	0.136
6	4	19	0.211
7	18	69	0.261
8	9	32	0.281
9	6	18	0.333
10	23	51	0.451
11	54	115	0.470
12	20	41	0.488
13	28	50	0.560
14	51	62	0.823
	(243)	(775)	

One possible model would be to take the x_i to be the numerical realisations of independent random variables $X_1..., X_m$, where, for $i = 1, ..., m, X_i$ possesses a binomial $B(\theta, n_i)$ distribution, with probability θ and sample size n_i. In this case θ may be estimated by $\widehat{\theta} = 243/775 = 0.314$. Alternatively, each X_i may be taken to possess a $B(\theta_i, n_i)$ distribution with θ_i

estimated by $\widehat{\theta}_i = x_i/n_i$, the appropriate entry to the last column of Table 1.1.

An alternative sampling model supposes that, conditional upon a random variable U_i, each X_i possesses a binomial $B(U_i, n_i)$ distribution. Then the unconditional probability mass function of X_i is

$$p(X_i = x_i) = ^{n_i}C_{x_i} E[U_i^{x_i}(1 - U_i)^{n_i - x_i}] \qquad (x_i = 0, 1, ..., n_i),$$

where the expectation is taken with respect to a common distribution for the U_i. If this common mixing distribution is assumed to be a discrete distribution, then it can be completely estimated from the data, using similar techniques to those indicated in Section 1.8, for mixtures of Poisson distributions. We indeed propose the mixing distribution which assigns probabilities 1/14, 4/14, 4/14, 4/14, and 1/14 to the respective values 0.020, 0.103, 0.257, 0.480, and 0.823, for the probability U_i of a binomial distribution $B(U_i, n_i)$, with probability U_i and sample size n_i.

This distribution reflects the heterogenous nature of our data. Further analysis by Leonard (1984) suggests that the occupations may be clustered into three groups of four, with two outlying proportions (0.000 and 0.823), as indicated by the double lines in Figure 1.1. However, the ninth occupation might provide a further, internal outlier.

Consider next the data in Table 1.2. These were reported by Duncan (1974) and relate to a multiple-choice test covering basic mathematical skills, taken at the University of California, Davis. There were 20 items on each test, each with five alternative answers. Each student was scored correct or incorrect on each item, and the ith student therefore received a total score (X_i) out of $n = 20$ $(i = 1, ..., N)$. A binomial distribution $B(\theta_i, n)$ for X_i can only be directly justified, based upon this description, if the ith student responds to each item independently and gives a correct response, with the same probability θ_i. There were two sections of examiners, with numbers of examinees $N = 195$ and $N = 150$. The second column in the first half of Table 1.2 provides observed frequencies for Group 1 $(N = 195)$. These denote the numbers of candidates out of 195, who obtained total scores $0, 1, .., 20$. In the second half of Table 1.2, similar observed frequencies are described for Group 2 $(N = 150)$.

Table 1.2 *Duncan's multiple-choice data*

Group 1				Group 2			
Total Score	Observed Frequency	BB	EF	Total Score	Observed Frequency	BB	EF
0	0	0.0	0.0	0	0	0.0	0.0
1	0	0.0	0.0	1	0	0.0	0.0
2	0	0.1	0.1	2	1	0.1	0.0
3	0	0.2	0.3	3	0	0.2	0.3
4	1	0.6	0.7	4	0	0.6	0.7
5	0	1.5	1.6	5	1	1.3	1.4
6	4	3.0	3.1	6	3	2.5	2.6
7	5	5.3	5.3	7	7	4.3	4.4
8	9	8.5	8.4	8	3	6.8	6.7
9	14	12.4	12.2	9	8	9.8	9.5
10	16	16.7	16.3	10	10	12.9	12.6
11	24	20.7	20.4	11	18	15.8	15.5
12	21	23.6	23.5	12	22	17.9	17.8
13	23	24.7	24.9	13	17	18.6	18.8
14	23	23.6	24.1	14	25	17.8	18.1
15	18	20.3	20.9	15	14	15.3	15.8
16	18	15.5	15.9	16	6	11.8	12.1
17	11	10.1	10.2	17	7	7.8	7.9
18	7	5.4	5.2	18	5	4.3	4.1
19	0	2.1	1.9	19	2	1.7	1.5
20	1	0.5	0.4	20	1	0.4	0.3

Duncan felt that the probability θ_i of a correct response was likely to vary from item to item. He represented this variability by taking the θ_i to be independent, with each θ_i possessing a beta distribution, with positive parameters α and β, mean $\xi = \alpha/\alpha + \beta$, and variance $\xi(1 - \xi)/(\gamma + 1)$, with $\gamma = \alpha + \beta$ and probability distribution function

$$B(u) \quad = \quad p(\theta_i \le u)$$
$$= \quad \text{area to the left of } u \text{ under the density curve } b,$$

where the density b is defined by

$$b(u) = \frac{\Gamma(\alpha + \beta)}{\Gamma(\alpha)\Gamma(\beta)} u^{\alpha-1}(1 - u)^{\beta-1} \qquad (0 < u < 1),$$

with $\Gamma(\alpha)$ again denoting the Gamma function. In this case the (marginal) probability mass function of X_i assumes the form

$$p(X_i = x) = C \frac{\Gamma(\alpha + x)\Gamma(\beta + n - x)}{\Gamma(x + 1)\Gamma(n - x + 1)} \qquad (x = 0, 1, ..., n),$$

where

$$C = \frac{\Gamma(n+1)\Gamma(\alpha+\beta)}{\Gamma(\alpha)\Gamma(\beta)\Gamma(\alpha+\beta+n)}.$$

Moreover, the (marginal) mean and variance of X_i are

$$E(X_i) = n\xi,$$

and

$$Var(X_i) = n\tau\xi(1-\xi),$$

with $\xi = \alpha/(\alpha+\beta)$ and $\tau = (n+\gamma)/(1+\gamma)$. In this case X_i is said to possess a beta-binomial distribution with parameters α and β.

Duncan calculated the observed sample mean and standard deviation of the $N = 195$ scores in his first sample to be $\bar{x} = 12.56$ and $s = 3.03$. Hence, reasonable estimates $\widehat{\xi}$ and $\widehat{\tau}$ for ξ and τ satisfy

$$12.56 = 20\widehat{\xi},$$

and

$$3.03^2 = 20\widehat{\tau}\widehat{\xi}(1-\widehat{\xi}).$$

Consequently, $\widehat{\xi} = 0.628$ and $\widehat{\tau} = 1.965$. A value for $\widehat{\tau}$ close to $\widehat{\tau} = 1$ would suggest that it is reasonable to take the X_i to constitute a random sample from a binomial distribution. However, our large estimated value $\widehat{\tau} = 1.965$ for the "overdispersion factor" τ gives some indication that a beta-binomial distribution might be more appropriate. The corresponding estimates for α and β are $\widehat{\alpha} = 11.79$ and $\widehat{\beta} = 6.98$, respectively.

In the third column of Table 1.2, are the fitted frequencies for this beta-binomial model with $\alpha = \widehat{\alpha} = 11.79$ and $\beta = \widehat{\beta} = 6.98$. The entries multiply the (marginal) probability mass function for the X_i, by $n = 20$. As these fitted frequencies are very close to the observed frequencies, the beta-binomial model provides an excellent fit to the data. We therefore conclude, with some confidence, that a beta-binomial model will be more appropriate.

For the second group of students ($N = 150$), $\bar{x} = 12.51$ and $s = 3.08$, so that $\widehat{\xi} = 0.6255$, $\widehat{\tau} = 2.025$, $\widehat{\alpha} = 10.89$, and $\widehat{\beta} = 6.51$. The fitted frequencies in the third column again provide an excellent fit to the data. The alternative fitted frequencies in the fourth column of Table 1.2 are described in the next section.

1.10 The discrete exponential family of distributions

As a further generalization of the binomial distribution consider a discrete random variable X, with

$$\phi_j = p(X = j) \qquad \text{for } j = 0, 1, ..., n,$$

where $\phi_0, \phi_1, ..., \phi_n$ are strictly positive and sum to unity. This is an opportunity to consider the *multivariate logit* transformation, i.e., parameters $\gamma_0, \gamma_1, ..., \gamma_n$ satisfying,

$$\phi_j = e^{\gamma_j} / \sum_{g=0}^{n} e^{\gamma_g} \qquad (j = 0, 1, ..., n),$$

so that

$$\gamma_j = \log \phi_j + D(\boldsymbol{\gamma}) \qquad (j = 0, 1, ..., n),$$

with

$$D(\boldsymbol{\gamma}) = \log \sum_{g=0}^{n} e^{\gamma_g}.$$

Note that the γ_j adjust the $\log \phi_j$ by the term $D(\boldsymbol{\gamma})$. This extra term ensures that the ϕ_j are strictly positive, and sum to unity, whatever decimal values are assumed for the γ_j. Hsu, Leonard, and Tsui (1991) next assume that

$$\gamma_j = \log(^nC_j) + \alpha_1 j + \alpha_2 j^2 + \cdots + \alpha_q j^q$$

for some $q < n$. For example, when $q = 1$, we have $\gamma_j = \log^n C_j + \alpha_1 j$, and

$$\begin{aligned} \phi_j &= (^nC_j)e^{j\alpha_1} / \sum_{g=0}^{n} (^nC_g)e^{g\alpha_1} \qquad (j = 0, 1, ..., n) \\ &= (^nC_j)\, e^{j\alpha_1} / (1 + e^{\alpha_1})^n. \end{aligned}$$

These are just the probabilities for a binomial $B(\theta, n)$ distribution, with $\theta = e^{\alpha_1}/(1 + e^{\alpha_1})$, so that $\alpha_1 = \log\theta - \log(1 - \theta)$ denotes the logistic parameter of this distribution. For general q,

$$\phi_j = (^nC_j)\exp\{\alpha_1 j + \alpha_2 j^2 + \cdots + \alpha_q j^q - \Lambda(\boldsymbol{\alpha})\},$$

where

$$\Lambda(\boldsymbol{\alpha}) = \log \sum_{g=1}^{n} (^nC_g)\exp\{\alpha_1 g + \alpha_2 g^2 + \cdots + \alpha_q g^q\}.$$

Let $x_1, ..., x_N$ denote independent and replicated observed values of X. Then, for fixed q, $\alpha_1, ..., \alpha_q$ may be estimated by maximization of the "log-likelihood function",

$$\log \ell(\alpha_1, ..., \alpha_q | \mathbf{x}) = \sum_{i=1}^{N} \log (^nC_{x_i}) + \alpha_1 t_1 + \cdots + \alpha_q t_p - N\Lambda(\boldsymbol{\alpha}),$$

where $t_k = \sum_{i=1}^{N} x_i^k$ is to the kth sample moment. An appropriate choice of q may be obtained by choosing q to maximise Akaike's information criterion,

$$AIC = \log \ell(\widehat{\alpha}_1, ..., \widehat{\alpha}_q | \mathbf{x}) - q,$$

which penalises the log-likelihood, according to the number of parameters in the model.

For Duncan's data (see Table 1.2 of Section 1.9), AIC suggests that $q = 2$ is the best choice for both samples, this again refuting a simple binomial assumption ($q = 1$). For the first sample, the estimates $\widehat{\alpha}_1 = -17.78$ and $\widehat{\alpha}_2 = 22.94$ were obtained with associated estimated standard errors of 2.94 and 2.39. For the second example the estimates $\widehat{\alpha}_1 = -18.90$ and $\widehat{\alpha}_2 = 23.77$ were obtained, with associated estimated standard errors of 3.22 and 2.64. The corresponding fitted frequencies in the fourth column of Table 1.2, again, suggest an excellent fit to the observed data.

In Table 1.3 we describe data reported by Keats (1964) and relating to the numbers of items correctly answered by $N = 1000$ candidates, out of $n = 30$ items, in a mental theory test. In the second column are described the observed frequencies of candidates attaining the possible scores out of 30, i.e., $0, 1, ..., 30$. In this case AIC suggested $q = 5$, with $\widehat{\alpha}_1 = 48.56$, $\widehat{\alpha}_2 = 14.68$, $\widehat{\alpha}_3 = 217.30$, $\widehat{\alpha}_4 = 259.14$, and $\widehat{\alpha}_5 = 112.26$. The corresponding fitted frequencies are described in the fourth column of Table 1.3, and provide a good fit. Hsu, Leonard, and Tsui (1991) shows that this is a superior fit when compared with many competitors in the literature, including the four parameter generalisation of the beta-binomial distribution proposed by Morrison and Brockway (1979). The fitted frequencies for the Morrison-Brockway model are described in the third column of Table 1.3. Hsu, Leonard, and Tsui also analyse the Matsumura data (Table 9.2), and provide an example where $q = 3$ is appropriate.

Table 1.3 Keats' multiple choice data

Raw Score	Observed Frequency	Four-Parameter Beta-Binomial	Five-Parameter Exponential Family
0	0	0.26	0.06
1	0	0.63	0.37
2	1	1.10	1.06
3	2	1.66	2.07
4	4	2.30	3.15
5	6	3.02	4.11
6	7	3.82	4.87
7	2	4.71	5.44
8	3	5.69	5.92
9	4	6.77	6.40
10	5	7.96	6.95
11	14	9.26	7.67
12	10	10.70	8.61
13	12	12.28	9.87
14	10	14.03	11.51
15	14	15.98	13.63
16	17	18.16	16.31
17	16	20.61	19.64
18	22	23.40	23.69
19	27	26.61	28.50
20	37	30.37	34.11
21	48	34.86	40.53
22	40	40.40	47.80
23	50	47.58	56.01
24	74	57.54	65.36
25	78	72.30	76.09
26	85	94.17	88.39
27	103	121.46	101.79
28	112	139.28	113.48
29	114	119.00	114.25
30	83	54.05	82.38

1.11 Generalising the multinomial distribution

Consider observed frequencies $X_1, ..., X_k$, which are initially taken to possess an $M(\xi_1, ..., \xi_k; n)$ multinomial distribution, given cell probabilities $\xi_1, ..., \xi_k$, summing to unity, and sample size n. There are several ways of generalising this assumption, parallelling the developments in Sections 1.8 through 1.10. See also Paul and Plackett (1978). The generalisation in the present section was reported by Leonard (1973) and Leonard and Hsu (1994). Similar ideas can be used to extend the Poisson and binomial assumptions of Sections 1.8 and 1.9.

Owing to the conditioning property of Theorem 1 of Section 1.7, our multinomial frequencies $X_1, ..., X_k$ satisfy the property of basis independence; i.e., they are effectively independent, apart from the constraint that they sum to n.

Definition 1.3: $X_1, ..., X_k$ *possess the property of basis independence if they possess the joint distribution obtained by conditioning independent random variables* $X_1, ..., X_k$ *upon* $X_1 + \cdots + X_k = a$, *for some constant* a.

This property is quite restrictive (see Aitchison, 1982; 1986). Consider, for example, the data in Table 1.4, which are observational, with no random sampling at the design stage. The frequencies denote the numbers of students obtaining different grades in mathematics at a London grammar school.

Table 1.4 *Observed grade frequencies in mathematics (at a London grammar school)*

Grade	1	2	3	4	5	6	Total
Frequency	3	8	11	13	3	7	45

Intuitively, one might expect each X_i for $i = 2, 3, 4,$ and 5 to be somewhat related to the adjacent cell frequencies X_{i-1} and X_{i+1}, but less closely related to the X for nonadjacent cells. One might envision the X_i assuming some sort of "time"-dependent structure, but with "time" replaced by grade level. A more flexible sampling model may be obtained by regarding the ξ_j in our multinomial assumption for $X_1, ..., X_k$, given $\xi_1, ..., \xi_k$, as random variables, rather than fixed constants. In particular, let us reconsider the *multivariate logits*, introduced in Section 1.10. Now suppose that

$$\gamma_j = \log \xi_j + D(\gamma) \qquad (j = 1, ..., k),$$

where

$$D(\gamma) = \log \sum_{j=1}^{q} e^{\gamma_j}.$$

The following set of assumptions leads to a broad generalisation of the multinomial distribution.

Assumption 1: Conditional on the ratios $\xi_1, ..., \xi_k$, the frequencies $X_1, ..., X_k$ possess a multinomial $M(\xi_1, ..., \xi_k; n)$ distribution.

Assumption 2: The ξ_j satisfy

$$\xi_j = \exp\{\gamma_j - D(\gamma)\} \qquad (j = 1, ..., k),$$

where the γ_j are realizations of random variables G_j, and G_ℓ is normally distributed with mean μ_j and σ_j^2, for $j = 1, ..., k$.

Assumption 3: The (linear) correlation between G_j and G_ℓ is

$$corr(G_j, G_\ell) = \rho_{j\ell} \qquad (j \neq \ell).$$

Assumption 4: Any linear combination $a_1 G_1 + \cdots + a_k G_k$ of the G_j is also normally distributed (so that $G_1, ..., G_k$ are characterised to possess a "multivariate normal distribution").

We describe the consequent unconditional distribution of $X_1, ..., X_k$ as a "logistic Gaussian multinomial mixture" distribution. The correlation $\rho_{j\ell}$ permit the modelling of interdependencies between $X_1, ..., X_k$. Leonard and Hsu (1994) describe full details of a procedure for obtaining approximate maximum likelihood estimates for all parameters in this distribution. In their example they have $k = 6$, and data from 40 London high schools. In particular, their estimate of the correlation matrix of the G_j indicates moderately high correlation for the logits corresponding to adjustment cells, and negative correlations for all cells, more than two cells apart. There is therefore some indication of the time series style structure described above. Tavaré and Altham (1983) and Fingleton (1984) discuss other models for counted data involving serial and spatial correlation. The presence of such correlations can substantially reduce the actual significance of apparently significant test results.

Exercises

1.1 Show that the probabilities of the hypergeometric distribution in Property S1 satisfy the recurrence relations

$$f(x+1) = \frac{(M-x)(N-M-x)}{(x+1)(n-x+1)} f(x)$$

$$\text{for } x = x^*, ..., \min(n, M) - 1$$

with $x^* = \max(0, n + M - N)$ and $f(x^*) = {}^m C_{x^*}^{N-M} C_{n-x^*} / {}^N C_n$. Hence, calculate these probabilities when $n = 10$, $M = 10$, and $N = 20$. Find the mean and variance of this distribution.

1.2 Show that the probabilities of the binomial distribution in Property

S2 satisfy the recurrence relations

$$f(x+1) = \frac{(n-x)}{(x+1)} \frac{\theta}{(1-\theta)} f(x) \qquad \text{for } x = 0, ..., n-1$$

$$\text{with } f(0) = (1-\theta)^n.$$

1.3 Consider a group of $N = 100$ students of whom $M = 15$ study statistics. You take a random sample of size n from the group, and let X equal the number of students in the sample studying statistics. How large a sample should you take to ensure that the coefficient of variation of X is less than 0.01, if the random sampling is (a) with replacement, (b) without replacement?

1.4 Consider a machine with $n = 10$ components, each of which fails independently. Each machine fails with probability $\theta = 0.01$ and does not fail with probability $1 - \theta$. Find:

(a) the probability that no components fail;
(b) the probability that at least one component fails;
(c) the probability that exactly three components fail;
(d) the expectation and standard deviation of the number of failures.

1.5 Consider n coincidences each of which might occur during the next week. Assume that each coincidence has probability A/n of occurring, where A is constant in n, and that difference coincidences occur independently. Show that the probability that at least one of these coincidences occurs during the next week is

$$1 - \left(1 - \frac{A}{n}\right)^n$$

and show that, for $n = 10^6$, this probability is approximated by $1 - e^{-A}$.

Hint: For large n, $(1 - \frac{A}{n})^n$ is approximated by e^{-A} where $e = 1 + \frac{1}{1!} + \frac{1}{2!} + \frac{1}{3!} + \cdots$ is approximately 2.718.

1.6 You observe the number X_1, out of a random sample of size 1000, of members of the population of Great Britain, who are women, and the number X_2 out of a random sample of size 10,000 of members of the population of China, who are women. If the random sampling is with replacement, carefully discuss whether it is reasonable to take $X_1 + X_2$ to possess a binomial distribution.

1.7 For $i = 1$ and 2, let $Z_i = 1$ if my ith daughter visits me next month, and zero otherwise. Assume that $p(Z_1 = 1) = 1/2$, and $p(Z_2 = 1) = 1/3$, and that Z_1 and Z_2 occur independently. Find the probability mass function of $X = $ number of my daughters who visit me next month, and show that X does not follow a binomial distribution.

1.8 You take a random sample of size $n = 400$ from the Brazilian population, and observe that $x = 331$ members of the population are football supporters.

   (a) Find an unbiased estimate of $\theta =$ proportion of the Brazilian population who are football supporters, together with the estimated standard error of your estimate.

   (b) Find approximate 95% and 99% confidence intervals for the unknown θ.

   (c) Assume that the Brazilian footballer Pele has previously proposed the null hypothesis that $\theta = 0.90$. Do the observed data support or refute this hypothesis?

   (d) Sketch the likelihood curve of θ and interpret this curve.

1.9 Consider a homogenous Poisson process with constraint rate λ, for arrivals in $(0, \infty)$. Show that the probability of no arrivals in the interval $(0, t)$ is $e^{-\lambda t}$. Show that the probability of exactly three arrivals in the interval $(0, 1)$ is $e^{-\lambda}\lambda^3/3!$. If X is a random variable denoting the time until the first arrival, show that

$$p(X \le x) = 1 - e^{-\lambda x} \qquad (0 < x < \infty).$$

Note: X is said to possess an exponential distribution with parameter λ. The mean and standard deviation of X are both λ, and X is an example of a continuous random variable (see Section 10.1; the density is $f(x) = \lambda e^{-\lambda x}$ for $0 < x < \infty$). The interarrival times in the process are all independent, and also possess exponential distributions with parameter λ.

1.10 Let X possess a Poisson distribution, with $p(X = 0) = 0.5$. Find the mean and variance of X. Use recurrence relations to evaluate $p(X = 1), p(X = 2), ..., p(X = 5)$.

1.11 For a nonhomogenous Poisson process on (a, b), with intensity function $\lambda(t)$, the joint probability mass function/density of n the number of arrivals in the interval (a, b), together with the arrival times $x_1, ..., x_n$, is

$$p(n; x_1, ..., x_n) = \prod_{i=1}^{n} \lambda(x_i) \exp\{- \int_a^b \lambda(t)dt\},$$

where the integral expression within the exponential is the area, under the intensity function, falling between a and b. In the special case where

$$\log \lambda(t) = \beta_0 + \beta_1 t,$$

show that this expression reduces to

$$\exp\{n\beta_0 + n\beta_1\bar{x} - e^{\beta_0} \int_a^b e^{\beta_1 t} dt\}.$$

Noting that $\int_a^b e^{\beta_1 t} dt = (e^{\beta_1 b} - e^{\beta_1 a})/\beta_1$, show how this yields an analytic expression for the likelihood of β_0 and β_1.

1.12   The number of people X in a population of size $N = 100,000$, who possess a rare disease D, is taken to possess a binomial distribution, with probability 0.0001, and sample size N. Find a Poisson approximation to the distribution of X and hence approximately evaluate $p(X \leq 10)$.

1.13   Blood counts are taken in two different samples. The expectations of the blood counts in the two samples are, respectively, 10 and 20. You are now, however, informed that the total of the two blood counts is 25. Stating all assumptions made, find your new expectation and variance of the blood count for the first sample, conditional on this fresh information.

1.14   Your observed blood count in a single sample is $x = 36$. Stating all assumptions made, find an approximate 95% confidence interval for μ =expected blood count in any similar sample, and state an estimated standard error for your estimate of μ. Sketch the likelihood of μ.

1.15   Ten balls are assigned at random to four boxes B_1, B_2, B_3, B_4. The probability that any particular ball is assigned to any particular box is 0.25. Let X_1, X_2, X_3, and X_4 denote the numbers of balls, totalling to ten, which are assigned to the respective boxes. Find the joint probability mass function of $X_1, ..., X_4$, and show that this multiplies a multinomial coefficient by $1/4^{10}$. Find the distribution, mean and variance of $X_1 + X_2$.

1.16   Let X_1, X_2, X_3, and X_4 denote independent Poisson variates, each with mean 2. Find, conditional on $X_1 + X_2 + X_3 + X_4 = 10$, the joint probability mass function of X_1, X_2, X_3, and X_4.

1.17   Write an essay discussing how the more general sampling models of Sections 1.8 through 1.11 should influence a statistician's judgement when drawing conclusions from data, using simpler binomial, Poisson, and multinomial sampling models.

CHAPTER 2

Two-by-Two Contingency Tables

2.1 Conditional probability and independence

A *statistical experiment* ε is some occurrence with an uncertain outcome. The *sample space* S is the set of all possible outcomes of ε (on a single repetition of ε). An *event* A is some subset of S (subject to some mathematical regularity conditions, when S either is a subset of Euclidean space containing all decimal numbers within its boundaries or is of similar or greater complexity). We let $p(A)$ denote the probability that the outcome of ε, which actually occurs, falls in the subset A of S. Also, for any two events A and B, with $p(B) > 0$, let

$$p(A|B) = p(A \cap B)/p(B)$$

denote the conditional probability that the outcome falls in A, given that it is known to fall in B. Here $A \cap B$ represents the intersection of A and B. Furthermore, let the complement A^C consist of all outcomes in S, not in A.

Then, the events A and B are said to be *independent*, if exactly one of the following six conditions holds, in which case the other five will also hold:

$$
\begin{array}{llrcll}
I1: & \text{(a)} & p(A \cap B) & = & p(A)p(B) & \\
& \text{(b)} & p(A \cap B^C) & = & p(A)p(B^C) & \\
& \text{(c)} & p(A^C \cap B) & = & p(A^C)p(B) & \\
& \text{(d)} & p(A^C \cap B^C) & = & p(A^C)p(B^C) & \\
I2: & & p(A|B) & = & p(A|B^C) & (= p(A)) \\
I3: & & p(B|A) & = & p(B|A^C) & (= p(B)) \\
\end{array}
$$

For example, let A denote the event that Prime Minister Blair eats an egg for breakfast tomorrow and B denote the event that President Clinton eats an egg for breakfast tomorrow. You judge that $p(A) = 1/3$ and $p(B) = 1/4$. You also judge that your probability of B would be unaffected by the knowledge that A either does or does not occur. Consequently, A and B are thought to be independent, by condition $I3$. By the equivalency of our various conditions you can now, for example, calculate $p(A|B) = 1/3$, $p(A \cap B) = 1/12$, and $p(A^C \cap B^C) = 1/2$.

2.2 Independence of rows and columns

Suppose that, for individuals in a population, either A or A^C occurs and either B or B^C occurs. For example, let A denote presence of a particular disease, and let B denote presence of a particular symptom. Then the table

$$
\begin{array}{c|cc|c}
 & A & A^C & \\
B & p(A \cap B) & p(A^C \cap B) & p(B) \\
B^C & p(A \cap B^C) & p(A^C \cap B^C) & p(B^C) \\
\hline
 & p(A) & p(A^C) & 1
\end{array}
$$

represents some of the important probabilities for A and B. If these are the probabilities for individuals chosen at random from the population, then they also represent corresponding population proportions. Note that $p(B)$ and $p(B^C)$ are the row totals and $p(A)$ and $P(A^C)$, the column totals. We will use algebraic symbols to describe the probabilities in the preceding table, as represented by the entries in the following table:

$$
\begin{array}{c|cc|c}
 & A & A^C & \\
B & \xi_{11} & \xi_{12} & \xi_{1*} \\
B^C & \xi_{21} & \xi_{22} & \xi_{2*} \\
\hline
 & \xi_{*1} & \xi_{*2} & 1
\end{array}
$$

For example, $\xi_{21} = p(A \cap B^C)$ is the probability that the individual is in the $(2,1)$ cell of the table, i.e., the second row and the first column. Also, $\xi_{1*} = \xi_{11} + \xi_{12} = p(B)$ is the probability that the individual is in the first row of the table, and $\xi_{*2} = \xi_{12} + \xi_{22} = A^C$ is the probability that the individual is in the second column. If A and B are independent events, then the rows and columns of our table are also said to be independent.

If A and B are not independent, then the *row variable A* and *column variable B* are said to be *associated*. This is a *positive association* if $\theta_1 = p(A|B) > \theta_2 = p(A|B^C)$ and a *negative* association if $\theta_1 < \theta_2$. Note that $\theta_1 = \xi_{11}/\xi_{1*}$ and $\theta_2 = \xi_{21}/\xi_{2*}$. There is equivalently a positive association if $\zeta_1 = p(B|A) > \zeta_2 = p(B|A^C)$. Equivalently, $\zeta_1 = \xi_{11}/\xi_{*1}$ and $\zeta_2 = \xi_{12}/\xi_{*2}$. We remark that $p(A|B) > p(A|B^C)$ implies that $p(B|A) > p(B|A^C)$, and vice versa, a very important result in medical diagnosis.

The quantities θ_1 and θ_2 will be referred to as "the conditional probabilities given the rows" and ζ_1 and ζ_2 will be referred to as "the conditional probabilities given the columns". The six equivalent conditions of independence, of Section 2.1, may be succinctly replaced by

$I1:$ $\xi_{ij} = \xi_{i*}\xi_{*j}$ for at least one of the possible pairs (i,j),
for $i = 1,2$ and $j = 1,2$.

$I2:$ $\theta_1 = \theta_2$

$I3:$ $\zeta_1 = \zeta_2$

As an example, consider the table based upon the Mendelian theory of inheritance, and relating to a population of pea plants.

		Texture		
		Round	Wrinkled	
Colour	Yellow	9/16	3/16	3/4
	Green	3/16	1/16	1/4
		3/4	1/4	1

Each of the four interior entries of this table is the product of the corresponding row and column totals. Consequently, texture is independent of colour, by the preceding property $I1$. This incorporates $I1$(a), (b), (c), and (d), of Section 2.1. Also, $\theta_1 = \theta_2 = 3/4$ and $\zeta_1 = \zeta_2 = 3/4$. Consider, however, the table

		Disease		
		Present	Absent	
Symptom	Present	0.005	0.095	0.10
	Absent	0.005	0.895	0.90
		0.01	0.99	1

Since $\zeta_1 = 0.5 > \zeta_2 = 0.096$, the row and column variables are not independent, and there is a positive association between the symptom and the disease. Equivalently, $\theta_1 = 0.05 > \theta_2 = 0.0056$.

2.3 Investigating independence, given observational data

Suppose now that n individuals are randomly sampled, with replacement, from the population of Section 2.2. Let y_{11}, y_{12}, y_{21}, and y_{22}, respectively, denote the numbers of individuals in the sample falling in categories, $A \cap B$, $A^C \cap B$, $A \cap B^C$, and $A^C \cap B^C$. Then, these data may be arranged in the following contingency table:

	A	A^C	
B	y_{11}	y_{12}	$n_1 = y_{1*}$
B^C	y_{21}	y_{22}	$n_2 = y_{2*}$
	$m_1 = y_{*1}$	$m_2 = y_{*2}$	n

As an illustrative example, consider the table

		Disease		
		Present	Absent	
Symptom	Present	10	40	50
	Absent	10	490	500
		20	530	550

How do we now investigate the null hypothesis of independence of rows and columns, when the corresponding population proportions ξ_{ij} are unknown? Once way of describing this null hypothesis is, of course,

$$H_0 : \xi_{ij} = \xi_{i*}\xi_{*j} \quad (i = 1, 2; \ j = 1, 2),$$

where ξ_{ij} is the population proportion underlying the (i,j)th cell of our table ($i = 1, 2; \ j = 1, 2$). If H_0 is not true, then we estimate each ξ_{ij} by the corresponding $\widehat{\xi}_{ij} = p_{ij} = y_{ij}/n$. However, if H_0 is true, then we instead use $\widehat{\xi}_{ij} = p_{i*}p_{*j}$. A standard way of investigating H_0 is via the *chi-squared goodness-of-fit* statistic

$$X^2 = \sum_{i=1,2} \sum_{j=1,2} (y_{ij} - e_{ij})^2 / e_{ij}$$

where

$$
\begin{aligned}
e_{ij} &= n_i m_j / n \\
&= y_{i*} y_{*j} / n \quad (i = 1, 2; \ j = 1, 2) \\
&= n p_{i*} p_{*j}
\end{aligned}
$$

Note that the e_{ij} are the fitted values for the y_{ij}, when H_0 is true, and that

$$\frac{e_{ij}}{n} = \left(\frac{y_{i*}}{n}\right)\left(\frac{y_{*j}}{n}\right)$$

is a sensible estimate for ξ_{ij} when H_0 is true, since the two components of the product on the right-hand side estimate ξ_{i*} and ξ_{*j}, respectively. In our example, we have $e_{11} = 50 \times 20/550$, $e_{12} = 50 \times 530/550$, $e_{21} = 500 \times 20/550$, and $e_{22} = 500 \times 530/550$. This gives the following table of fitted values e_{ij}.

		Disease		
		Present	Absent	
Symptom	Present	1.818	48.182	50
	Absent	18.182	481.82	500
		20	530	550

The four components $(y_{ij} - e_{ij})^2 / e_{ij}$ of X^2 are therefore given in the table

		Disease	
		Present	Absent
Symptom	Present	36.82	1.39
	Absent	3.68	0.14

$$(X^2 = 42.03)$$

Whenever H_0 is true, the probability distribution of X^2, when n is large, is approximated by a distribution known as a "chi-squared distribution with one degree of freedom". The 95th and 99th percentiles of this distribution are 3.841 and 6.635. Whenever the observed value of X^2 satisfies $X^2 \geq$ 3.841, the chi-squared goodness-of-fit test rejects H_0: independence of rows and columns, at the 5% level of significance. If $X^2 \geq 6.635$, rejection also occurs at the 1% level of significance. In this case there is said to be "strong evidence of an association between the row and column variable". In our example, $X^2 = 42.03$ is far in excess of 6.635. There is, therefore, said to be strong evidence in the data of an association between disease and symptom.

Statistical significance tests investigate *statistical significance*. Statistical significance does not always imply significance in real-life terms. It is also important to investigate *practical significance*, which for medical data, is referred to as *clinical significance*. In our example, one way of considering practical significance is to note that the fitted values, or *fitted frequencies* e_{ij}, differ from the observed frequencies y_{ij} by quantities $y_{ij} - e_{ij}$. These equal 8.182 in magnitude for each of the four cells in our table. Indeed, moving eight individuals from the (present, present) cell to the (present, absent) cell, and eight individuals from the (absent, absent) cell to the (absent, present) cell, in our observed table, would yield a table giving a virtually perfect fit to our independence hypothesis. Therefore, out of the $n = 550$ individuals in our sample, we are only about 16 individuals away from an overprecise fit to independence. In practical terms, we need only seek an explanation for, say 10 or 12 possibly misplaced individuals out of 550. This does not seem to be a particularly extreme difference from independence, and our strongly statistically significant result should therefore be treated with considerable caution.

The independence hypothesis H_0 can also be investigated via its alternative form

$$H_0 : \theta_1 = \theta_2,$$

where

$$\theta_1 = p(A|B) = p(\text{Disease}|\text{Symptom}),$$

and

$$\theta_2 = p(A|B^C) = p(\text{Disease}|\text{No symptom}).$$

The two-sample binomial test addresses the parameter of interest $\theta_1 - \theta_2$, since H_0 can be expressed as $H_0 : \theta_1 - \theta_2 = 0$. Now $\theta_1 - \theta_2$ can be unbiasedly estimated by $q_1 - q_2$, where $q_1 = y_{11}/n_1$ and $q_2 = y_{21}/n_2$. We also refer to the pooled probability,

$$q^* = \frac{n_1 q_1 + n_2 q_2}{n_1 + n_2} = m_1/n.$$

Under H_0, the estimated standard error of $q_1 - q_2$ is

$$s_e = \sqrt{\left(\frac{1}{n_1} + \frac{1}{n_2}\right) q^*(1 - q^*)}.$$

We then refer to an approximate normal test statistic

$$Z_0 = (q_1 - q_2)/s_e.$$

In our example, we have $q_1 = 0.2$, $q_2 = 0.02$, $q^* = 0.364$ and $s_e = 0.0278$. Consequently, $Z_0 = 6.483$. Note the surprising fact that

$$X^2 = Z_0^2,$$

a result which is indeed algebraically true (Fienberg, 1987, p. 10 and Exercises 2.3 and 2.4). The (two-sided) sample binomial test for investigating the null hypothesis $H_0 : \theta_1 - \theta_2 = 0$, the alternative hypothesis $H_1 : \theta_1 - \theta_2 \neq 0$, rejects H_0 at the 5% level if $|Z_0| \geq 1.960$ and at the 1% level if $|Z_0| \geq 2.576$. The critical values 1.960 and 2.576 are, respectively, the 97.5th and 99.5th percentile of the standard normal distribution. As $|Z_0| = 6.483$ exceeds 2.576, there again appears to be overwhelmingly strong evidence to suggest an association between rows and columns.

However, $1.960^2 = 3.841$ (when the percentage points are evaluated to greater numerical accuracy) and $2.576^2 = 6.635$. Consequently, the chi-squared goodness-of-fit test, and our two-sided two-sample binomial test , will always give exactly the same answers. By interchanging rows and columns of our contingency table, and investigating the equivalent null hypothesis of independence $H_0 : \zeta_1 - \zeta_2 = 0$, it is straightforward to formulate a second two-sided two-sample binomial test, but which addresses the parameter $\zeta_1 - \zeta_2$, rather than $\theta_1 - \theta_2$. However, both two sample binomial tests will always give exactly the same answers, together with our chi-squared goodness-of-fit test. As discussed in Chapter 4, θ_1 and $1 - \theta_2$ are sometimes referred to as the *positive* and *negative predictive values*, and ζ_1 and $1 - \zeta_2$ as the *sensitivity* and *specificity*, particularly when we are evaluating a medical diagnostic procedure.

All three tests just described should be used with extreme caution, for a variety of reasons. One reason is that other test statistics can possess the same probability distributions, under H_0, when n is very large, and can yet give quite different numerical results when applied to practical data. For example, the statistic

$$X_*^2 = \sum_{i=1,2} \sum_{j=1,2} (y_{ij} - e_{ij})^2 / \max(y_{ij}, e_{ij}),$$

with $e_{ij} = n_i m_j / n$, also possesses, under H_0, a distribution, which for large enough n is "chi-squared with one degree of freedom". However, $X_*^2 \leq X^2$ always, and the differences between X_*^2 and X^2 can be quite remarkable. In our preceding symptom/disease example, we have $X_*^2 = 11.90$, compared

with $X^2 = 42.03$, substantially reducing the apparent statistical significance.

The path-breaking theorem in Section 2.4 demonstrates that the X^2 test
may not be logically founded. Owing to its equivalence with our pair of two-
sample binomial tests , the X^2 test effectively addresses the association
between rows and columns by consideration of the parameters $\theta_1 - \theta_2$ and
$\zeta_1 - \zeta_2$.

2.4 Edwards' theorem

Let us reconsider our table of population proportions from Section 2.2,

	A	A^C	
B	ξ_{11}	ξ_{12}	ξ_{1*}
B^C	ξ_{21}	ξ_{22}	ξ_{2*}
	ξ_{*1}	ξ_{*2}	1

Remembering that $\theta_i = \xi_{i1}/\xi_{i*}$ for $i = 1, 2$, and $\zeta_j = \xi_{1j}/\xi_{*j}$, for $j = 1, 2$,
we consider three propositions relating to the concept of a *measure of as-
sociation* η, that is, some single numerical value summarising the discrep-
ancies of the ξ_{ij} from the null hypothesis H_0 of independence. Here we
invoke a hidden assumption that it is appropriate to summarise these dis-
crepancies by a single measure. Without this hidden assumption, it might
be realistic to consider the *directional deviances* (Jean-Marc Bernard, personal communication):

$$\tau_{ij} = \left(\xi_{ij} - \xi_{i*}\xi_{*j} \right) / \left(\xi_{i*}\xi_{*j} \right)^{\frac{1}{2}} \qquad (i = 1, 2; \ j = 1, 2),$$

which more fully represent the three distinct parameters in the model. However, under our hidden assumption, we refer to the equivalent conditions of
I_1, I_2, and I_3, independence of rows and columns, outlined in Section 2.2.

Proposition A: η *should be some (unspecified) function $\eta = g(\theta_1, \theta_2)$ of
the conditional row probabilities θ_1 and θ_2, only.*

Proposition B: η *should be some function $\eta = h(\zeta_1, \zeta_2)$ of the conditional
column probabilities ζ_1 and ζ_2, only.*

Proposition C: *The functions g and h should be identical, i.e., $\eta =
g(\theta_1, \theta_2) = g(\zeta_1, \zeta_2)$, for some function g, not depending further upon the
ξ_{ij}.*

Proposition A says that we can measure the association between rows
and columns by comparing just θ_1 and θ_2. This appears quite reasonable
since $\theta_1 = \theta_2$ and $\zeta_1 = \zeta_2$ both give independence. Proposition B says that
we can alternatively measure the association between rows and columns
by comparing ζ_1 and ζ_2. Proposition C suggests that we should use the

same criterion, when comparing θ_1 with θ_2, as when comparing ζ_1 with ζ_2. This is again very reasonable, since we would surely wish to retain the same criterion upon interchanging rows and columns in our table. Quite remarkably, A and B together imply C, although a careful scrutiny of a proof by Antony Edwards is needed to demonstrate this.

Theorem 2.1: *(Corollary to Antony Edwards, 1963). Subject to Propositions A and B, any measure of association η must be some function of the cross-product ratio*

$$\lambda = \xi_{11}\xi_{22}/\xi_{12}\xi_{21} \ ,$$

and proposition C automatically holds.

Before examining the proof of this theorem, let us consider some of its consequences. One convenient function of λ is its natural logarithm,

$$
\begin{aligned}
\eta &= \log \lambda \\
&= \log \xi_{11} + \log \xi_{22} - \log \xi_{12} - \log \xi_{21} \\
&= \log \theta_1 - \log(1 - \theta_1) - \log \theta_2 + \log(1 - \theta_2) \\
&= \log \zeta_1 - \log(1 - \zeta_1) - \log \zeta_2 + \log(1 - \zeta_2) \\
&= \alpha_1 - \alpha_2 \\
&= \beta_1 - \beta_2 \ ,
\end{aligned}
$$

where

$$\alpha_i = \log\{\theta_i/(1 - \theta_i)\} \quad (i = 1, 2) \ ,$$

and

$$\beta_i = \log\{\zeta_i/(1 - \zeta_i)\} \quad (i = 1, 2) \ .$$

The chi-squared goodness-of-fit test of Section 2.3 does not address λ, $\log \lambda$, or any function of λ. The two-sample binomial test for comparing θ_1 with θ_2 addresses $\theta_1 - \theta_2$. However, $\theta_1 - \theta_2$ is not a function of $\alpha_1 - \alpha_2$, the difference between the logits (the logit α_i is also referred to as the *logistic* transformation of the probability θ_i, or alternatively as the *log-odds*). Consequently, this test is not consistent with our propositions. The two-sample binomial test for comparing ζ_1 with ζ_2 is similarly inconsistent with our propositions, since it addresses $\zeta_1 - \zeta_2$, which is not a function of $\beta_1 - \beta_2$. In Section 2.6, we instead describe a test which addresses $\eta = \log \lambda$, as a log-contrast of the ξ_{ij} (the above linear combination with coefficients summing to unity). This expression of our log measure of association as a log-contrast in the ξ_{ij} provides an initiative justification for the notion of log-linear models (see Chapter 7). Note that $\eta = \log \lambda = 0$ corresponds to independence, or no association, $\eta = \log \lambda > 0$ gives a positive association, and $\eta = \log \lambda < 0$ gives a negative association.

Proof of Theorem 2.1 (paralleling Edwards, 1963): Let $\theta_i = \xi_{i1}/\xi_{i*}$ for $i = 1, 2$, and $\zeta_j = \xi_{ij}/\xi_{*j}$, for $j = 1, 2$, where, for the mathematical purposes of this proof, the ξ_{ij} are nonnegative, but not necessarily constrained to sum to unity. Let Propositions A and B hold. Then,

$$
\begin{aligned}
\eta &= g(\theta_1, \theta_2) \\
&= g\left(\frac{\xi_{11}}{\xi_{11} + \xi_{12}}, \frac{\xi_{21}}{\xi_{21} + \xi_{22}}\right) \\
&= g\left(\frac{1}{1 + \xi_{12}/\xi_{11}}, \frac{1}{1 + \xi_{22}/\xi_{21}}\right) \\
&= f(\xi_{12}/\xi_{11}, \xi_{22}/\xi_{21}),
\end{aligned}
$$

where

$$
f^*(x, y) = g\left(\frac{1}{1+x}, \frac{1}{1+y}\right).
$$

This quantity is unaffected by multiplying both ξ_{22} and ξ_{21} by any positive factor K.

Furthermore

$$
\begin{aligned}
\eta &= h(\zeta_1, \zeta_2) \\
&= h\left(\frac{\xi_{11}}{\xi_{11} + \xi_{21}}, \frac{\xi_{12}}{\xi_{12} + \xi_{22}}\right) \\
&= f(\xi_{21}/\xi_{11}, \xi_{22}/\xi_{12}),
\end{aligned}
$$

where

$$
f^*(x, y) = h\left(\frac{1}{1+x}, \frac{1}{1+y}\right).
$$

Multiplying ξ_{22} and ξ_{21} by any positive factor K tells us that

$$
\begin{aligned}
\eta &= f(\xi_{12}/\xi_{11}, \xi_{22}/\xi_{21}) \\
&= f^*(K\xi_{21}/\xi_{11}, K\xi_{22}/\xi_{12}).
\end{aligned}
$$

This can only occur, for all positive K, if η is a function of the ratio of ξ_{22}/ξ_{12} and ξ_{21}/ξ_{11} only, i.e., if η is a function of $\lambda = \xi_{11}\xi_{22}/\xi_{12}\xi_{22}$ only. [In general, if $f^*(x, y)$ is a function of positive arguments x and y which is unchanged by multiplying x and y by any positive K, then $f^*(x, y)$ must be representable as a function of x/y alone.] Since $\lambda = \{\theta_1/(1 - \theta_1)\}/\{\theta_2/(1 - \theta_2)\} = \{\zeta_1/(1 - \zeta_1)\}/\{\zeta_2/(1 - \zeta_2)\}$, proposition C immediately holds. Q.E.D.

Edwards' remarkably simple proof is the basis for a logical approach to contingency table analysis, based upon the dual concepts of measures of association and log-linear models. When developing appropriate statistical procedures, a general result for log-contrasts of multinomial cell frequencies is required.

2.5 Log-contrasts and the multinomial distribution

Consider the situation introduced in Section 1.7, where frequencies $X_1, ..., X_k$, possess a multinomial distribution with k cells, strictly positive cell probabilities $\xi_1, ..., \xi_k$, summing to unity, and sample size n, i.e.,

$$X_1, ..., X_k \sim M(\xi_1, ..., \xi_k; n).$$

Consider for example, a population partitioned into k subpopulations $A_1, A_2, .., A_k$, with proportions $\xi_1, ..., \xi_k$ of the population belonging to the corresponding subpopulations. We then choose n individuals at random, with replacement, from the population, and let $X_1, ..., X_k$ denote the numbers of individuals in the sample, who have been selected from $A_1, A_2, ..., A_k$, respectively. Then, $X_1, ..., X_k$ will follow our multinomial distribution exactly. If instead, the random sampling is without replacement, our multinomial distribution can provide an excellent approximation, but only if the population size is large compared with the sample size n.

Consider the log-contrast

$$\eta = \sum_{i=1}^{k} a_i \log \xi_i \;,$$

where the a_i are fixed specified values, not depending upon the ξ_i, and satisfying $a_1 + a_2 + \cdots + a_k = 0$. Consider the corresponding log-contrast

$$U = \sum_{i=1}^{k} a_i \log X_i,$$

but calculated in terms of the cell frequencies $X_1, ..., X_k$. We also refer to the random variable

$$V = \sum_{i=1}^{k} a_i^2 X_i^{-1},$$

which should be interpreted as an estimator of the variance of U. Then, the standardized variate

$$W = (U - \eta)/V^{\frac{1}{2}}$$

possesses a distribution, which is approximately standard normal, when n is large. This key result can be stated with complete mathematical precision, in the sense that, as $n \to \infty$, with $\xi_1, ..., \xi_k$, and k fixed, W converges in distribution to a standard normal variate (i.e., the cumulative distribution function of W converges pointwise to the standard normal distribution function).

In the more realistic situation where n is finite, suppose also that $\xi_1, ..., \xi_k$ are unknown, and that numerical values $x_1, ..., x_k$ are observed for $X_1, ..., X_k$. Then, one consequence of our approximate standard normal distribution for W, is that an approximate 95% confidence interval for η is

$$(u - 1.96v^{\frac{1}{2}}, u + 1.96v^{\frac{1}{2}}),$$

where $u = \sum a_i \log x_i$, and $v = \sum a_i^2 x_i^{-1}$. Furthermore, an approximately normal test statistic for investigating $H_0 : \eta = 0$ versus $H_1 : \eta \neq 0$ is $z_0 = u/v^{\frac{1}{2}}$, and tests of size 5% and 1% compare $|z_0|$ with 1.960 and 2.576, respectively.

The above-stated normal approximation to the distribution of W promises much greater accuracy than the types of normal approximations to cell frequencies which underpin chi-squared goodness-of-fit and two-sample binomial tests. For example, a log transformation is employed, together with a denominator $V^{\frac{1}{2}}$ which depends upon the X_i. See Efron and Hinkley (1978) for a discussion of some related approximations. Indeed complex calculations by Leonard, Hsu, and Tsui (1989), and others, suggest that the preceding confidence intervals and significance tests will give adequate accuracy if $x_i \geq 5$, for $i = 1, ..., k$.

Consider an example where $k = 3$, $a_i = 1$, $a_2 = -1/2$, $a_3 = -1/2$ and $n = 45$, so that

$$\eta = \log\{\xi_1/(\xi_2\xi_3)^{\frac{1}{2}}\}.$$

Suppose that we observe $x_1 = 20$, $x_2 = 5$, and $x_3 = 20$. Then $u = \log 2, v = 9/80$. Consequently, our approximate 95% confidence interval for η is $0.693 \pm 1.96 \times 0.335 = (0.036, 1.351)$, and our normal test statistic for investigating $H_0 : \xi_1 = (\xi_2\xi_3)^{\frac{1}{2}}$ versus $H_1 : \xi_1 \neq (\xi_2\xi_3)^{\frac{1}{2}}$ is $0.693/0.335 = 2.067$.

2.6 The log-measure-of-association test

Consider the situation and notation described in Section 2.3, where the overall total n is fixed. Assume that, for $i = 1, 2$ and $j = 1, 2$, the y_{ij} are regarded as the numerical realizations of random variables Y_{ij}, summing to n. Suppose, further, that it is regarded as appropriate to make the assumption

$$Y_{11}, Y_{12}, Y_{21}, Y_{22} \sim M(\xi_{11}, \xi_{12}, \xi_{21}, \xi_{22}; n),$$

where the ξ_{ij} are the corresponding unconditional cell probabilities, summing to unity, and all strictly positive. For example, n individuals might be randomly sampled from a much larger population, and then categorised into a two by two table, according to the presence or absence of factors A and B. In this situation we have a *single multinomial model*.

Now consider the log measure of association, as justified in Section 2.4,

$$\eta = \log \xi_{11} + \log \xi_{22} - \log \xi_{12} - \log \xi_{21}.$$

Applying the main results of Section 2.5, let

$$U = \log Y_{11} + \log Y_{22} - \log Y_{12} - \log Y_{21},$$

and

$$V = Y_{11}^{-1} + Y_{22}^{-1} + Y_{12}^{-1} + Y_{21}^{-1}.$$

Then, the standardized variate,

$$W = (U - \eta)/V^{\frac{1}{2}},$$

possesses a distribution which is approximately standard normal, when n is large. Consequently, under $H_0 : \eta = 0$ (independence of rows and columns), the random variable

$$B = U/V^{\frac{1}{2}}$$

approximately possesses a standard normal distribution, and the test statistic

$$
\begin{aligned}
B^2 &= U^2/V \\
&= \frac{(\log Y_{11} + \log Y_{22} - \log Y_{12} - \log Y_{21})^2}{Y_{11}^{-1} + Y_{22}^{-1} + Y_{12}^{-1} + Y_{21}^{-1}}
\end{aligned}
$$

approximately possesses a , with one degree of freedom. In the numerical example of Section 2.3 ($y_{11} = 10, y_{12} = 40, y_{21} = 10, y_{22} = 490$), the numerical realization of U is the natural logarithm,

$$
\begin{aligned}
u &= \log\left(\frac{10 \times 490}{10 \times 40}\right) \\
&= \log(12.25) \\
&= 2.506.
\end{aligned}
$$

As u is positive, the data indicate a possible positive association between rows and columns. The numerical realization of V is the estimated variance

$$v = 10^{-1} + 490^{-1} + 40^{-1} + 10^{-1} = 0.2270.$$

Therefore, the numerical realization of our B^2 statistic is

$$b^2 = u^2/v = 27.65.$$

This provides the alternative we recommend to the chi-squared goodness-of-fit statistic X^2. Again, b^2 should be compared with the 95th percentiles, 3.841 and 99th percentile 6.635 of the chi-squared distribution with one degree of freedom. The statistical significance can be more precisely judged via the approximate significance probability,

$$\alpha_p = 2\{1 - \Phi(|b|)\},$$

where $b = u/v^{\frac{1}{2}}$ and Φ denotes the cumulative distribution function of the standard normal distribution (calculate using the Splus command *pnorm*; for example, the command *pnorm (5.258)* gives output 0.9999999). In our example, $b = 5.258$, so that u falls over five standard errors above zero, and α_p is virtually zero, again a very strongly statistically significant result.

An advantage of the log-measure-of-association approach, when compared with many other procedures for investigating independence of rows and columns, lies in the availability of appropriate confidence intervals for η and the cross-product ratio $\lambda = e^\eta = \xi_{11}\xi_{22}/\xi_{12}\xi_{21}$. An approximate 95% confidence interval for η is

$$(u - 1.96v^{\frac{1}{2}}, u + 1.96v^{\frac{1}{2}}) = (1.572, 3.439).$$

Taking exponentials of both limits, we find that a 95% confidence interval for λ is (4.81, 31.17). The width of the confidence interval can also be used to judge practical significance in cases where the point estimate for $\widehat{\lambda} = y_{11}y_{22}/y_{12}y_{21}$ for λ satisfies $\lambda > 1$. In our example, $\lambda = 12.25$, while the independence hypothesis corresponds to $\lambda = 1$. However, as the confidence interval for λ is quite wide, this suggests that the information in the data regarding λ is not particularly precise. Therefore, the immense statistical significance of our association between rows and columns should be somewhat down-weighted (if $\widehat{\lambda} < 1$, the width of the corresponding confidence interval for λ^{-1} should instead be considered. Remember that λ^{-1} is the measure of association for the same table, but with rows or columns reversed). The results indeed suggest that further data should be collected, to confirm the association. This would be particularly important if there were any doubt concerning the reasonability of our underlying multinomial assumption. In general, it is quite important to try to replicate the experiment, i.e., to try to repeat similar results under similar conditions. If our experiment involves random sampling, replications can protect against an unlucky randomization, e.g., all members of our sample happening by chance to belong to a particular ethnic or age group.

The above results can also be interpreted via the 95% interval (2.19, 5.58) for the ratio $\lambda^{\frac{1}{2}}$ of the geometric means $(\xi_{11}\xi_{22})^{\frac{1}{2}}$ and $(\xi_{12}\xi_{21})^{\frac{1}{2}}$. Our above numerical results are available from our Splus function *prog1*, which can also be applied more generally to an $r \times s$ table. The command *prog1( )* on Splus creates requests for the numbers of rows (r) and columns (s). On entering $r = 2$ and $s = 2$, you are required to enter your table row by row. The output of prog1 includes a statement of all the prog1 main results you need, including the observed log measure of association, its estimated standard error, the observed measure of association 95% and 99% confidence intervals for the cross-product ratio measure of association, the values of b^2, X^2, and the likelihood ratio statistic (LRS):

$$\text{LRS} = 2\sum_{ij} y_{ij}\log(y_{ij}/e_{ij}),$$

where $e_{ij} = n_i m_j / n$. In our example LRS = 23.75, comparing with the values $b^2 = 27.65$, $X^2 = 42.03$, and $X_*^2 = 11.90$ (see Section 2.3). The LRS is quite appealing and not obviously inconsistent with Edwards' theorem.

Clearly, this methodology does not work well if one of the cell frequencies is zero, and it is less likely to be accurate if one of the cell frequencies is less than five. If all of the cell frequencies are small, then attention should be confined to Fisher's exact test (see Section 2.9), but with grave concern regarding potential practical significance. However, a number of *ad hoc* devices are available which permit a modification to the log-measure-of-association test, in situations where one cell frequency is small, and the remainder are moderate to large. For example, each of the log y_{ij}, in the calculation of b, may be replaced by

$$\log(y_{ij} + \tfrac{1}{2}) - 3/2(y_{ij} + \tfrac{1}{2}),$$

and each of the y_{ij}^{-1}, in the calculation of v, may be replaced by $(y_{ij} + 1/2)^{-1}$. The option for this adjustment is made available during our prog1 input.

2.7 The product binomial model

Suppose that n_1 individuals are chosen from category B, e.g., patients receiving a new drug, and n_2 individuals are chosen from category B^C, e.g., patients receiving a placebo. Let y_{11} denote the number of individuals in B who also fall in category A, e.g., those patients who recover, and let y_{21} denote the number of individuals in B^C who also fall in A. Then the data can be arranged in a 2×2 contingency table, but now with both row totals, n_1 and n_2, fixed.

	A	A^C	
B	y_{11}	$y_{12} = n_1 - y_{11}$	n_1
B^C	y_{21}	$y_{22} = n_2 - y_{21}$	n_2

The *product binomial model* regards y_{11} and y_{21} as realizations of independent random variables Y_{11} and Y_{21}, with

$$Y_{i1} \sim B(\theta_i, n_i) \quad (i = 1, 2).$$

The parameters θ_1 and θ_2 are again the "conditional row probabilities" and the only meaningful probabilities in the model, if n_1 and n_2 are indeed fixed in advance. The product binomial assumption, could, with considerable caution, be made subjectively. It, however, particularly relates to the following two situations:

(A) There are two populations B and B^C with population sizes much larger than n_1 and n_2, respectively. Random samples without replacement are taken from the two populations, separately. Proportions θ_1

and θ_2, of populations B and B^C, possess some characteristic A, and y_{11} out of n_1, and y_{21} out of n_2, members, of the respective samples, possess characteristic A.

(B) The overall total $n = n_1 + n_2$ only is fixed, and the single multinomial model

$$Y_{11}, Y_{21}, Y_{21}, Y_{22} \sim M(\xi_{11}, \xi_{12}, \xi_{21}, \xi_{22}; n)$$

is thought to hold. Then, conditional on

$$Y_{11} + Y_{12} = n_1$$

and

$$Y_{21} + Y_{22} = n_2,$$

probability theory tells us that our product binomial model holds, with

$$\theta_1 = \xi_{11}/(\xi_{11} + \xi_{12})$$

and

$$\theta_2 = \xi_{21}/(\xi_{21} + \xi_{22}).$$

Property (B) tells us that even if n only is fixed in advance, we can still analyse our results as if both n_1 and n_2 were fixed. We might wish to do this in situations where the conditional row probabilities $\theta_1 = p(A|B)$ and $\theta_2 = p(A|B^C)$ are of primary interest, together with the independence hypothesis, $\theta_1 = \theta_2$.

As an example of this conditioning result, when the ξ_{ij} are specified, consider the Mendelian hypothesis where

$$Y_{11}, Y_{12}, Y_{21}, Y_{22} \sim M\left(\frac{9}{16}, \frac{3}{16}, \frac{3}{16}, \frac{1}{16}; n\right).$$

Then, conditional on fixing the row totals, n_1 and n_2, it follows that Y_{11} and Y_{21} are independent, and possess binomial $B(3/4, n_1)$ and $B(3/4, n_2)$ distributions, respectively. Nevertheless, in some situations n_1 and n_2 are genuinely fixed in advance. Consider, for example, the following data on cases and controls, reported by Breslow and Day (1980).

| | Alcohol Consumption | | |
	≥ 80 grams/day	< 80 grams/day	Total
Cancer cases	96	104	200
Controls (cancer free)	109	666	775

Under our product binomial model, we are interested in checking whether the first conditional row proportion $96/200 = 0.480$ is indeed significantly different from the second conditional row proportion $109/775 = 0.141$ and in investigating the measure of association between these variables. Note that, if $H_0 : \theta_1 = \theta_2$ is not known to be true, then we would estimate each θ_i by the corresponding $\widehat{\theta}_i = q_i = y_{i1}/n_i$. However, under $H_0 : \theta_1 = \theta_2$, we would instead use $\widehat{\theta}_i = q^* = m_1/n$, where $m_1 = y_{1*}$ and $n = y_{**}$. We refer to the following approximations for binomial logits and their differences. These are special cases/extensions of the results for log-contrasts, as described in the multinomial situation of Section 2.5.

Normal Approximations for Binomial Logits: Under the above product binomial model, with n_1 and n_2 fixed, let

$$
\begin{aligned}
U_i &= \log(Y_{i1}/(n_i - Y_{i1})), \\
V_i &= Y_{i1}^{-1} + (n_i - Y_{i1})^{-1},
\end{aligned}
$$

and

$$\alpha_i = \log\theta_i - \log(1 - \theta_i), \text{ for } i = 1, 2.$$

Then, when n_i is large, the distributions of

$$(U_i - \alpha_i)/V_i^{\frac{1}{2}}$$

are approximately standard normal, for $i = 1, 2$. When both n_1 and n_2 are large, the distribution of

$$(U - \eta)/V^{\frac{1}{2}}$$

is approximately standard normal, where

$$
\begin{aligned}
\eta &= \alpha_1 - \alpha_2, \\
U &= U_1 - U_2,
\end{aligned}
$$

and

$$V = V_1 + V_2.$$

Let u_i, v_i, u, and v denote the observed values of U_i, V_i, U, and V, respectively. Then the preceding results tell us that:

(a) u_1 and u_2 are point estimates of the logits α_1 and α_2, with respective estimated standard errors $v_1^{\frac{1}{2}}$ and $v_2^{\frac{1}{2}}$. In our numerical example we have

$$
\begin{aligned}
u_1 &= \log(96/104) = -0.080, \\
u_2 &= \log(109/666) = -1.810, \\
v_1 &= 0.020, v_1^{\frac{1}{2}} = 0.142, \\
v_2 &= 0.011, v_2^{\frac{1}{2}} = 0.103.
\end{aligned}
$$

Then $u_i \pm 1.960 \, v_i^{\frac{1}{2}}$ is an appropriate 95% confidence interval for α_i for $i = 1, 2$.

(b) $u = u_1 - u_2$ is a point estimate for the measure of association η with estimated standard error $v^{\frac{1}{2}} = (v_1 + v_2)^{\frac{1}{2}}$. In our example $u_1 - u_2 = 1.730$, $v = 0.031$, and $v^{\frac{1}{2}} = 0.175$.

(c) $u \pm 1.960 v^{\frac{1}{2}}$ is an approximate 95% confidence interval for the measure of association η. In our example, this interval is $(1.387, 2.073)$. Taking exponentials, we find that the corresponding interval for the cross-product ratio $\lambda = e^{\eta} = \theta_1(1 - \theta_2)/\theta_2(1 - \theta_1)$ is $(4.001, 7.952)$. Therefore, even with these moderately large sample sizes, the data do not contain precise information about λ, as our confidence interval is still quite wide. The interval, of course, contains the point estimate $\widehat{\lambda} = y_{11}(n_2 - y_{21})/y_{21}(n_1 - y_{11}) = 96 \times 666/109 \times 104 = 5.640$. However, the value $\lambda = 1$, corresponding to our independence hypothesis, is well outside this interval.

(d) The independence hypothesis, $H_0 : \eta = 0$ or $\lambda = 1$, may be tested by reference to the approximate normal statistic $b = u/v^{\frac{1}{2}}$, or by comparing $b^2 = u^2/v$ with the chi-squared values 3.841 and 6.635. In our example, $b = 9.87$ and $b^2 = 97.45$, strongly refuting H_0. The significance probability $\alpha_p = 2(1 - \Phi|b|)$ is again virtually zero.

In this example, the fitted cell frequencies under independence differ by ± 54 from the observed frequencies. We conclude that the increase in alcohol consumption with the occurrence of cancer is of immense practical and clinical, as well as statistical, significance. This presumes that the product binomial assumption can be justified at the design stage, e.g., by appropriate random sampling, and that the population of controls is chosen in a fair and meaningful way.

Equivalence of Procedures: Observe that, with reference to our estimates, standard errors, confidence intervals, and tests, for the measures of association η and $\lambda = e^{\eta}$, we have obtained exactly the same results, both algebraically and numerically, for the product binomial model, as those described in Section 2.6, for the single multinomial model. It therefore does not really matter, for the purposes of an association analysis, whether or not we regard the row totals as fixed. We might base this choice upon our specific parameters of interest, i.e., whether we wish to parameterise our model by the conditional probabilities θ_1 and θ_2, or by the unconditional probabilities $\xi_{11}, \xi_{12}, \xi_{21}$, and ξ_{22}.

2.8 The independent Poisson model

Suppose that we observe $n = 113$ cars entering the Channel Tunnel during a particular 5-minute period, and record whether or not each car is red, and whether or not each car is British. Suppose that our aggregate data are recorded as follows

	Red	Not Red	
British	31	32	63
Not British	20	30	50
	51	63	113

Denote the cell frequencies, as before, by y_{ij}, for $i = 1, 2$ and $j = 1, 2$, and let the y_{ij} be numerical realizations of random variables Y_{ij}. Then, the independent Poisson model is defined by taking Y_{11}, Y_{12}, Y_{21}, and Y_{22} to be independent and Poisson distributed, with respective means, say, $\mu_{11}, \mu_{12}, \mu_{21}$, and μ_{22}.

This model would be precisely justified if the cars in the four categories were known to arrive according to four independent Poisson processes, with possibly different, and possibly time-varying, intensity functions. This is a consequence of the developments in Section 1.4 and the fact that the number of arrivals in any particular interval, for a possibly time-varying Poisson process, is Poisson distributed.

Under these assumptions, the row totals $Y_{i*} = Y_{i1} + Y_{i2}$ are independent and Poisson distributed with means $\mu_{i*} = \mu_{i1} + \mu_{i2}$, for $i = 1, 2$. Furthermore, the column totals $Y_{*j} = Y_{1j} + Y_{2j}$ are independent and Poisson distributed, with means $\mu_{*j} = \mu_{1j} + \mu_{2j}$, for $j = 1, 2$. Finally, the overall total $N = Y_{**}$ is Poisson distributed with mean $\mu_{**} = \mu_{11} + \mu_{12} + \mu_{21} + \mu_{22}$. Consequently, none of the totals in this table is fixed.

Definition 2.1 *The row variable and column variable are said to be independent (i.e., there is no association between the row and column variables) if*

$$\mu_{ij} = \mu_{i*}\mu_{*j}/\mu_{**} \quad (i = 1, 2).$$

Lemma 2.1 *The row and column variables are independent if, and only if, the measure of association*

$$\lambda = \mu_{11}\mu_{22}/\mu_{12}\mu_{21}$$

is equal to unity.

Under $H_0 : \lambda = 1$, we would estimate each μ_{ij} by the corresponding $\widehat{\mu}_{ij} = y_{i*}y_{*j}/y_{**}$. If H_0 is not known to be true, we would instead use $\mu_{ij} = y_{ij}$. We can investigate H_0, under our independent Poisson model, by considering the log measure of association

$$\eta = \gamma_{11} + \gamma_{22} - \gamma_{12} - \gamma_{21},$$

where

$$\gamma_{ij} = \log \mu_{ij} \quad (i = 1, 2; \ j = 1, 2).$$

If each of the μ_{ij} is greater than five, the distribution of

$$Y_{ij}^{\frac{1}{2}} (\log Y_{ij} - \gamma_{ij})$$

may be taken to be approximately standard normal. Therefore, an approximate 95% confidence interval for γ_{ij} is

$$(\log y_{ij} - 1.960 y_{ij}^{-\frac{1}{2}}, \log y_{ij} + 1.960 y_{ij}^{-\frac{1}{2}}).$$

It is also a consequence of the current normal approximation that all the methodology in Section 2.6 for investigating $H_0 : \eta = 0$ in the single multinomial case, and based upon the definitions of

$$U = \log Y_{11} + \log Y_{22} - \log Y_{12} - \log Y_{21}$$

and

$$V = Y_{11}^{-1} + Y_{22}^{-1} + Y_{12}^{-1} + Y_{21}^{-1},$$

becomes applicable to our current situation. The methodology, however, now becomes appropriate as the μ_{ij} increase in magnitude, rather than as n gets large. In particular, $W = (V - \eta)/V^{\frac{1}{2}}$ still possesses an approximate standard normal distribution, $B^2 = U^2/V$ is still approximately chi-squared distributed, under H_0, with one degree of freedom, an approximate 95% confidence interval for η is $u \pm 1.96 \, v^{\frac{1}{2}}$, where u and v represent the observed U and V, and prog1 can be applied in exactly the same way as before.

In the preceding numerical example (British and red cars),

$$
\begin{aligned}
u &= \log(31 \times 30/20 \times 32) \\
&= \log(1.453) \\
&= 0.374,
\end{aligned}
$$

$v = 0.147$, and $v^{\frac{1}{2}} = 0.383$. Consequently, $b = 0.975$ and the significance probability of our test for $H_0 : \eta = 0$, against a general alternative is

$$
\begin{aligned}
\alpha_p &= 2(1 - \Phi(0.975)) \\
&= 0.330.
\end{aligned}
$$

Also, $b^2 = 0.951$ is less than d.f. $= 1$, the approximate expectation of B^2, if H_0 is true. The data possess insufficient evidence to suggest that British cars are more likely to be red.

The precise agreement of our procedures under the single multinomial model, the product binomial model, and now the independent Poisson model, suggests that it really does not matter whether we regard only the overall total as fixed, no totals as fixed, just the row totals as fixed, or, indeed (another product binomial model is available by conditioning on the columns), just the column totals as fixed. These properties are not surprising, given the following correspondences between the models (see Theorem 1.1 and Corollary 1.1, of Section 1.7):

(A) If the Poisson model holds, with cell means $\mu_{11}, \mu_{12}, \mu_{21}$, and μ_{22}, then conditioning the Y_{ij} upon fixed row totals $Y_{i*} = n_i$, for $i = 1, 2$, gives the product binomial model, with parameters θ_1 and θ_2, where

$$\theta_i = \mu_{i1}/\mu_{i*} \quad (i = 1, 2).$$

If we, instead, condition the Y_{ij} upon fixed column totals $Y_{*j} = m_j$, for $j = 1, 2$, then we get an alternative product binomial model, where Y_{11} and Y_{12} are conditionally independent, with

$$Y_{1j} \sim B(\zeta_j, m_j) \quad (j = 1, 2)$$

and

$$\zeta_j = \mu_{1j}/\mu_{*j} \quad (j = 1, 2).$$

If we, instead, condition on a fixed overall total $N = Y_{**} = n$, then we get our single multinomial model, with unconditional cell probabilities satisfying

$$\xi_{ij} = \mu_{ij}/\mu_{**} \quad (i = 1, 2; j = 1, 2).$$

(B) If the single multinomial model, with unconditional cell probabilities $\xi_{11}, \xi_{12}, \xi_{21}$, and ξ_{22}, is appropriate, then conditioning on the row totals gives the product binomial model of Section 2.7, with

$$\theta_i = \xi_{i1}/\xi_{i*} \quad (i = 1, 2).$$

If we, instead, condition on the column totals, then we get the alternative product binomial model, with

$$\zeta_j = \xi_{1j}/\xi_{*j} \quad (j = 1, 2).$$

As an example of (A), suppose that the cars in our four categories are all thought to enter the Channel Tunnel at the same rate of 30 per minute. Therefore, Y_{11}, the number of red British cars, has a Poisson distribution with mean and variance both equal to 30. We are now, however, informed that exactly $n_1 = 70$ British cars entered the tunnel during this period. Conditioning on this information, we find that our new distribution for Y_{11} is $B(0.5, 70)$, so that Y_{11} now has conditional mean 35 and variance 17.5. If we were instead informed that a total of $n = 150$ cars entered the tunnel, then the four cell frequencies would possess a conditional distribution which is multinomial $M(0.25, 0.25, 0.25, 0.25; 150)$. Therefore, Y_{11} would instead be $B(0.25, 150)$ distributed, with mean 37.5 and variance 28.125.

As an example of (B) consider the ξ_{ij} represented in the table

		Eye Colour		
		Blue	Not Blue	
Hair colour	Blonde	1/2	1/2	7/12
	Not Blonde	1/6	1/4	5/12
		2/3	1/3	1

Then, under our multinomial assumptions, with $n = 100$, say,

$$Y_{11} = \text{ number of individuals in sample with}$$
$$\text{blue eyes and blonde hair}$$
$$\sim \ B(1/2, 100),$$

and

$$Y_{21} = \text{ number of individuals in sample with}$$
$$\text{blue eyes, but not blonde hair}$$
$$\sim \ B(1/6, 100),$$

but Y_{11} and Y_{21} are not independent. We are, however, now informed that $n_1 =$ number of individuals in sample with blonde hair $= 70$, so that $n_2 = 30$. Conditionally on this new information, Y_{11} and Y_{21} become independent, with $Y_{11} \sim B(6/7, 70)$, and $Y_{21} \sim B(2/5, 30)$. If we are instead informed that $m_1 =$ number of people in sample with blue eyes $= 60$, then Y_{11} and Y_{21} become independent, with $Y_{11} \sim B(3/4, 60)$, and $Y_{21} \sim B(1/4, 60)$.

Consider now Mendel's pea-breeding data (e.g., Fisher, 1936, Leonard; 1977b) for peas from $n = 556$ plants

		Texture		
		Round	Wrinkled	
Colour	Yellow	315	101	416
	Green	108	32	140
		423	133	556

The following two hypotheses are worthy of consideration. Note that H_0 is implied by H_0^*.

H_0 : No association between the row and column variables
H_0^* : The unconditional cell probabilities satisfy

$$\xi_{11} = 9/16, \ \xi_{12} = 3/16, \ \xi_{21} = 3/16, \ \text{and} \ \xi_{22} = 1/16.$$

Our function prog1 can be used to test H_0 against a general alternative. This gives $b^2 = 0.116$ with one degree of freedom, and a significance probability of 73.31%, e.g., under our independent Poisson assumptions. However, our fitted values under H_0 are (316.49, 99.51, 106.51 and 33.49); these are suspiciously close to the observed data. The corresponding fitted cell probabilities (e.g., $\widehat{\xi}_{11} = 316.49/556 = 0.569$) are only slightly different from their values under H_0^* (e.g., $\widehat{\xi}_{11} = 9/16 = 0.5625$).

We now develop a test for H_0^*, against a general alternative; under our independent Poisson model, consider, in general, the statistic,

$$B_*^2 = \sum_{i=1}^{2} \sum_{j=1}^{2} Y_{ij} [\log(Y_{ij}/e_{ij})]^2,$$

where the $e_{ij} \geq 5$ are completely specified. Under $\widetilde{H}_0 : \mu_{ij} = e_{ij}$ ($i = 1, 2; j = 1, 2$) the distribution of B_*^2 will be approximately chi-squared with four degrees of freedom. However, under $H_0^\dagger : \mu_{ij} = K\xi_{ij}$ ($i = 1, 2; j = 1, 2$), where the ξ_{ij} are completely specified, and sum to unity, the distribution of B_*^2, with $e_{ij} = N\xi_{ij}$, where $N = Y_{**}$, is approximately chi-squared, under H_0^*, with three degrees of freedom.

Multiplying each ξ_{ij} by $n = 556$ gives our appropriate e_{ij}. Our observed test statistic on three degrees of freedom is therefore

$$
\begin{aligned}
b_*^2 &= 315[\log(315/312.75)]^2 \\
&\quad + 101[\log(101/104.25)]^2 \\
&\quad + 108[\log(108/104.25)]^2 \\
&\quad + 32[\log(32/34.75)]^2 \\
&= 0.470.
\end{aligned}
$$

This yields a significance probability of 92.54%. Fisher (1936) noticed similarly high significance probabilities for several tables of this type, originally reported by Mendel. He concluded that it would be extremely unlikely to observe statistical results so close to the Mendelian hypothesis, if this hypothesis were assumed true and standard sampling assumptions made. The data were quite possibly collected, by Mendel's monks, in a manner which was biased towards the null hypothesis.

2.9 Fisher's exact test

Fisher's "exact" test can also be used to investigate the association in a 2×2 table. It is, however, only really exact in the unusual situation where all marginal totals (the row totals n_1 and n_2 and the column totals m_1 and m_2) are regarded as fixed. In this case, it is, of course, enough to describe the conditional distribution of Y_{11}, given the fixed totals, since $Y_{12} = n_1 - Y_{11}$, $Y_{21} = m_1 - Y_{11}$, and $Y_{22} = n_2 - m_1 + Y_{11}$.

The following results are consequences of either our single multinomial model, our two product binomial models, or our independent Poisson model.

In any of these four cases, conditioning on fixed marginal totals $n_1, n_2, m_1,$ and m_2, together with $H_0 : \eta = 0$, gives a hypergeometric $H(n_1, m_1, n)$ distribution for Y_{11}, with probabilities

$$p(Y_{11} = y) = (^{n_1}C_y)(^{n_2}C_{m_1-y})/(^nC_{m_1}),$$

for $y = \max(0, m_1 - n_2), ..., \min(n_1, m_1)$. As an example, consider the table

	Nosebleed	Other	
Drug	y	$5-y$	5
Placebo	$5-y$	y	5
	5	5	10

Then,

$$
\begin{aligned}
p(Y_{11} = y) &= \left(^5C_y\right)\left(^5C_{5-y}\right)/\left(^{10}C_5\right) \\
&= \left(^5C_y\right)^2/\left(^{10}C_5\right) \quad (y = 0, 1, ..., 5).
\end{aligned}
$$

This probability mass function is described in the following table $\left(^{10}C_5 = 252\right)$.

y	0	1	2	3	4	5
$252p(Y_{11} = y)$	1	25	100	100	25	1

For the two-sided version of Fisher's exact test we should consider the significance probability

$$\alpha_p = 2\min\{p(Y_{11} \leq y), p(Y_{11} \geq y)\},$$

where y is the value of Y_{11} actually observed. For example, when $y = 0$ or 5, we have, based upon a total sample size of $n = 10$,

$$\alpha_p = 1/126 < 0.01,$$

suggesting a strongly statistically significant association between rows and columns. Whether or not this result is of strong practical significance is, of course, open to doubt. It is quite startling that, when treating ten patients with nose bleeds, we might be influenced to recommend strongly a new drug, when just five patients receiving the new drug recover within 10 minutes and a further five patients, receiving the placebo, do not recover within 10 minutes.

Whenever $n < 200$, the two-sided significance probability may be obtained by applying our special Splus command fisher.exact, and entering the table

$$
\begin{array}{cc}
3 & 50 \\
1 & 100
\end{array}
$$

gives the response "p-value = 0.118". Replacing the entry $y_{21} = 1$ by $y_{21} = 0$ gives "p-value = 0.04". Further replacing $y_{11} = 3$ by $y_{11} = 5$ gives "p-value = 0.005", a strongly significant result.

As a further example, consider the data

		Arterial Complication		
		Present	Absent	
Heart Condition	Present	50	110	160
	Absent	2	35	37
		52	145	197

These data were specific to patients of a particular consultant at Edinburgh Royal Infirmary, and the two samples, 160 patients with the condition and 37 patients for whom the condition was completely absent, were chosen separately from large groups of patients. In this case $\alpha_p = 0.07\%$, suggesting a strongly significant association, which is, of course, positive. However, the parameter of interest is really $\theta_1 = p$ (arterial complication present|heart condition). Using the Splus command theta.zero we find that our 95% confidence interval for θ_1 is $(0.245, 0.387)$. The corresponding 95% interval for $\theta_2 = p$(arterial condition present|heart condition completely absent) is $(0.011, 0.162)$.

Quite interestingly, Lehmann (1994, p. 145) provides an expression permitting the calculation of the power function of Fisher's exact test, when all marginal totals are indeed fixed, in terms of the cross-product ratio measure of association λ. Therefore, Fisher's exact test does indeed address the measure of association λ, as required by Edwards' theorem. This point is also highlighted by a duality between Fisher's exact test and an inferential procedure for the measure of association, discovered by Altham (1969).

2.10 Power properties of our test procedures

In this section, we in particular address the product binomial model, with parameters θ_1 and θ_2, where the row totals n_1 and n_2, only, are regarded as fixed. Consider fixed-size tests which reject a null hypothesis, H_0, if the significance probability does not exceed, say, 5% or 1%. Such tests control the probability of the Type I error, i.e., the probability of rejecting H_0, if H_0 is true. It is, however, also important to report the probability of the Type II error , i.e., the probability of accepting H_0, if H_0 is false. One minus the probability of the Type II error is

$$\beta = \text{Power} = p(\text{Rejecting } H_0 | H_0 \text{ is false}).$$

The terminology *reject, accept,* and *power,* is, of course, statistical and without the usual English language meanings. Indeed, *reject* means "enough evidence in the data to suggest refuting H_0", *accept* means *don't reject,* and *power* should simply be identified with its probabilistic definition.

In the product binomial situation, the two-sided version of Fisher's exact test has the best finite-sample power properties available, when compared with any other test procedure. It is also a theoretical fact that the two-sided significance probability for our b^2 log-measure-of-association test will closely approximate the exact probability from Fisher's test, unless one of the cell frequencies is quite small. However, it would be futile to investigate the power of the log-measure-of-association test, owing to its inadequacies when one of the cell frequencies is small.

Nevertheless, paralleling the normal approximations for binomial logits, as described in Section 2.7, which underpin our development of the log-measure-of-association test, in this case, it is possible to use related approximations, which will then approximate the power of Fisher's exact test (rather than the log-measure-of-association test itself). The approximate power for a 5% level test is

$$\beta = \beta(\theta_1, \theta_2) = 1 - \Phi\left[1.96 - w(\theta_1, \theta_2)\right] + \Phi\left[-1.96 - w(\theta_1, \theta_2)\right],$$

where

$$w(\theta_1, \theta_2) = (\alpha_1 - \alpha_2)/[n_1^{-1}w^*(\theta_1) + n_2^{-1}w^*(\theta_2)]^{\frac{1}{2}},$$

with $\alpha_i = \text{logit}(\theta_i)$, and

$$w^*(\theta_i) = 1/\theta_i(1 - \theta_i), \text{ for } i = 1, 2.$$

The power, or power function, is a function of the probabilities θ_1 and θ_2. It is particularly useful, at the design stage, when making an appropriate choice of sample size. Suppose, for example, that you judge that θ_1 and θ_2 are likely to be about 0.5 and 0.2, and assume equal sample sizes $n_1 = n_2 = n_*$. Then, these choices of θ_1 and θ_2 give

$$w = w(0.5, 0.2) = 0.433n_*^{\frac{1}{2}}.$$

For example, when $n_* = 20$, then $\beta = 0.491$, but when $n_* = 100$, then $\beta = 0.991$. This illustrates that, although small sample sizes can yield statistically significant results, moderate to large sample sizes can give much greater power. Power calculations for the two sample binomial test are described by Donner (1984). Some exact power calculations for Fisher's exact test are provided by Bennett and Hsu (1960).

Exercises

2.1 You observe a family with three children, where for each child either a boy (B) or girl (G) is equally likely. Show that eight outcomes of the form BBB, BGB, BBG, BGG, GBB, GGB, GBG, GGG can be judged equally likely, each with probability 1/8. Without assuming independence of A_1 and A_2 show that

$$p(A_1 \cap A_2) = p(A_1)p(A_2),$$

where

$$
\begin{aligned}
A_1 &= \{\text{first two children are girls}\} \\
A_2 &= \{\text{third child is a boy}\}.
\end{aligned}
$$

Hence, show that $p(A_2|A_1) = p(A_2) = 1/2$.

2.2   Consider the unconditional cell probabilities in the following contingency table

	A	A^C
B	1/4	1/6
B^C	1/12	1/2

Give numerical values for $p(A^C \cap B)$, $p(B^C)$, $p(A|B)$, $p(A|B^C)$, $p(B|A)$, and $p(B|A^C)$. Show that the row and column variables are not independent.

2.3   Express the expected frequencies e_{ij}, under the hypothesis of independent rows and columns in a 2×2 table, in the forms,

$$
\begin{aligned}
e_{11} &= n_1(y_{11} + y_{21})/(n_1 + n_2) \\
e_{12} &= n_1(y_{12} + y_{22})/(n_1 + n_2) \\
e_{21} &= n_2(y_{11} + y_{21})/(n_1 + n_2)
\end{aligned}
$$

and

$$e_{22} = n_2(y_{12} + y_{22})/(n_1 + n_2).$$

Hence, show that the X^2 goodness-of-fit statistic, for this hypothesis, can be arranged as

$$X^2 = \frac{[y_{11}(n_2 - y_{21}) - y_{21}(n_1 - y_{11})]^2/(n_1 + n_2)}{(y_{11} + y_{21})(y_{12} + y_{22})n_1 n_2}.$$

2.4   Using the notation of Section 2.3, show that the squared Z_0^2 of the two-sample binomial statistic Z_0 is equal to the expression for X^2 in Exercise 2.3. Under $H_0 : \theta_1 = \theta_2$ the distribution of Z_0 is approximately $N(0,1)$. Find an approximate distribution for Z_0 under $H_0 : \theta_1 \neq \theta_2$, and hence describe the power function of a two-sample binomial test of size α.

2.5   A random variable Z has a standard normal distribution with density (see also Section 10.1),

$$\phi(z) = e^{-\frac{1}{2}z^2}/\sqrt{2\pi} \qquad (-\infty < z < \infty)$$

and cumulative distribution function (c.d.f.)

$$\Phi(z) = p(Z \le z).$$

Show that the c.d.f. of $U = Z^2$ is

$$\begin{aligned} F(u) &= p(U \le u) \\ &= \Phi(u^{\frac{1}{2}}) - \Phi(-u^{\frac{1}{2}}) \qquad (0 < u < \infty). \end{aligned}$$

The density $f(u)$ of U is the slope (or first derivative) of the c.d.f. $F(u)$ at the point u. Show that

$$\begin{aligned} f(u) &= \frac{1}{2} u^{-\frac{1}{2}} \{ \phi(u^{\frac{1}{2}}) + \phi(-u^{\frac{1}{2}}) \} \\ &= u^{-\frac{1}{2}} e^{-\frac{1}{2}u} / \sqrt{2\pi} \qquad (0 < u < \infty). \end{aligned}$$

This is known as the density of the chi-squared distribution with one degree of freedom.

2.6 Resolving the Pearson - Fisher Controversy (Fisher, 1925, Lancaster, 1969):

Professor Karl Pearson thought that, under H_0 : the rows and columns of a 2×2 table are independent, the distribution of X^2 is approximately chi-squared with three degrees of freedom. Sir Ronald Fisher felt that there was instead just a single degree of freedom, and the controversy became bitter. Read Exercises 2.3, 2.4, and 2.5, and describe how you think this controversy might be resolved.

2.7 Yule's Q (see Yule, 1900) can be written in the form

$$Q = \frac{\xi_{11}\xi_{22} - \xi_{12}\xi_{21}}{\xi_{11}\xi_{22} + \xi_{12}\xi_{21}}.$$

Show that Yule's Q can be expressed as a function of the measure of association λ.

2.8 Show that the directional deviances

$$\tau_{ij} = \frac{\xi_{ij} - \xi_{i*}\xi_{*j}}{(\xi_{i*}\xi_{*j})^{\frac{1}{2}}} \qquad (i = 1, 2; j = 1, 2)$$

cannot be expressed as functions of λ alone.

2.9 Let $X_1, ..., X_7$ possess a multinomial $M(\xi_1, ..., \xi_7; n)$ distribution, and denote by $X_1, ..., X_7$ the numbers of students out of $n = 100$, who obtain grades A, AB, B, BC, C, D and F on a test. We observe, moreover, $X_1 = 8$, $X_2 = 15$, $X_3 = 23$, $X_4 = 5, X_5 = 9, X_6 = 23$, and $X_7 = 17$. Find approximate 95% confidence intervals for the log-contrasts

$$\eta = \log \xi_1 - \frac{1}{6} (\log \xi_2 + \log \xi_3 + \cdots + \log \xi_7)$$

and

$$\eta = \log \xi_6 - \log \xi_7$$

Perform a significance test to investigate whether or not substantially more students obtain a D rather than an F.

2.10 Consider the cancer case data of Section 2.7. Perform the calculations for the B^2 test (a) using prog1 and (b) using a hand calculator. Also perform the calculations for X^2, X_*^2, and LRS.

2.11 Let $Y \sim B(\theta, n)$ denote a single binomial frequency, and let $U = \log\{Y/(n-Y)\}$, $\alpha = \log\{\theta/(1-\theta)\}$, and $\omega(\theta) = \theta^{-1}(1-\theta)^{-1}$. Then, when n is large, the distribution of U is approximately normal with mean α and variance $n^{-1}\omega(\theta)$. When $n = 900$ and $\theta = 0.5$, use this result to find an approximation to $p(Y \geq 460)$.

With $n = 900$ you observe that $x = 480$. Would this observation refute a hypothesis that $\theta = 0.5$? Show that $Z = (U - \alpha)/n^{-\frac{1}{2}}\omega^{\frac{1}{2}}(\theta)$ has a distribution which is approximately standard normal. Why is this compatible with an approximate standard normal distribution for $Z^* = (U - \alpha)/V^{\frac{1}{2}}$, where $V = Y^{-1} + (n-Y)^{-1}$?

2.12 Consider the observed table

	A	A^C	
B	$225 + K$	$75 - K$	300
B^C	$75 - K$	$25 + K$	100
	300	100	400

Find X^2 as a multiple of K^2. How large a value of K would you need to ensure that the chi-squared test rejects independence of rows and columns at the 1% level? How large a value of K would you need to ensure that the B^2 test draws a similar conclusion?

2.13 In Exercise 2.10 find an approximate 95% confidence interval for the measure of association, with each of the two values of K you have calculated. Interpret your results in relation to practical significance.

2.14 If $Y \sim P(\mu)$, then, for large μ, $\log Y$ is approximately normally distributed with mean $\gamma = \log \mu$ and variance μ^{-1}. If $\mu = 25$, use this result to find an approximation to $p(Y \geq 35)$. Suppose that you observe $Y = 15$. Would this observation refute a hypothesis that $\mu = 25$, again a two-sided alternative?

2.15 Under independent Poisson assumptions, you observe the table

	A	A^C
B	$900K$	$300/K$
B^C	$300/K$	$100K$

Express the B^2 statistic as a function of K. For which values of K

would a B^2 refute a hypothesis of independence of rows and columns, at the 1% level?

2.16 Perform Fisher's exact test (two-sided) for the table

$$
\begin{array}{ccc}
 & A & A^C \\
B & 5 & 0 \\
B^C & 0 & 5
\end{array}
$$

using both Splus and by direct calculation. Does the significance of your result concern you in practical terms?

2.17 Sketch, as a function of θ_2, an approximate power function for Fisher's exact test (two-sided and at the 1% level), when $n_1 = n_2 = 100$ and $\theta_1 = 2\theta_2$. Interpret your results.

2.18 *Challenge Question (Age Discrimination)*. Company X is observed to appoint 23 out of those 54 applicants who are less than 50 years old, but to only appoint 8 out of those 42 applicants who are more than 50 years old. Under the "four-fifths rule", age discrmination occurs if the employment rate in any age group is significantly less than four-fifths of the employment rate of all remaining applicants. Construct a significance test which will help us to investigate whether or not age discrimination has occurred. How would you interpret the current data?

2.19 In an age discrimination case, with different figures, in Wisconsin, the plaintiff believed that a state institution was appointing applicants within his age group at 2/5 of the rate of applicants in other age groups. How large a sample size would you suggest for the purpose of adequately investigating whether or not the four-fifths rule has been significantly violated? The plaintiff's assertion proved to be true based upon data presented by the state for a several-month period. However, the expert witness for the state showed that the significance probability was only as low as 2%, and the court found for the state. How should the plaintiff have pursued the issue?

CHAPTER 3

Simpson's Paradox and 2^3 Tables

3.1 Probability theory

Consider a situation where $p(A|B) > p(A|B^C)$ so that there is a positive association between A and B. As an example, a company may employ 60% of all male applicants and only 52.2% of female applicants. Then, with $A = \{applicant\ is\ employed\}$, and $B = \{applicant\ is\ male\}$, we have $p(A|B) = 0.6$ and $p(A|B^C) = 0.525$, for a randomly selected applicant, suggesting possible gender discrimination against females. However, let D denote some other event. Then, it is quite logical, regardless of the above positive association, for our probabilities to satisfy both

$$p(A|B, D) < p(A|B^C, D)$$

and

$$p(A|B, D^C) < p(A|B^C, D^C),$$

so that there is a negative association between A and B, both given that D occurs and given that D does not occur! This phenomenon is known as "Simpson's Paradox", see Simpson (1951).

Continuing our gender example, let D denote the event that the applicant possesses some designated skill. Then, with $p(A|B) = 0.6 > p(A|B^C) = 0.525$, it is, for example, quite possible that

$$p(A|B, D) = 0.7 < p(A|B^C, D) = 0.9,$$

and

$$p(A|B, D^C) = 0.3 < p(A|B^C, D^C) = 0.4,$$

in which case the gender discrimination appears to be in favour of females! To see this, note that

$$p(A|B) = \alpha p(A|B, D) + (1 - \alpha)p(A|B, D^C),$$

and

$$p(A|B^C) = \beta p(A|B^C, D) + (1 - \beta)p(A|B^C, D^C),$$

where $\alpha = p(D|B)$ and $\beta = p(D|B^C)$. If B and D were independent, then $\alpha = \beta$, and it would be impossible to obtain the inequality reversal described above. However, if α and β were unequal, then this reversal can occur. In our example $\alpha = 3/4$ and $\beta = 1/4$ appropriately matches the specified conditional probabilities. If, instead, $\alpha = 2/3$ and $\beta = 1/3$, then our conditional specifications, yielding negative associations, given both D and D^C, would give $p(A|B) = p(A|B^C) = 0.567$, suggesting no overall association. At another extreme $\alpha = 1$ and $\beta = 0$, gives $p(A|B) = 0.7$ and $p(A|B^C) = 0.4$.

Next, note that

$$p(A|D) = \gamma p(A|B, D) + (1 - \gamma)p(A|B^C, D)$$

and

$$p(A|D^C) = \delta p(A|B, D^C) + (1 - \delta)p(A|B^C, D^C),$$

where $\gamma = p(B|D)$ and $\delta = p(B|D^C)$. In our example assume, for illustrative purposes, that $p(B) = p(male) = p(B^C) = p(female) = 0.5$. If, say, $\alpha = 3/4$ and $\beta = 1/4$, then $\gamma = 3/4$, $\delta = 1/4$, so that

$$p(A|D) = \frac{3}{4} \times 0.7 + \frac{1}{4} \times 0.9 = 0.75$$

and

$$p(A|D^C) = \frac{1}{4} \times 0.3 + \frac{3}{4} \times 0.4 = 0.375,$$

so that

$$p(A|D) > p(A|D^C).$$

Then,

$$
\begin{aligned}
\gamma &= p(B|D) \\
&= \frac{p(D|B)p(B)}{p(D|B)p(B) + p(D|B^C)p(B^C)} \\
&= \frac{\frac{1}{2} \times \alpha}{\frac{1}{2} \times \alpha + \frac{1}{2} \times \beta} = \frac{\alpha}{\alpha + \beta},
\end{aligned}
$$

and $p(D) = 1/2(\alpha + \beta)$, so that

$$
\begin{aligned}
\delta &= p(B|D^C) \\
&= \frac{p(D^C|B)p(B)}{p(D^C)} \\
&= \frac{\frac{1}{2}(1 - \alpha)}{1 - \frac{1}{2}(\alpha + \beta)} = \frac{1 - \alpha}{2 - \alpha - \beta}.
\end{aligned}
$$

This suggests that our apparent paradox (inequality reversal) has occurred because the company is strongly in favour of employing applicants with a designated skill D, in a situation where many more male than female applicants happen to possess skill D. This conclusion might, of course, be modified upon conditioning upon some fourth event.

Lemma 3.1: *For any $p(A|B) > p(A|B^C)$, both contained in $(0,1)$, it is possible to find P_1, P_2, Q_1, and Q_2 lying in the interval $(0,1)$, such that $P_1 < P_2$ and $Q_1 < Q_2$ with*

$$p(A|B) = \alpha P_1 + (1 - \alpha)Q_1$$

and

$$p(A|B^C) = \beta P_2 + (1 - \beta)Q_2,$$

for some α and β, both in the closed interval $[0, 1]$.

Proof. Let $\alpha = 1$ and $\beta = 0$. Then $p(A|B) = P_1$ and $p(A|B^C) = Q_2$. Let P_2 denote any value greater than $p(A|B)$ and Q_1 any value less than $p(A|B^C)$. Then all conditions described in the Lemma hold. Q.E.D.

[A slight extension tells us that α and β need only lie in the open interval $(0,1)$. If $p(A|B)$ and $p(A|B^C)$ fall well inside the interval $(0,1)$, then far less extreme values than $\alpha = 1$ and $\beta = 0$ are required.]

Lemma 3.1 tells us that the inequality reversal described above can occur even if $p(A|B)$ and $p(A|B^C)$ are very different, e.g., 0.999 and 0.002, so that there is a very strong association between A and B, but which might, however, be regarded as a "spurious association" for interpretation purposes. Similarly, if $p(A|B) = p(A|B^C)$, suggesting no association, it is quite possible for associations between A and B to exist, given both D and D^C, which are either both positive or both negative.

3.2 The Cornish pixie/Irish leprechaun example

Following an ancient legend, a green cloud containing the "Andromeda Strain" hits the western coasts of the British Isles, and, in particular, infects 4000 Irish leprechauns and 4000 Cornish pixies. Two treatments - Treatment 1: Wizard's Elixir, and Treatment 2: Auntie Em's Poppyseed - are available. Let the first variable denote treatment ($T1$ or $T2$), the second variable relate to recovery (R or R^C), and the third variable denote nationality (Irish or Cornish). When the Irish and Cornish patients are pooled, the performances of the treatments are summarised as follows:

Pooled Table

	R	R^C	
$T1$	2053	1947	4000
$T2$	1697	2303	4000
	3750	4250	8000

$$(\widehat{\theta}_1 = 0.513 > \widehat{\theta}_2 = 0.424, \quad \widehat{\lambda} = 1.431 > 1)$$

There is clearly a substantial positive association, with treatment 1 giving a higher recovery rate than treatment 2. Consider, however, the following two subtables, when we split the data, based on the third variable, our *lurking variable* (or *confounding variable*, or *confounder*), that is, nationality. The entries in our two subtables add up to the corresponding entries in the preceding pooled table.

Irish Leprechauns

	R	R^C	
$T1$	1802	1198	3000
$T2$	698	302	1000
	2500	1500	4000

$$(\theta_1 = 0.601 < \widehat{\theta}_2 = 0.698, \quad \widehat{\lambda} = 0.651 < 1)$$

Cornish Pixies

	R	R^C	
$T1$	251	749	1000
$T2$	999	2001	3000
	1250	2750	4000

$$(\widehat{\theta}_1 = 0.251 < \widehat{\theta}_2 = 0.333, \quad \widehat{\lambda} = 0.671 < 1).$$

This is an example of *Simpson's paradox* (see Simpson, 1951) and, at first sight, appears to be illogical. The pooled table apparently suggests a positive association between the row and column variables. However, the two subtables both suggest a negative association, indicating that the positive association in the pooled table should be interpreted as a *spurious association*. The *spurious association* is created by the *lurking variable*, nationality. Observe that the paradox cannot occur if the proportion of Irish receiving treatment 1 is set equal to the proportion of Cornish receiving treatment 1 (this can be proved via the probabilistic arguments of the previous section, and relates to the situation where the sets A and D, as described there, are independent).

Simpson's paradox creates considerable problems with statistical interpretation, and all statisticians should remain continuously aware of this paradox and its ramifications. As the paradox appears to defy common-sense many scientists will try to ignore the paradox, and keep to their "common-sense" interpretation of the pooled table, and then obtain spurious results. The paradox is, of course, less serious if possible lurking variables can be identified before collecting the data. A more complete data collection and analysis can then be performed, by reference to a 2^m contingency table, e.g., the analyses for 2^3 tables (one lurking variable present) described later in this chapter. However, an unknown lurking variable can always exist, and this can always threaten our conclusions, in particular when no random sampling has been introduced at the design stage.

Suppose, for example, with the above numerical data, our first variable denotes "smoking or not", and the second variable "lung cancer or not", so that the pooled table indicates a strong positive association between smoking and lung cancer. Then, there could exist some mysterious gene Z, associated with both smoking and lung cancer, such that, just like nationality in our example, splitting the pooled table according to the presence or absence of gene Z reenacts the above paradox. This argument was used by the U.S. Tobacco Institute, for many years, to defend itself against data suggesting a strong association between smoking and lung cancer. However, the mysterious gene was never found.

Just as it is a very useful part of the scientific process to contemplate possible lurking variables which have not been observed, we regard medical, rather than standard statistical, interpretation as "the contemplation of further variables of medical interest, which may have influenced the statistical results, and of variables which can definitely be excluded from the current medical situation."

3.3 Interpretation of Simpson's paradox

This paradox is, in fact, quite logical. Using the notation and probability theory of Section 3.1, let

$$
\begin{aligned}
A &= \{\text{random patient recovers}\}, \\
B &= \{\text{random patient receives treatment 1}\}, \\
&\quad \text{and} \\
D &= \{\text{random patient is Irish}\},
\end{aligned}
$$

where the patient is chosen at random from all $n = 8000$ patients involved. Then, our pooled table tells us that

$$p(A|B) = 0.513$$

and

$$p(A|B^C) = 0.424,$$

with $p(B) = 0.5$. The first subtable tells us that

$$p(A|B, D) = 0.601$$

and

$$p(A|B^C, D) = 0.698,$$

with $\alpha = p(D|B) = 0.75$, and the second subtable gives

$$p(A|B, D^C) = 0.251$$

and

$$p(A|B^C, D^C) = 0.333,$$

with $\beta = p(D|B^C) = 0.25$. These numbers satisfy the laws of total probability, as stated in Section 3.1, and are therefore quite logical.

It is possible to protect against lurking variables, if appropriate randomisation can be performed at the design stage. In our example, simply choose the $n_1 = 4000$ patients, receiving treatment 1, at random without replacement, from the total collection of $n_1 + n_2 = 8000$ patients, and then assign the remaining $n_2 = 4000$ patients to treatment T_2 (n_1 and n_2 need not in general be equal). This tends to equate $p(B|D)$ and $p(B|D^C)$, and hence also to equate $\alpha = p(D|B)$ and $\beta = p(D|B^C)$, as defined in Lemma 3.1.1. The approximate equality reduces the likelihood of the paradox occurring, when the lurking variable is "nationality". However, the random sampling also tends to equate $p(B|G)$ and $p(B|G^C)$ for any other event G, and hence to reduce the likelihood of the paradox occurring, for any further lurking variable, whether anticipated in advance, or not. Of course, if we are unable to randomise the treatment allocations, then, however many lurking variables we consider, there may always be another lurking variable, which might create the paradoxical situation. This creates considerable problems when interpreting observational data and typically encourages scientists to imagine creatively all lurking variables which might influence their results. This is part of our *Inductive Synthesis*, and catalyses scientific discovery.

If the preceding randomisation is possible, we may protect against an unlucky randomisation (e.g., all patients receiving treatment 1 happening by extreme chance to possess green ears) by replication. Where feasible, we should repeat the experiment several times, under identical conditions, and hope to obtain similar results on each replication.

3.4 The three-directional approach

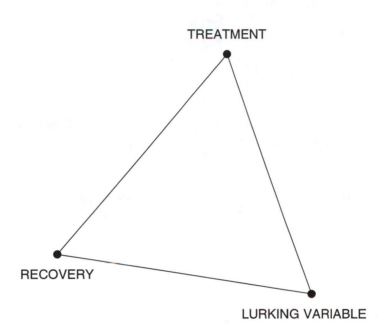

Figure 3.1 *The three directions*

In Section 3.3, we showed, by a cross-classification of recovery against treatment, that there was an apparent positive association between treatment and recovery. This was, however, made spurious by the presence of a lurking or confounding variable, nationality (see Figure 3.1). A fuller analysis of these data may, however, be performed by closer consideration of the association between treatment and nationality, and between recovery and nationality. All conclusions will, of course, be conditional on the absence of further lurking variables. Note that our data may be arranged into a 2^3 contingency table, as represented symbolically by Figure 3.2.

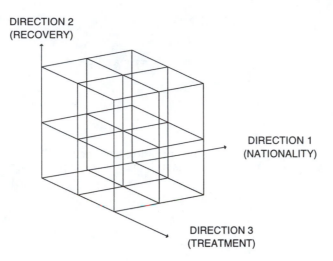

Figure 3.2 *The three-directional approach*

We have so far analysed the data via a split of the table in Direction 1 (nationality). We should however also refer to all conclusions which might be obtained via splits in Direction 2 (Recovery), and Direction 3 (Treatment). Splitting in Direction 2, and then pooling across this direction, gives the rearranged data

	Pooled		Recover		Do Not Recover	
	T1	T2	T1	T2	T1	T2
Irish	3000	1000	1802	698	1198	302
Cornish	1000	3000	251	999	749	2001

Consideration of the pooled table gives us a positive association, where 75% of the Irish receive T1, while only 25% of Cornish receive T1. Out of patients who recover, 72.08% of Irish receive T1, compared with 20.08% of Cornish. Out of patients who do not recover, 79.87% of Irish receive T1, compared with 27.24% of Cornish. Therefore, our positive association between nationality and treatment is not invalidated by a split on the recovery variable.

Splitting in Direction 3, and then pooling across this direction, gives the rearranged data

| | Pooled | | Treatment 1 | | Treatment 2 | |
	R	R^C	R	R^C	R	R^C
Irish	2500	1500	1802	1198	698	302
Cornish	1250	2750	251	749	999	2001

Overall, 62.5% of Irish recover, compared with 31.25% of Cornish. For patients receiving treatment 1, 60.07% of Irish recover, compared with 25.10% of Cornish. For patients receiving treatment 2, 69.80% of Irish recover, compared with 33.30% of Cornish.

Our main conclusions can be summarised as follows:

Direction 1: The apparent positive association (T1>T2) is spurious and Simpson's paradox has occurred.

Direction 2: Irish have a much higher propensity to receive T1 than T2.

Direction 3: Irish have a much higher propensity to recover largely independent of treatment. These two conclusions, for directions 2 and 3 explain why, in our pooled table for direction 1, there is an illusion that T1 is better.

Resolution: Considering our direction 3 tables in greater detail, observe that Irish patients receiving treatment 1 have a lower propensity to recover (60.07% compared with 69.80%) than Irish patients receiving treatment 2. The same is true for Cornish patients (25.10% compared with 33.30%). This leads to the conditional conclusion, in the absence of further lurking variables, that treatment 2 is better than treatment 1, and that there is, after all, a meaningful association between our two main variables, treatment and recovery. This is, however, now a negative association, rather than the positive association originally envisioned.

Observe that, in direction 1, the ratio of the measures of association, for our two split tables is $0.651/0.671 = 0.970$. This ratio is the same $(10.275/10.598$ and $4.489/4.630)$, for the split tables in directions 2 and 3. The log of this ratio is sometimes referred to as the "second-order interaction" or "overall measure of association for the 2^3 table". Its difference from zero measures the differences between the log-measures of association for the subtables, on each of our three splits. Procedures enabling us to judge more fully the statistical significance of the conclusions drawn from a three-dimensional approach are described in the next section. However, when considering the following example, proportions and conditional proportions should be considered rather than statistical significance.

Consider the data in Table 3.1, for $n = 226$ defendants in murder trials, presented by Radelet (1981), together with the rearrangements needed for a three-directional approach. The event D denotes "imposition of the death penalty", for defendants in this category.

Table 3.1 *Racial characteristics and imposition of death penalty.*

Direction 1	**Overall**			
	D	D^C		
White Defendant	19	141		
Black Defendant	17	149		
	White Victim		**Black Victim**	
	D	D^C	D	D^C
White Defendant	19	132	0	9
Black Defendant	11	52	6	97
Direction 2	**Overall**			
	D	D^C		
White Victim	30	184		
Black Victim	6	106		
	White Defendant		**Black Defendant**	
	D	D^C	D	D^C
White Victim	19	132	11	52
Black Victim	0	9	6	97
Direction 3	**Overall**			
	White Victim	Black Victim		
White Defendant	151	9		
Black Defendant	63	103		
	Death Penalty		**No Death Penalty**	
	White Victim	Black Victim	White Victim	Black Victim
White Defendant	19	0	132	9
Black Defendant	11	6	52	97

The following conclusions can be drawn from these data, via our three-directional approach. In any particular table, let $\widehat{\theta}_1$ and $\widehat{\theta}_2$ denote the conditional proportions given the rows.

Direction 1: The apparent positive association ($\widehat{\theta}_1 = 0.119 > \widehat{\theta}_2 = 0.102$) between colour of defendant and imposition of death penalty in the overall table is made spurious by negative associations in the two subtables ($\widehat{\theta}_1 = 0.126 < \widehat{\theta}_2 = 0.175$ when the victim is white, and $\widehat{\theta}_1 = 0 < \widehat{\theta}_2 = 0.058$ when the victim is black) when the data are split based upon colour of victim.

Direction 2: The overall table suggests a positive association, where defendants with white victims ($\widehat{\theta}_1 = 0.140$) are more likely to receive death penalty than defendants with black victims ($\widehat{\theta}_2 = 0.054$). This positive association remains true for both subtables, and therefore holds irrespective of colour of defendant. For white defendants $\widehat{\theta}_1 = 0.126 > \widehat{\theta}_2 = 0$, and for black defendants, $\widehat{\theta}_1 = 0.175 > \widehat{\theta}_2 = 0.058$. There is, therefore, a positive association in the data between death penalty and colour of victim, which could only be invalidated by a further confounding variable (apart from colour of victim), such as socioeconomic status of defendant.

Direction 3: There is a positive association between colour of defendant and colour of victim. For white defendants, a very high proportion $\widehat{\theta}_1 = 0.944$ of the victims were white, whereas for black defendants a proportion $\widehat{\theta}_2 = 0.380$ of the victims were white (the difference between $\widehat{\theta}_1$ and $1 - \widehat{\theta}_2 = 0.620$ is also interesting, and suggests that black defendants in the sample have a greater propensity than white defendants to choose a victim of the opposite colour). The increased propensity for white defendants to have white victims combines with the increased propensity (direction 2) for defendants with white victims to receive the death penalty, to create the illusion (see Simpson's paradox in direction 1) that white defendants are more likely to receive the death penalty. The lurking variable is "colour of victim".

Resolution: Our analysis in direction 1 and 2 also tells us that, among defendants with white victims, 12.58% of white defendants receive the death penalty, which is less than the 17.46% of black defendants who receive the death penalty. Moreover, among defendants with black victims, these percentages switch to 0% for white defendants, which is less than 5.83% for black defendants. We conclude that there is a negative association between colour of defendant and imposition of the death penalty, which reverses the conclusion from the original overall table.

3.5 Measure of association analysis for 2^3 tables

Let Y_{ijk} denote the cell frequency for the (i, j, k)th cell ($i = 1, 2; j = 1, 2,$ and $k = 1; 2$) of a 2^3 table. Let μ_{ijk} denote the corresponding cell mean, and

$$\xi_{ijk} = \mu_{ijk}/\mu_{***} \, ,$$

with

$$\mu_{***} = \sum_{ijk} \mu_{ijk} \, ,$$

denote the corresponding unconditional cell probability. The current methodology relates to either the independent Poisson model where

$$Y_{ijk} \sim P\left(\mu_{ijk}\right) \qquad (i = 1, 2; j = 1, 2; k = 1, 2),$$

or the single multinomial model, with $2^3 = 8$ cells, where the Y_{ijk} possess multinomial distribution, with fixed sample size

$$n = \sum_{ijk} Y_{ijk},$$

and where each $n\xi_{ijk}$ denotes the expectation of the corresponding Y_{ijk}. The single multinomial model can, of course, be obtained from the independent Poisson model, by conditioning on the observed value of n. Let $i = 1, 2$ according to the presence or absence of factor A, $j = 1, 2$ according to the presence or absence of factor B, and $k = 1, 2$ according to the presence or absence of factor D.

Consider now the cross-product ratio

$$\tau = [\xi_{111}\xi_{221}/\xi_{121}\xi_{211}]/[\xi_{112}\xi_{222}/\xi_{122}\xi_{212}].$$

Note that τ is the ratio of the measures of association between A and B, when D is present and when D is absent. It can also be rearranged as the ratio of the measures of association between B and D, when A is present and when A is absent. It can furthermore be rearranged as the ratio of the measures of association between D and A, when B is present and B is absent.

The hypothesis $H_0 : \tau = 1$ is therefore of some interest, since if true, the measures of association would be equal for each of the two subtables, when splitting the table in any of the three ways indicated by the three-directional approach of Section 3.4. However, H_0 does not correspond to any hypothesis involving independence of A, B, and D, or conditional independence, e.g., of A and B, given D. No sensible algebraically explicity estimates exist for the ξ_{ijk}, under H_0. Observe that when H_0 is not assumed true, the maximum likelihood estimate $\hat{\eta}$ of the log-contrast

$$\begin{aligned} \eta &= \log\tau = \log\xi_{111} + \log\xi_{221} - \log\xi_{121} - \log\xi_{211} \\ &\quad - \log\xi_{112} - \log\xi_{222} + \log\xi_{122} + \log\xi_{212}, \end{aligned}$$

is given by

$$\begin{aligned} \hat{\eta} &= U = \log Y_{111} + \log Y_{221} - \log Y_{121} - \log Y_{211} \\ &\quad - \log Y_{112} - \log Y_{222} + \log Y_{122} + \log Y_{212}, \end{aligned}$$

and that $\hat{\eta} = U$ has estimated variance

$$V = \sum_{i,j,k} Y_{ijk}^{-1}.$$

Furthermore, the test statistic,

$$G = U/V^{\frac{1}{2}},$$

possesses a distribution, which under H_0 is approximately standard normal. In the Irish/Cornish example of Section 3.2, the observed values of U and $V^{\frac{1}{2}}$ are

$$u = \log(0.970) = -0.0305$$

and

$$v^{\frac{1}{2}} = 0.1138$$

yielding an observed G value of $g = u/v^{\frac{1}{2}} = -0.2676$. There is therefore insufficient evidence to refute our hypothesis H_0 that the *three-way interaction* η is zero.

In situations where $H_0 : \eta = 0$ is taken to be true, the following three tables summarise all information in the data about the remaining parameters (y_{ijk} is just the numerical realisation of Y_{ijk}, and $*$ again denotes summation with respect to the corresponding subscript).

	B	B^C
A	y_{11*}	y_{12*}
A^C	y_{21*}	y_{22*}

	D	D^C
B	y_{*11}	y_{*12}
B^C	y_{*21}	y_{*22}

	D	D^C
A	y_{1*1}	y_{1*2}
A^C	y_{2*1}	y_{2*2}

These are just the pooled tables, for the three directions indicated in Section 3.4. Hence, the collection of marginal totals of the form y_{ij*}, y_{*jk}, or y_{i*k}, is said to be "sufficient" for the unknown parameters in the model, when $\eta = 0$. Consider also the hypothetical data

D present

	B	B^C
A	40	10
A^C	10	40

D absent

	B	B^C
A	80	10
A^C	10	20

which give $\widehat{\eta} = \log(16/16) = 0$. Then, our three pooled tables are

	B	B^C
A	120	20
A^C	20	60

	D	D^C
B	50	90
B^C	50	30

	D	D^C
A	50	90
A^C	50	30

In situations where η is taken to be equal to zero, Simpson's paradox can still occur (see Section 3.6). It might therefore be misleading to just analyse these three tables separately, e.g., using the log-measure-of-association methodology of Chapter 2. Quite interestingly, the theory of log-linear models (see Chapter 10) would involve iteratively fitting a complicated model to the entire 2^3 table. This may not be particularly useful. Therefore, unless the zero three-way interaction hypothesis is of immediate interest, we instead recommend versions of the three-directional approach of Section 3.4, which involves repeated application of our B^2 test for two-way tables (see Sections 3.6 through 3.8). These difficulties in interpreting the zero three-way interaction model will also recur when considering more general three-way tables with larger dimensions. Edwards (1963) also discusses these problems. For these reasons we do not recommend the analysis of the current section as central to our general approach.

3.6 Medical example

Ku and Kullback (1974) and Everitt (1992, p. 87) report two 4×4 tables each cross-classifying medical patients according to blood pressure and serum cholesterol level. The first table relates to the 93 patients, out of a sample of $n = 1330$ patients, who possess coronary heart disease, and the second table relates to the 1237 patients in the sample without coronary heart disease. We condense and simplify the data into a 2^3 table as follows. The boundaries between the Low and High categories are 147 units for blood pressure and 220 units for serum cholesterol. Note that 2×2 tables may frequently be obtained by dichotomising continuous variables in this manner. This method can be very useful in situations where the continuous variables are noisy and difficult to model.

Disease Present

Serum Cholesterol

		Low	High	
Blood	Low	10	11	21
Pressure	High	38	34	72
		48	45	93

Disease Absent

Serum Cholesterol

		Low	High	
Blood	Low	421	132	553
Pressure	High	494	190	684
		915	322	1237

The observed measure of association for the first table is $\widehat{\lambda} = 0.813$, while for the second table $\widehat{\lambda} = 1.227$. This gives a slight indication that, while cholesterol level and blood pressure might be positively associated among patients without the coronary disease, they may be negatively associated for patients with the disease. However, these conclusions are not statistically significant based upon this data set alone (our B^2 test gives significance probabilities of 67.75% and 11.96% when investigating association in these subtables).

Quite importantly, the ratio $\widehat{\tau} = 0.663$ of these two measures of association is not significantly different from unity. Using the notation and methodology of Section 3.5, we find that $u = \log \widehat{\tau} = -0.411$ with estimated standard error $v^{\frac{1}{2}} = 0.514$, yielding a value $g = 0.800$ for our normal test statistic and a significance probability of 42.4% when testing $H_0 : \eta = \log \tau = 0$ against a general alternative. Consider the three pooled tables

		Serum Cholesterol		
		Low	High	
Blood Pressure	Low	431	143	574
	High	532	224	756
		963	367	1330

$(b = 1.904$, sig. prob. $= 5.69\%$, $\widehat{\lambda} = 1.269)$

		Heart Disease		
		Yes	No	
Serum Cholesterol	Low	48	915	963
	High	45	322	367
		93	1237	1330

$(b = -4.508$, sig. prob. $= 0.00\%$, $\widehat{\lambda} = 0.375)$

		Heart Disease		
		Yes	No	
Blood Pressure	Low	21	553	574
	High	72	684	756
		93	1237	1330

$(b = -4.006$, sig. prob. $= 0.01\%$, $\widehat{\lambda} = 0.361)$

In summary, the positive overall association between the blood pressure and serum cholesterol reading is not quite significant (significance probability $= 5.69\%$). There are, however, strongly significant associations between (high) serum cholesterol and the presence of heart disease (significance probability $= 0.00\%$) and between (high) blood pressure and the presence of heart disease (significance probability $= 0.01\%$). The first of the strongly significant associations ($\widehat{\lambda} = 0.375$) is not made spurious by splitting the table based upon low or high blood pressure, since the two split tables (see Section 3.7), respectively, yield $\widehat{\lambda} = 0.285$ and $\widehat{\lambda} = 0.429$. The second of these strongly significant association ($\widehat{\lambda} = 0.361$) is not made spurious by a split based upon high or low serum cholesterol since the split two tables (see Section 3.7), respectively, yield $\widehat{\lambda} = 0.309$ and $\widehat{\lambda} = 0.466$.

We have completed a three-directional approach because the "three-way order interaction test" and its ramifications do not appear to provide a complete approach to the analysis of 2^3 tables. Consider, for example, the fictitious data

	D Present				D Absent				Overall	
	B	B^C			B	B^C			B	B^C
A	900	200		A	100	500		A	1000	700
A^C	500	100		A^C	200	900		A^C	700	1000

Note that the measure of association is $\widehat{\lambda} = 0.9 < 1$ for each of the two subtables (D present and D absent), while $\widehat{\lambda} = 2.04 > 1$ overall. Therefore,

Simpson's paradox can occur even when our three-way interaction test suggests that $\tau = 1$, and when the measures of association in our two subtables are equal.

3.7 Testing equality for two 2×2 tables

Consider the first two 2×2 tables (disease present and disease absent) reported in Section 3.6. Their entries may be rearranged in the following 2×4 contingency table:

| | Blood Pressure/Serum Cholesterol | |
	(Low, Low)	(Low, High)
Disease Present	10	11
Disease Absent	421	132

| | Blood pressure/Serum Cholesterol | |
	(High, Low)	(High, High)
Disease Present	38	34
Disease Absent	494	190

We wish to test whether the unconditional cell proportions in the first 2×2 table (disease present) are significantly different from the corresponding proportions when the disease is absent. This is equivalent to testing equality of the conditional row proportions of our 2×4 table. However, this in turn is equivalent to testing independence of rows and columns of our 2×4 table. One appropriate test is therefore a "likelihood ratio test" on three degrees of freedom. Upon entering our 2×4 table into prog1 we find that

$$\text{LRS} = 37.023$$

with significance probability $= 0.00\%$, thus refuting equality of the unconditional cell probabilities of our two tables. We can similarly consider the table:

		Blood Pressure/Disease			
Serum Cholesterol	Low	10	421	38	494
	High	11	132	34	190

This gives LRS$= 21.006$ and significance probability $= 0.0001$, suggesting significant differences between the unconditional probabilities of the following two subtables:

Low Serum Cholesterol Level

| | | Disease | |
		Present	Absent
Blood Pressure	Low	10	421
	High	38	494

High Serum Cholesterol Level

		Disease	
		Present	Absent
Blood Pressure	Low	11	132
	High	34	190

Consider the split in a third direction, together with the table:

		Serum Cholesterol/Disease			
Blood Pressure	Low	10	421	11	132
	High	38	494	34	190

This gives LRS = 22.190 and significance probability = 0.0001, suggesting significance differences between the unconditional probabilities of the following two subtables:

Low Blood Pressure

		Disease	
		Present	Absent
Serum Cholesterol	Low	10	421
	High	11	132

High Blood Pressure

		Disease	
		Present	Absent
Serum Cholesterol	Low	38	494
	High	34	190

To complete our "three-directional analysis" (which does not condition on $\tau = 1$) observe that prog1 gives the values $b = -3.250, -2.094, -2.801$, and -3.363, for the last four 2 × 2 tables reported, together with significant probabilities, 0.0012, 0.0362, 0.0051, and 0.0008. This indicates a somewhat significant association between the diagnostic factor and the disease for each of these subtables. In terms of percentages, the first 2 × 4 table of the current section tells us that the following combinations of categories for blood pressure and serum cholesterol give us the attached propensity for heart disease:

(Low, Low)	(Low, High)	(High, Low)	(High, High)
2.32%	7.69%	7.14%	15.16%

In particular, high blood pressure and high serum cholesterol are both associated with an increased propensity for heart disease. An alternative to the preceding analysis involves the three B^2 tests on one degree of freedom indicated in Exercise 3.3. A procedure for investigating equality of the conditional probabilities of two 2 × 2 tables, e.g., with row totals fixed, is described in Exercise 3.2.

3.8 The three-directional approach to the analysis of 2^3 tables (summary)

This procedure may in general be summarised as follows. Note that your practical intuition and knowledge of the scientific background of the data should be incorporated at every stage.

(A) Use the likelihood ratio test for 2×4 tables, and your practical judgement, to investigate equality of the unconditional cell probabilities of the two subtables, according to splits in each of the three available directions.

(B) For each direction in which you judge the unconditional cell probabilities of the two subtables are unequal, analyse the two subtables separately, e.g., by comparing conditional and unconditional percentages and performing a log-measure-of-association (B^2) test. Also, compare the results in your two subtables.

(C) For each direction in which you consider the unconditional cell probabilities of the two subtables to be equal, analyse the overall table, e.g., by considering conditional and unconditional probabilities.

(D) When interpreting your results, try to incorporate results from all three directions (e.g., when explaining Simpson's paradox).

(E) Report results and insights, e.g., using percentages, which might be useful in the scientific context of the data. When reporting percentages you can also report the "exact" confidence intervals of Section 1.3.4.

For applications of this approach to the Edinburgh childrens' head injury data, see Leonard (1999). The three main variables are injury category, helmet usage, and age. Two further variables, helmet ownership and poverty level, are also considered. It is shown that children under eight are at greater risk of head injury if they do not wear a helmet, particularly if they own a helmet.

Exercises

3.1 Show that the following data give a further real-life example of Simpson's paradox. The data compare two treatments for the removal of kidney stones. These are open surgery (O.S.) and perontaneous nephrolithotomy (P.N.). The data were reported by Charig et al. (1986). Fully analyse the data using a three-directional approach. Also perform the three-way interaction test.

	Overall		Stones < 2 cm		Stones > 2 cm	
	Success	Failure	Success	Failure	Success	Failure
O.S.	273	77	81	6	192	71
P.N.	289	61	234	36	55	25

3.2   Consider the following two contingency tables, with row totals fixed:

	Males				Females		
	R	R^c	Total		R	R^c	Total
T1	75	25	100	T1	65	15	100
T2	50	50	100	T2	40	60	100

(a) Perform a B^2 test on the 2×2 table combining the first rows of the above tables, to investigate equality of the conditional probabilities θ_1.

(b) Perform a B^2 test on the 2×2 table combining the second rows of the above tables to investigate equality of the conditional probabilties θ_2.

3.3   Apply the two B^2 tests of Exercise 3.2 to the two split tables in the kidney stone example of Exercise 3.1. Show that a further B^2 test on the row totals combines with your first two tests to provide an alternative procedure for investigating equality of the unconditional probabilities of the two split tables.

3.4   The data in the following table were described by Moore (1991, p. 25) in the context of accident and prevention.

	Front Seat	
	Restrained	Not Restrained
Injured	121	2125
Uninjured	981	9679

	Back Seat	
	Restrained	Not Restrained
Injured	76	1719
Uninjured	788	11,502

The observed measures of association between the row and column variables in the preceding 2×2 tables are 0.5618 (front seat) and 0.662 (back seat). Would you judge this difference to be of practical significance?

3.5   Apply the LRS test of Section 3.7 to investigate possible differences between the unconditional cell probabilities of the two 2×2 tables (front seat and back seat) described in Exercise 3.4.

3.6   Perform a full three-directional analysis of the data in Exercise 3.4. Does Simpson's paradox occur?

3.7   You are informed, for a particular disease D and Symptom S, for a randomly chosen patient that $p(D|S) = 0.99$, while $p(D|S^C) = 0.05$. Use the developments of Section 3.1, Lemma 3.1, to show that these may be a mysterious gene Z, such that $p(D|S, Z) < p(D|S^C, Z)$, and $p(D|S, Z^C) < p(D|S^C, Z^C)$. Describe all values of $\alpha = p(Z|S)$ and $\beta = p(Z|S^C)$ such that this can occur.

3.8   In a gender discrimination case, Company X has appointed 67 out of 503 male applicants, but only 25 out of 404 female applicants.

(a) As an attorney for a plaintiff, how would you use these data as evidence to suggest that gender discrimination has occurred? How would you respond to issues that are likely to be raised by the defense? How would you handle the problem of potential confounding variables?

(b) As an attorney for Company X, how would you try to defend the case? Which confounding variables might be suggested? Is it appropriate to state an objectively interpretable significance probability?

Hint: How would you interpret these results, if for one employment grade, there were 100 applicants, all male, of whom 60 were appointed?

CHAPTER 4

The Madison Drug and Alcohol Abuse Study

By Orestis Papasouliotis and Thomas Leonard

4.1 Experimental design

We report a study completed between the summers of 1994 and 1996, for the
U.S. National Institute of Drug Abuse. Details of this and a related study
have been reported by Brown et al. (1997; 1998; 1999), and the project was
completed with our co-workers Richard Brown and Laura Saunders of the
Department of Family Medicine, University of Wisconsin-Madison.

Our 1994 research proposal to the U.S. National Institutes of Health
stated the objective: The goals of this study are to produce and validate
a brief questionnaire, consisting of no more than five items, that screens
conjointly for alcohol and drug abuse among primary care patients of di-
verse gender and race. In Phase I, focus groups of professionals, previous
substance abusers, and current substance abusers will suggest and critique
potential questionnaire items.

In Phase 2, the discriminant validity of up to twenty questionnaire items
will be assessed initially on 300 known substance abusers in treatment and
300 nonabusers in primary care practices. In Phase 3, the discriminant validity of the most discriminating items from Phase 2 will be assessed for 300
substance abusing and 600 non-abusing primary care patients. For Phases
2 and 3, the Composite International Diagnostic Instrument-Substance
Abuse Modules (Cidi-Sam) will be used as the chief criterion measure of
substance abuse. Agreement by all primary care subjects to undergo urine
drug screens after questionnaire administration, as determined by 1-in-4
random draw, will enhance the accuracy of self-report.

Owing to practical constraints our samples at Phase 2, as collected in
1995, finally consisted of 190 substance (i.e., drug or alcohol or both)
abusers attending one of three substance abuse treatment centres (Hope
Haven, Share, and Women and Children's) in Madison and 323 nonabusers
in primary care in one of three clinics (North-East, Wingra, and Verona).
At Phase 3, a further 261 patients at these clinics, were characterised as
substance abusers, and 552 further patients at these clinics were diagnosed

as nonabusers. The choices of recommended sample size were motivated by power calculations (see Section 3.10 and Exercise 4.1; Donner, 1984).

In all cases a diagnosis of current substance abuse was made using the international Cidi-Sam questionnaire (up to 837 items). Our objective was to be able screen patients using far fewer items. However, the Cidi-Sam questionnaire is regarded as the most accurate method of diagnosis available.

There was considerable debate during the design stage regarding a previously proposed "multivariate analysis approach"; i.e., should we attempt to ask each of our subjects several hundred questions and then try to discern from the data which items best indicated a positive diagnosis? The answer should clearly be "No!", if only because several hundred questions would probably confuse our subjects at the screening stage. This criticism can, of course, also be made regarding the Cidi-Sam diagnostic procedure. We were, however, also concerned with retaining a simple statistical analysis. We therefore decided at this stage to use contingency table analysis and logistic regression as our analytic techniques for much simpler data sets. As a result of discussions with our focus groups, just nine initial items were recommended. These are listed in Table 4.1.

Table 4.1 *Nine Items*

Please respond on a Four-Point Scale: Never, Rarely, Sometimes, Often, and in relation to the last year.

1. How many times have you not remembered things that happened while you were drinking or using drugs?
2. Have you ever drunk or used drugs more than you meant to?
3. Have you been bothered by someone complaining about your drinking or drug use?
4. Have you felt that you wanted or needed to cut down on your drinking or drug use?
5. Have you had problems related to your drinking or drug use?
6. Has anyone ever been concerned about your drinking or drug use?
7. Have you drunk or used nonprescription drugs to deal with your feelings, stress, or frustration?
8. As a result of your drinking or drug use, did anything happen that you wish didn't happen?
9. Do you think you have a problem with your use of alcohol or drugs?

Of the three focus groups, previous substance abusers were the most helpful. The professionals possessed less real-life experience of substance abuse, and the current abusers seemed too closely in contact with their current problems. The previous substance abusers confirmed with us that many people would give dishonest responses, and this aspect influenced our subsequent analysis. Furthermore, random urine tests were included in the study in the hope of both detecting dishonest responses and encouraging honest responses.

As the study began, it soon became apparent that proper random sampling (e.g., choosing one per person at random from every three candidates) for choice of interviewee would be impossible. The clinics imposed time constraints on the interviewers. There was pressure on each interviewer to complete as many interviews as possible, without being slowed down by random sampling. As each interviewee received $15, there was pressure on the interviewers to interview particular people. Although the sample was not taken at random, a large number of variables were observed for each interviewee including demographic variables, smoking habits, dietary habits, current medications, and social desirability variables. It turned out that none of these further variables or choice of interviewer, or treatment centre, substantially influenced the primary conclusions of the study. We therefore regard the samples taken as possessing reasonably high quality.

The purpose of Phase 2 was to ensure that the questions were good enough to detect previously identified abusers. The questions were judged according to their observed *sensitivity* (the proportion of previously identified substance abusers who responded positively to the questions). By "positively" we mean known substance abusers who did not answer "never" to the question, but gave one of another three possible responses. The questions were also judged according to their observed *specificity* (the proportion of non-abusing primary care patients who responded negatively, i.e., "never" to the question). Primary care patients diagnosed by the Cidi-Sam questionnaire as substance abusers were not included in this part of the study. The sensitivities and specificities are listed in Table 4.2, and indicate that all questions work well in situations where the subjects have nothing to lose by admitting that they are substance abusers.

Table 4.2 *Results of Phase 2 of Study*

Question	Sensitivity	Specificity
1	85.26%	91.95%
2	97.37%	82.97%
3	94.74%	96.59%
4	98.42%	92.26%
5	97.89%	95.98%
6	97.37%	95.12%
7	85.79%	83.90%
8	96.32%	95.67%
9	99.47%	96.28%

4.2 Statistical results (phase 3) of study

It is important to realise that Phase 3 of the study was confined to primary care patients only, whether substance abusers or not. Therefore, less extreme sensitivities were contemplated when compared with Phase 2 of the study. After 434 patients were interviewed, questions 3, 5, 6, and 9 were dropped from the study. Their observed (Phase 3) sensitivities were, respectively, 32.43%, 28.83%, 32.43% and 37.84% with observed specificities 96.59%, 95.98%, 94.12% and 96.28%. The low sensitivities indicate that primary care patients experiencing substance abuse may be quite unwilling to admit to this abuse. The remaining questions, numbers 1, 2, 4, 7, and 8, were referred by the same labels for the remainder of the study. These were also evaluated by positive and negative predictive values, as defined after Tables 4.3 through 4.7. All reported B^2 are on one degree of freedom, with extremely small significance probabilty.

Table 4.3 *Responses to question 1*

		Diagnosis		
		No	Yes	
Screening Question	No	809	152	961
	Yes	66	109	175
		875	261	1136

$$B^2 = 147.00$$

Sensitivity = 41.76%   Specificity = 92.46%
Positive Predictive Value = 62.29%   Negative Predictive Value = 84.18%

Table 4.4 *Responses to question 2*

		Diagnosis		
		No	Yes	
Screening Question	No	708	78	786
	Yes	167	183	350
		875	261	1136

$$B^2 = 205.46$$

Sensitivity = 70.11%   Specificity = 80.91%
Positive Predictive Value = 52.29%   Negative Predictive Value = 90.08%

Table 4.5 *Responses to question 4*

		Diagnosis		
		No	Yes	
Screening Question	No	802	114	816
	Yes	73	147	220
		875	261	1136

$$B^2 = 230.25$$

Sensitivity = 56.32%   Specificity = 91.66%
Positive Predictive Value = 66.82%   Negative Predictive Value = 87.55%

Table 4.6 *Responses to question 7*

		Diagnosis		
		No	Yes	
Screening Question	No	760	119	879
	Yes	115	142	257
		875	261	1136

$$B^2 = 167.52$$

Sensitivity = 54.41%   Specificity = 86.86%
Positive Predictive Value = 55.25%   Negative Predictive Value = 86.46%

Table 4.7 *Responses to question 8*

		Diagnosis		
		No	Yes	
Screening Question	No	840	154	994
	Yes	35	107	142
		875	261	1136

$$B^2 = 173.64$$

Sensitivity = 41.00%   Specificity = 96.00%
Positive Predictive Value = 75.35%   Negative Predictive Value = 84.51%

Upon viewing the results in Tables 4.3 through 4.7 we see that questions 2 and 4 possess the highest sensitivities (70.11% and 56.32%). All specificities are quite high. We also report the positive predictive values, i.e., the proportions of positive screened patients with positive diagnoses, and the negative predictive values, i.e., the proportions of negatively screened patients with negative diagnoses. The positive predictive values are quite low, but this does not really matter. We are simply positively screening about twice as many patients as necessary. Further informal screening, or discussions with the doctor, will frequently limit the numbers of patients needing to receive treatment.

How can we best increase the sensitivity while combining the responses to two or more questions? Remembering the advice from our second focus group that patients may not tell the truth, we found that it was best, in terms of sensitivity and specificity, to combine questions 2 and 4 alone, and to do this by positively screening a patient if and only if the patient did not answer "No" (at the bottom of a four-point scale) to each of questions 2 and 4 (Table 4.8). The inclusion of the responses to further questions increased the sensitivity (up to 86.21% for at least one nonnegative response to questions 1, 2, 4, 7, and 8 but decreased the specificity, e.g., to 67.43% in this five-question situation).

Table 4.8 *Combined responses to questions 2 and 4*

		Diagnosis		
		No	Yes	
Combination of Screening	No	682	54	736
Questions 1 and 4	Yes	193	207	400
		875	261	1136

$$B^2 = 226.41$$

Sensitivity = 79.31%　　　　　　　　　Specificity = 77.94%

Positive Predictive Value = 51.75%　　Negative Predictive Value = 92.66%

This is the main result of our study, which should be contrasted with the state of the art, i.e., the 837-item diagnostic questionnaire, and also a "Cageaid" questionnaire, which was previously investigated by interviewing a sample of 373 primary care patients (Table 4.9).

Table 4.9 *Responses to Cageaid questionnaire*

		Diagnosis		
		No	Yes	
Combination of Screening	No	227	26	253
Question A and B	Yes	65	55	120
		292	81	373

$$B^2 = 52.32$$

Sensitivity = 67.90%　　　　　　　　　Specificity = 77.74%

Positive Predictive Value = 45.83%　　Negative Predictive Value = 89.72%

On the Cageaid questionnaire, the best two questions were

A. Have you ever felt that you ought to cut down on your drinking or drug use?

B. Have you ever had drink or drugs first thing in the morning to steady your nerves or to get rid of a hangover?

Again, a patient was positively screened if and only if the patient responded positively to at least one of these two questions. However, the sensitivity is only 67.90%. Surprisingly, a urine test assigned at random to the patients on our current study gives much less sensitivity when screening for substance abuse. In Table 4.10 we describe the results for a random urine test at Phase 3 of the study for our new questionnaire.

Table 4.10 *Urine test results*

		Diagnosis		
		No	Yes	
Urine Test	Negative	155	40	195
	Positive	21	15	36
		176	55	321

$B^2 = 7.11$(significance probability $= 0.0077$)

Sensitivity $= 27.27\%$ Specificity $= 88.07\%$

Positive Predictive Value $= 41.67\%$ Negative Predictive Value $= 79.49\%$

The low performance of the urine test is quite remarkable. The percentage 11.93%, 19.93%, of nonabusers who are nevertheless positive on the urine test might raise some general concerns regarding the use of urine tests to detect substance abusers.

4.3 Further validation of results

Our Phase 3 results were firstly analysed after the first 434 patients had been interviewed (Table 4.11).

Table 4.11 *Questions 2 and 4 (first 434 patients)*

		Diagnosis		
		No	Yes	
Combination of Screening	No	261	21	282
Questions 2 and 4	Yes	62	90	152
		323	111	434

$B^2 = 106.33$

Sensitivity $= 81.08\%$ Specificity $= 80.80\%$

Positive Predictive Value $= 59.21\%$ Negative Predictive Value $= 92.55\%$

A full statistical analysis was performed at this stage, and the minor importance of many further variables was confirmed. We then completed the total sample of 1136 patients (see Table 4.8) by interviewing 702 further patients (Table 4.12). Our study is therefore effectively *replicated*, i.e., repeated under as similar conditions as permitted by practical considerations.

Table 4.12 *Questions 2 and 4 (next 702 patients)*

		Diagnosis		
		No	Yes	
Combination of Screening	No	421	33	454
Question 1 and 4	Yes	131	117	248
		552	150	702

$B^2 = 121.16$

Sensitivity $= 78.00\%$ Specificity $= 76.27\%$
Positive Predictive Value $= 47.18\%$ Negative Predictive Value $= 92.73\%$

The remarkably close correspondence between the results in Tables 4.11 and 4.12 considerably validates the conclusions of our study. Our further analysis of these data included the logistic regression techniques of Chapter 8, which were used to investigate the possible effects of other variables. No further variables, i.e., demographic variables and social desirability substantially affected our key conclusion that primary care patients can be efficiently screened using a two-item questionnaire. By using the terminology of Chapter 8, one excellent fitting regression model ($X^2 = 26.85$ on 25 degrees of freedom) took the form:

$$\alpha = -0.426 + 0.622x_2 + 0.748x_4 + 0.569x_7 + 0.282G + 0.283A - 0.208Ax_4,$$

where

$$x_i = \begin{cases} +1 & \text{if response to question } i \text{ is positive} \\ -1 & \text{otherwise} \end{cases} \quad (\text{for } i = 2, 4 \text{ and } 7),$$

$$G = \begin{cases} +1 & \text{if subject is male} \\ -1 & \text{if subject is female,} \end{cases}$$

and

$$A = \begin{cases} +1 & \text{if largest daily alcohol consumption in previous} \\ & \text{30 days is less than three drinks} \\ -1 & \text{otherwise.} \end{cases}$$

For example, the performance of our screening procedure, if we screen for substance abuse whenever $\alpha > -1.33$, is described in Table 4.13.

Table 4.13 *Screening by Regression*

		Diagnosis		
		No	Yes	
Screening by Regression	No	701	54	755
	Yes	174	207	381
		875	261	1136

$$B^2 = 245.46$$

Sensitivity $= 79.31\%$ Specificity $= 80.11\%$
Positive Predictive Value $= 54.33\%$ Negative Predictive Value $= 92.85\%$

This performance, based upon five explanatory variables, only slightly improves upon the results described in Table 4.8 for the much simpler screening procedure based upon questions 2 and 4 alone. We therefore prefer the latter for screening by a medical expert. We now report a split of the results in Table 4.8, based upon gender (Tables 4.14 and 4.15).

Table 4.14 *Questions 2 and 4 (male subjects)*

		Diagnosis		
		No	Yes	
Combination of Screening	No	181	21	202
Question 2 and 4	Yes	63	100	163
		244	121	365

$$B^2 = 82.64$$

Sensitivity = 83.64%   Specificity = 74.18%

Positive Predictive Value = 61.35%   Negative Predictive Value = 89.60%

Table 4.15 *Questions 2 and 4 (female subjects)*

		Diagnosis		
		No	Yes	
Combination of Screening	No	501	33	534
Question 2 and 4	Yes	130	107	237
		631	140	781

$$B^2 = 129.27$$

Sensitivity = 76.43%   Specificity = 79.40%

Positive Predictive Value = 45.15%   Negative Predictive Value = 93.82%

The differences between the performances of the screening procedure for males and females are not sufficient to be able to recommend different simple screening procedures according to gender. However, the prevalence of abuse for females is $140/781 = 17.93\%$, compared with $121/365 = 33.15\%$ for males. Furthermore, the positive predictive value for females is 45.15% compared with 61.35% for males. This suggests that positively screened females should be more carefully considered, before being subjected to the full diagnostic procedure.

At a final stage of the investigation, 106 of the Phase 3 patients were asked the same five questions about a year later; out of these, 86.79% gave exactly the same responses to questions two and four, as before.

Exercises

4.1 Use the methodology of Section 2.10 to find the approximate power for a 5% level B^2 test when $n_1 = 400$, $n_2 = 736$, $\theta_1 = 0.8$, and $\theta_2 = 0.2$. Repeat your calculations for a 1% level B^2 test. Do you think that Phase 3 of our study was well designed?

4.2 A simple application of conditional probability tells us that for any events A and B, with $p(A) > 0$,

$$p(B|A) = \frac{p(A|B)p(B)}{p(A|B)p(B) + p(A|B^C)p(B^C)} .$$

Use this formula to express the positive predictive value, in terms of the sensitivity, specificity and prevalence, of the medical condition. Since $p(B^C|A^C) = 1 - p(B|A^C)$ for any events A and B, express the negative predictive value in terms of similar quantities.

4.3 To determine the rate of drug abuse at the University of Wisconsin-Madison, a questionnaire was mailed to all students. With a response rate of about 55%, about 10% of the students stated that they had taken drugs during the previous month. A Statistics 421 student (Connie Wang) interviewed a sample of about 200 students, chosen subjectively to represent the student population reasonably. With a full response rate, about 1/3 of the students stated that they had taken drugs during the previous month. During an informal discussion with the Statistics 421 class, it was suggested that the true prevalence rate may be closer to 75%. How would you interpret these observations?

4.4 Use prog1 to obtain 95% confidence intervals for the measures of association for the data in Tables 4.4, 4.5, 4.8, and 4.10. Discuss the practical significance of the results indicated by these tables.

4.5 (a) Do you think that questionnaires with lots of items reasonably provide more information? Discuss.

(b) Do you think that responses on a seven-point ordinal scale, e.g., completely dissatisfied, very dissatisfied, quite dissatisfied, neutral, quite satisfied, very satisfied, completely satisfied, necessarily provide more information than responses on a three point scale? Discuss.

(c) Dr. Toby Mitchell once proposed the philosophy, "The greater the amount of information the less you know". Do you agree or disagree with this philosophy? Discuss.

(d) Do you think that we should have investigated several hundred rather than nine initial questions, during the Madison Drug and Alcohol Study? Discuss.

4.6 (a) Use the G test of Section 3.5 to investigate equality of the measures of association of Tables 4.14 and 4.15. Fully discuss the practical significance of your results.

(b) Use the LRS test of Section 3.7 to investigate equality of the unconditional cell probabilities of Tables 4.14 and 4.15, and use prog1 to report the b_{ij} test statistics for the corresponding 2×4 table. Fully interpret all your results.

(c) Perform a three-directional analysis of the three-way table (gender, screening variable, diagnostic variable) obtained from the two 2×2 tables, Tables 4.14 and 4.15. Fully report all conclusions drawn.

CHAPTER 5

Goodman's Full-Rank Interaction Analysis

5.1 Introductory example (no totals fixed)

The hair/eye colour data were reported by Snee (1974) and analysed in a variety of complex ways by a number of authors including Efron and Diaconis (1985) and several contributors to the written discussion following their paper.

Table 5.1 *The hair/eye colour data*

		\multicolumn{4}{c}{Hair Colour}			
		Black	Brunette	Red	Blonde	
	Brown	68	119	26	7	220
Eye Colour	Blue	20	84	17	94	215
	Hazel	15	54	14	10	93
	Green	5	29	14	16	64
		108	286	71	127	592

Table 5.1 is an example of an $r \times s$ contingency table, with $r = 4$ and $s = 4$. Many contingency tables of this type can be analysed by a full-rank interaction analysis (Goodman, 1964). This approach, which is programmed on prog1, can help you to combine your data analysis, your intuition/inductive thought process, and your knowledge regarding the scientific/medical/social background of the data, to infer appropriate real-life conclusions of the data. It hence plays a central role in our implementation of "Aitken's Inductive Synthesis". You primarily need to consider the significant "interaction effects", together with any pattern of significant interactions across the table, and then use your intuition to develop conclusions based upon your common sense. In this chapter, we assume that our $r \times s$ table has more than $2 \times 2 = 4$ cells.

A mathematical definition of the (i,j)th interaction effect $\lambda_{ij}^{A\beta}$ will be provided in Section 5.2. For the moment, note that:

(a) For $i = 1, ..., r$, and $j = 1, ..., s$, the λ_{ij}^{AB} measures the deviation of the (i,j)th cell frequency y_{ij} from the model of independence of the row and column factors (in this case, eye colour and hair colour). When the independence model holds, the fitted frequency for the (i,j)th cell is $e_{ij} = y_{i*}y_{*j}/y_{**}$.

(b) As they are measured in log space, interaction effects play a similar role to the log-measure-of-association in a 2×2 table, but where λ_{ij}^{AB} is specific to the (i,j)th cell. Indeed, λ_{ij}^{AB} possesses a rather similar interpretation, in qualitative terms, to a quarter of the log-measure-of-association for the 2×2 table, obtained by collapsing the observed frequencies as follows:

$$
\begin{array}{cc|c}
y_{ij} & y_{i*} - y_{ij} & y_{i*} \\
y_{*j} - y_{ij} & u_{ij} & y_{**} - y_{i*} \\
\hline
y_{*j} & y_{**} - y_{*j} & y_{**}
\end{array}
$$

The entry in the $(2,2)$th cell of this collapsed table is $u_{ij} = y_{ij} - y_{i*} - y_{*j} + y_{**}$. For example, a collapsed table with $(1,1)$th cells corresponding to the $(3,3)$th cell in Table 5.1.1, is

		Hair Colour		
		Red	Not Red	
Eye Colour	Hazel	14	79	93
	Not Hazel	57	442	499
		71	521	592

The log-measure-of-association in this table is log $(1.374) = 0.318$.

The b^2 statistic, from prog1, is $b^2 = 0.973$, yielding a significance probability of 32.40%.

(c) Interaction effects are, however, defined in such a way that their row totals λ_{i*}^{AB} and column totals λ_{*j}^{AB}, across the $r \times s$ table, are all set equal to zero. This may affect the way you interpret them.

Running the full 4×4 hair/eye colour table on prog1 gives a value for the likelihood ratio statistic of LRS $= 146.44$ on nine degrees of freedom with significance probability $= 0.00\%$. In general, the degrees of freedom for the likelihood ratio statistic are $(r-1)(s-1)$. In our example, the test result confirms a significant overall departure from independence of rows and columns. The prog1 output also gives the following estimates for the interaction effects λ_{ij}:

Estimates $\widehat{\lambda}_{ij}$ of the Interaction Effects

0.975	0.277	0.055	−1.306
−0.399	−0.222	−0.520	1.141
0.105	0.127	0.077	−0.309
−0.681	−0.182	0.389	0.474

together with their estimated standard errors

Standard Errors $v_{ij}^{\frac{1}{2}}$ of the Interaction Effects

$$
\begin{array}{cccc}
0.156 & 0.121 & 0.165 & 0.236 \\
0.175 & 0.115 & 0.173 & 0.143 \\
0.197 & 0.137 & 0.193 & 0.216 \\
0.275 & 0.162 & 0.202 & 0.202
\end{array}
$$

The ratios $b_{ij} = \widehat{\lambda}_{ij}^{AB} / v_{ij}^{\frac{1}{2}}$ provide normal test statistics, for investigating whether particular interactions are equal to zero. These highlight the important cells in the table. They are given on the prog1 output as

Normal Test Statistics b_{ij}

$$
\begin{array}{rrrr}
6.272 & 2.293 & 0.331 & -5.533 \\
-2.275 & -1.937 & -3.001 & 7.990 \\
0.532 & 0.931 & 0.397 & -1.429 \\
-2.478 & -1.124 & 1.931 & 2.347
\end{array}
$$

Clearly, the (blue, blonde) cell gives the most significant interaction, followed by the (brown, black) cell. The (brown, blonde) cell gives the most significant negative interaction.

Summary of Interaction Analysis

$$
\begin{array}{cccc}
\oplus & + & 0 & \ominus \\
- & -? & - & \oplus \\
0 & 0 & 0 & 0 \\
- & 0 & +? & +
\end{array}
$$

Circled cells have strongly significant interactions. Zeros denote that the interactions for these cells are not judged to be significantly different from zero at the 5% level, and that this judgement is not close. The interaction analysis highlights the main results in the table; these may be further validated by collapsing the data into 2×2 contingency tables. Two important 2×2 tables are as follows:

		Hair Colour		
		Blonde	Not Blonde	
Eye Colour	Blue	94	121	215
	Not Blue	33	344	377
		127	465	592

and

		Hair Colour		
		Black	Not Black	
Eye Colour	Brown	68	152	220
	Not Brown	40	332	372
		108	484	592

For example, students in the sample with blue eyes are $(94/215)/(33/377)=$
4.99 times more likely to have blonde hair, than students without blue eyes.
Students with blonde hair are $(94/127)/(121/465) = 2.84$ times more likely
to have blue eyes, than students without blonde hair. These are the main
conclusions to be drawn from this data set. It is easy to miss the apparently obvious conclusions, when concentrating on a complicated analysis.
The methodology described in this section holds, for example, under an
independent Poisson model with cell means μ_{ij} (no totals fixed). However,
in the following six sections we will develop the preceding methodology
(this will be referred to as Goodman's full-rank interaction analysis) under three different sampling schemes. The limitations of these sampling
schemes (Chapter 1) still influence the degree of objectivity of our results.

5.2 Methodological developments (no totals fixed)

Consider the independent Poisson model, where, for $i = 1, ..., r$ and $j =
1, ...s$, the observed cell frequencies y_{ij} are numerical realisations of ran-
dom variables Y_{ij}, which possess independent Poisson distributions, with
respective means μ_{ij}. Then the maximum likelihood estimate of μ_{ij} is

$$\widehat{\mu}_{ij} = y_{ij},$$

since this value "maximises the probability of obtaining the value y_{ij} of Y_{ij}
actually observed". In mathematical terms, $\widehat{\mu}_{ij}$ maximises

$$p(Y_{ij} = y_{ij}) = e^{-\mu_{ij}} \mu_{ij}^{y_{ij}} /y_{ij}! \, ,$$

as a function of μ_{ij}, when y_{ij} is fixed to its observed numerical value. We
now introduce a "log-linear model". By this, we mean a linear model for
the natural logarithms

$$\gamma_{ij} = \log \mu_{ij} \qquad (i = 1, ..., r; j = 1, ..., s),$$

of the cell means. Note that we currently have $r \times s$ unknown parameters
in the model. However, assume that

$$\gamma_{ij} = \lambda + \lambda_i^A + \lambda_j^B + \lambda_{ij}^{AB} \qquad (i = 1, ..., r; j = 1, ...s),$$

where λ is the *overall effect*, λ_i^A is the *row effect* for the ith row, λ_j^B is the
column effect, for the jth column, and λ_{ij}^{AB} is the *interaction effect* for the
(i, j)th cell. There are now a total of $1 + r + s + rs$ parameters in the model,
but only rs distinct observations. The number of distinct parameters can,

however, be equated to the number of distinct observations, by imposing the constraints

$$\lambda_{.}^{A} \;=\; 0 \quad \lambda_{.}^{B} = 0,$$
$$\lambda_{i.}^{AB} \;=\; 0 \quad (i = 1, ..., r),$$

and

$$\lambda_{.j}^{AB} = 0 \quad (j = 1, ..., s),$$

where the dot notation denotes "average with respect to that subscript", so that

$$\lambda_{.}^{A} \;=\; r^{-1} \sum_{i=1}^{r} \lambda_{i}^{A},$$

$$\lambda_{.}^{B} \;=\; s^{-1} \sum_{j=1}^{s} \lambda_{j}^{B},$$

$$\lambda_{i.}^{AB} \;=\; s^{-1} \sum_{j=1}^{s} \lambda_{ij}^{AB},$$

and

$$\lambda_{.j}^{AB} = r^{-1} \sum_{i=1}^{r} \lambda_{ij}^{AB}.$$

There are $2 + r + s - 1 = 1 + r + s$ distinct constraints, since $\lambda_{..}^{AB} = 0$ derives both from averaging $\lambda_{i.}^{AB} = 0$ across $i = 1, ..., r$, and from averaging $\lambda_{.j}^{AB} = 0$ across $j = 1, ...s$. There are consequently $1 + r + s + rs - r - s - 1 = rs$ distinct parameters in the model, when these constraints are imposed. As this matches the number of distinct observations, we have a *full-rank* model. The log-likelihood of all the parameters in our model is

$$\log \ell(\boldsymbol{\lambda}|\mathbf{y}) \;\equiv\; y_{**}\lambda + \sum_{i} y_{i*}\lambda_{i}^{A} + \sum_{j} y_{*j}\lambda_{j}^{B} + \sum_{ij} y_{ij}\lambda_{ij}^{AB}$$
$$-\Omega(\boldsymbol{\lambda}) - \sum_{ij}(\log y_{ij}!),$$

where

$$\Omega(\boldsymbol{\lambda}) = \sum_{ij} e^{\lambda + \lambda_{i}^{A} + \lambda_{j}^{B} + \lambda_{ij}^{AB}}.$$

It is tedious to maximise the log-likelihood directly subject to the constraints described above. However, notice that, subject to these constraints, the sets of effects can be represented in terms of the $\gamma_{ij} = \log \mu_{ij}$ by

$$
\begin{aligned}
\lambda &= \gamma_{..}\,, \\
\lambda_i^A &= \gamma_{i.} - \gamma_{..} \quad (i = 1, ..., r), \\
\lambda_j^B &= \gamma_{.j} - \gamma_{..} \quad (j = 1, ..., s), \\
\lambda_{ij}^{AB} &= \gamma_{ij} - \lambda - \lambda_i^A - \lambda_j^B, \\
&= \gamma_{ij} - \gamma_{i.} - \gamma_{.j} + \gamma_{..}\,.
\end{aligned}
$$

We now refer to a well-known invariance property of maximum likelihood estimates. The maximum likelihood estimate of γ_{ij} is $\widehat{\gamma}_{ij} = \log \widehat{\mu}_{ij} = \ell_{ij}$, where $\ell_{ij} = \log y_{ij}$. Consequently, the maximum likelihood estimates of the overall, row, column, and interaction effects are the following linear combinations of the ℓ_{ij}:

$$
\begin{aligned}
\widehat{\lambda} &= \ell_{..}, \\
\widehat{\lambda}_i^A &= \ell_{i.} - \ell_{..} \quad (i = 1, ..., r), \\
\widehat{\lambda}_j^B &= \ell_{.j} - \ell_{..} \quad (j = 1, ..., s), \\
\widehat{\lambda}_{ij}^{AB} &= \ell_{ij} - \ell_{i.} - \ell_{.j} + \ell_{..} \quad (i = 1, ..., r; j = 1, ..., s).
\end{aligned}
$$

As $\widehat{\gamma}_{ij} = \widehat{\lambda} + \widehat{\lambda}_i^A + \widehat{\lambda}_j^B + \widehat{\lambda}_{ij}^{AB} = \log y_{ij}$ the full-rank model perfectly fits the data whenever the estimated effects are all finite. However, the estimated effects will all be either infinite or undetermined if any of the cell frequencies are zero. We, however, proceed under the assumption that $y_{ij} \geq 5$ for each cell. If this is not the case, then the exact Bayesian procedures proposed by Leonard, Hsu, and Tsui (1989) will be required.

Next refer to the result (Section 2.8) that, with $L_{ij} = \log Y_{ij}$ and $U_{ij} = Y_{ij}^{-1}$

$$
U_{ij}^{-\frac{1}{2}} (L_{ij} - \gamma_{ij})
$$

is approximately standard normally distributed, whenever $\mu_{ij} \geq 5$. Consider any linear combination,

$$
W = \sum_{ij} a_{ij} L_{ij},
$$

of the L_{ij}, together with the corresponding linear combination $\eta = \sum a_{ij} \gamma_{ij}$ of the parameters. Then, as a restatement of the results in Section 2.8,

$$
(W - \eta)/V^{\frac{1}{2}}
$$

is approximately standard normally distributed, where $V = \sum_{ij} a_{ij}^2 V_{ij}$. As a special case of this result, it is possible to show after considerable algebra that, with $\Lambda_{ij}^{AB} = L_{ij} - L_{i.} - L_{.j} + L_{..}$,

$$
(\Lambda_{ij}^{AB} - \lambda_{ij}^{AB})/ \{V_{ij}^{AB}\}^{\frac{1}{2}}
$$

is approximately normally distributed, where

$$
\begin{aligned}
V_{ij}^{AB} &= (1 - 2/r)(1 - 2/s)U_{ij} \\
&+ (1 - 2/r)U_{i*}/s^2 \\
&+ (1 - 2/s)U_{*j}/r^2 \\
&+ U_{**}/r^2 s^2.
\end{aligned}
$$

Therefore, under the hypothesis $H_0^{ij} : \lambda_{ij}^{AB} = 0$, the statistic

$$
B_{ij} = \Lambda_{ij}^{AB} / \{V_{ij}^{AB}\}^{\frac{1}{2}}
$$

possesses a standard normal distribution. If an initial overall test for H_0 : $\lambda_{ij}^{AB} = 0$ $(i = 1, ..., r; j = 1, ..., s)$ suggests rejection of H_0, we can then search for specific differences from H_0 by consideration of the observed (approximately) normal test statistics $b_{ij} = \widehat{\lambda}_{ij}^{AB} / \{v_{ij}^{AB}\}^{\frac{1}{2}}$, where v_{ij}^{AB} replaces the U_{ij} in the preceding expression for V_{ij}^{AB}, by the corresponding $v_{ij} = y_{ij}^{-1}$. Our preferred overall test for H_0 is the likelihood ratio test on $(r-1)(s-1)$ degrees of freedom, incorporated into prog1. The corresponding test statistic can also be described as the *residual deviance*.

Now consider the null hypothesis H_0 : all interactions zero, in greater detail. Under this hypothesis, we have

$$
\gamma_{ij} = \lambda + \lambda_i^A + \lambda_j^B \qquad (i = 1, ..., r; j = 1, ..., s)
$$

but subject to $\lambda_.^A = 0$ and $\lambda_.^B = 0$. This hypothesis is equivalent to the independence hypothesis

$$
H_0 : \mu_{ij} = \frac{\mu_{i*}\mu_{*j}}{\mu_{**}} \qquad (i = 1, ..., r; j = 1, ..., s),
$$

where the μ_{ij} are related to the model parameters, by the equations

$$
\lambda = r^{-1} \sum_{k=1}^{r} \log \mu_{k*} + s^{-1} \sum_{g=1}^{s} \log \mu_{*g} - \log \mu_{**},
$$

$$
\lambda_i^A = \log \mu_{i*} - r^{-1} \sum_{k=1}^{r} \log \mu_{k*},
$$

and

$$
\lambda_j^B = \log \mu_{*j} - s^{-1} \sum_{g=1}^{s} \log \mu_{*g}.
$$

In fact, under H_0, the maximum likelihood estimates for λ, λ_i^A, and λ_j^B are quite different from the more general estimates previously described, and only depend on the marginal totals in the table. In particular

$$\widehat{\lambda}_i^A = \log y_{i*} - r^{-1} \sum_{k=1}^r \log y_{k*} ,$$

which is a different expression, when compared with the linear combination $\ell_{i.} - \ell_{..}$, of the $\ell_{ij} = \log y_{ij}$. Furthermore,

$$\widehat{\lambda}_j^B = \log y_{*j} - s^{-1} \sum_{g=1}^s \log y_{*g} ,$$

which is a different expression, when compared with the estimate $\ell_{.j} - \ell_{..}$ previously assigned.

5.3 Numerical example (a four-corners model)

The data in Table 5.2 are taken from the 1984 General Social Survey of the U.S. National Data Program and cross-classifies the job satisfaction expressed by $n = 901$ respondents, against income level. Both row and column variables relate to an ordinal scale.

Table 5.2 *Cross Classification of Job Satisfaction by Income*

	Job Satisfaction			
Income	Very Dissatisfied	Slightly Dissatisfied	Moderately Dissatisfied	Very Satisfied
<$6,000	20	24	80	82
$6,000 - $15,000	22	38	104	125
$15,000 - $25,000	13	28	81	113
>$25,000	7	18	54	92

Our log-measure-of-association analysis (prog1) gives LRS = 12.037 as our overall test statistic on nine degrees of freedom, with significance probability 21.12%. There is therefore insufficient information in the data to refute a hypothesis of independence of income and job satisfaction. Once this conclusion is reached from an overall test, we are not permitted to draw statistically significant conclusions from tests for individual differences. This is standard statistical practice and avoids "data snooping", i.e., a hunt for apparently significant results, which might in reality be appearing totally by chance, even in situations where the hypothesised model is in fact true.

However, our b_{ij} statistics for the individual cells are as follows:

$$\begin{array}{rrrr}
1.943 & -0.696 & 0.093 & -2.326 \\
0.691 & 0.375 & -0.397 & -1.348 \\
-0.630 & 0.270 & 0.075 & 0.727 \\
-1.364 & 0.087 & 0.163 & 2.468
\end{array}$$

These results suggest that the cells with the more significant interactions lie in the four-corners of the table. Note that the individual test statistics for the (1,1) and (4,4) cells are positive, while those for the (1,4) and (4,1) cells are negative. This would be consistent with a conclusion that "individuals with low salaries tend to have low job satisfaction, while individuals with high salaries tend to have high job satisfaction". We have, however, demonstrated that the obvious conclusion is not even weakly statistically significant given the current data, and moderate sample size, despite two apparently weakly significant values (-2.326 and 2.468) for our normal test statistics.

For many two-way tables with ordinal scales, this pattern is indeed observed, but with a significant overall test and significant values for the b_{ij} in the four corners of the table. This phenomenon is sometimes referred to as "a four-corners model".

5.4 Methodological developments (overall total fixed)

Consider now the single multinomial model, with $r \times s$ cells where the cell frequencies Y_{ij} sum to n across the $r \times s$ table, and the unconditional cell probabilities ξ_{ij} satisfy $\xi_{**} = 1$. The collection $\{Y_{ij}\}$ of cell probabilities $(i = 1, ..., r \, ; j = 1, ..., s)$ is taken to possess a multinomial distribution with corresponding collection of cell probabilities $\{\xi_{ij}\}$, and sample size n. This model would, of course, be a consequence of conditioning the independent Poisson model, for the Y_{ij} of Section 5.2, upon $Y_{**} = n$, in which case $\xi_{ij} = \mu_{ij}/\mu_{**}$ $(i = 1, ..., r; j = 1, ..., s)$.

For the single multinomial model, consider multivariate logits γ_{ij} satisfying

$$\xi_{ij} = e^{\gamma_{ij}} / \sum_{kg} e^{\gamma_{kg}},$$

and consider the linear model,

$$\gamma_{ij} = \lambda_i^A + \lambda_j^B + \lambda_{ij}^{AB},$$

subject to the constraints $\lambda_.^A = \lambda_.^B = 0$, $\lambda_{i.}^{AB} = 0$ $(i = 1, ..., r)$, and $\lambda_{.j}^{AB} = 0$ $(j = 1, ..., s)$. As discussed in Section 5.2, λ_i^A is the ith row effect, λ_j^B is the jth column effect, and λ_{ij}^{AB} is the interaction effect for the (i, j)th cell. As the Y_{ij} are subject to the single constraint of summing to n, there are now $rs - 1$ distinct observations in the model, and this is the same as the number of distinct parameters.

Note that ξ_{ij} is unchanged by adding the same constant K to each γ_{ij}. For this reason, no overall effect λ is needed in our linear model for the γ_{ij}, since its value would not influence the unconditional probability ξ_{ij}.

However, as before,

$$\lambda_i^A = \gamma_{i.} - \gamma_{..}, \quad (i = 1, ..., r)$$
$$\lambda_j^B = \gamma_{.j} - \gamma_{..}, \quad (j = 1, ..., s)$$

and $\qquad \lambda_{ij}^{AB} = \gamma_{ij} - \gamma_{i.} - \gamma_{.j} + \gamma_{..} \quad (i = 1, ..., r; j = 1, ..., s).$

The maximum likelihood estimates for the ξ_{ij} are the corresponding $\hat{\xi}_{ij} = p_{ij} = y_{ij}/n$. Consequently, the maximum likelihood estimates for the γ_{ij} are the corresponding $\ell_{ij} + K$, where $\ell_{ij} = \log y_{ij}$ and K is an arbitrary constraint, not depending upon i and j. However, as the row, column, and interaction affects are contrasts in the γ_{ij}, the arbitrary constant K vanishes when we consider their maximum likelihood estimates. These estimates and their estimated standard errors are exactly the same as reported in Section 5.2. This follows from the approximate normality result for the distribution of a multinomial log-contrast, as described in Section 2.5. Furthermore, exactly the same test procedures are appropriate, i.e., the likelihood ratio statistic LRS for investigating the overall hypothesis $H_0 : \lambda_{ij}^{AB} = 0$ for all i, j, and the b_{ij} statistics for investigating the individual hypothesis $H_0^{(i,j)} : \lambda_{ij}^{AB} = 0$, for a specific i and j.

Let us now consider the overall hypothesis H_0 in greater detail. This is clearly equivalent to $H_0 : \gamma_{ij} = \lambda_i^A + \lambda_j^B$ for all i, j. In this case,

$$
\begin{aligned}
\xi_{ij} &= e^{\gamma_{ij}} / \sum_{kg} e^{\gamma_{kg}} \\
&= e^{\lambda_i^A + \lambda_j^B} / \sum_{kg} e^{\lambda_k^A + \lambda_g^B} \\
&= e^{\lambda_i^A + \lambda_j^B} / (\sum_k e^{\lambda_k^A})(\sum_g e^{\lambda_g^B}) \\
&= \phi_i^A \phi_j^B,
\end{aligned}
$$

where

$$\phi_i^A = e^{\lambda_i^A} / \sum_k e^{\lambda_k^A} \quad (= \xi_{i*}),$$

and

$$\phi_j^B = e^{\lambda_j^B} / \sum_g e^{\lambda_g^B} \quad (= \xi_{*j}).$$

This proves the result that the overall hypothesis $H_0 : \lambda_{ij}^{AB} = 0$ for all i and j is equivalent to the usual hypothesis of independence of rows and columns, i.e., $H_0 : \xi_{ij} = \xi_{i*}\xi_{*j}$ for all i and j. It also shows that the λ_i^A and λ_j^B are, under H_0, multivariate logit transformations of the ϕ_i^A and the ϕ_j^B, respectively. The preceding piece of algebra provides an overwhelming justification for the use of the multivariate logit transformations in contingency table analysis, since the equivalence of the two preceding statements of H_0 would not be available, using a linear model of the form $\lambda_i^A + \lambda_j^B + \lambda_{ij}^{AB}$, for any other transformation of the ξ_{ij}.

5.5 Business school example (overall total fixed)

In the previous section, we showed that the prog1 methodology of Section 5.1 for our independent Poisson model with cell means μ_{ij} (no totals fixed) also holds for a single multinomial model with unconditional cell probabilities ξ_{ij} (overall total n fixed). We may wish to condition on n, if we are more interested in the ξ_{ij} than the μ_{ij}. Consider the data described in Table 5.3. These were collected in 1995 by Kubulay Gok, a business student at the University of Wisconsin - Madison, and relate to $n = 1824$ journal articles, selected from 3500 articles (discovered by computer search), according to key words "School Based Management", "School Leadership", "School Reform", and "Shared Decision Making". Only articles with a U.S. first author attending a U.S. university were selected, and the university was then classified according to U.S. region (West, East, Midwest, South). Because of the manner in which the data were collected, it appears unreasonable to take the overall total to be Poisson distributed. We therefore condition on the overall total being fixed.

Table 5.3 *Classification of authors by journal and region*

Region				Journal					
	1	2	3	4	5	6	7	8	
West	52	87	52	100	100	54	98	65	608
East	22	40	28	48	54	25	51	36	304
Midwest	60	109	64	102	106	128	38	57	664
South	14	18	16	46	48	41	21	44	248
Total	148	254	160	296	308	248	208	202	1824

The overall test on prog1 for independence of rows and columns gives LRS = 109.93 on (4-1)(8-1) = 21 degrees of freedom, suggesting a highly significant association. The normal test statistics b_{ij} for the 32 cells were

Interaction Analysis

	1	2	3	4
West	0.807	1.223	−0.062	−0.356
East	−0.339	0.404	0.509	−0.553
Midwest	1.552	2.998	1.238	−0.743
South	−1.228	−2.800	−1.175	1.366

	5	6	7	8
West	−0.910	−3.171	3.736	−1.193
East	0.038	−2.890	3.530	−0.118
Midwest	−0.884	4.776	−4.861	−2.843
South	1.330	2.613	−1.162	3.630

This analysis enables us to discover the main features in the data. The significant interactions are all strongly significant and may be summarised as follows:

Summary

	1	2	3	4	5	6	7	8
West	0	0	0	0	0	⊖	⊕	0
East	0	0	0	0	0	⊖	⊕	0
Midwest	0	⊕	0	0	0	⊕	⊖	⊖
South	0	⊖	0	0	0	⊕	0	⊕

Based upon this summary, note that Journal 2 is more likely than typical (i.e., $109/254 = 42.9\%$ versus $664/1824 = 36.4\%$) to possess authors, in the area designated by the key words, from the Midwest, and less likely than typical ($18/254 = 7.1\%$ versus $248/1824 = 13.6\%$) to possess authors in this area from the South. For Journal 8, the reverse is true (Midwest 28.2%, South 21.8%). For Journal 6, the percentages of relevant authors in the West, East Midwest, and South are 21.8%, 10.1%, 51.6%, and 16.5%. These percentages contrast sharply with the corresponding percentages for Journal 7, namely, 47.1%, 24.5%, 18.3%, and 10.1%. The percentages stated in the current paragraph highlight the major statistically significant conclusions to be drawn from these data, since they have been indicated to us by the strongly significant results in the interaction analysis.

5.6 Methodological developments (row totals fixed)

Suppose now that the r row totals $n_1, ..., n_r$ of our $r \times s$ table are regarded as fixed. For $i = 1, ..., r$ and $j = 1, ..., s$, let θ_{ij} denote the probability that an individual, selected at random from the n_i individuals in the ith row, also belongs to the jth column. Then, the row totals of the θ_{ij} satisfy the r constraints $\theta_{i*} = 1$, for $i = 1, ..., r$. Furthermore, if the observed cell frequencies y_{ij} are regarded as numerical realizations of random variables Y_{ij}, then we have $Y_{i*} = n_i$, for $i = 1, ..., r$. A *product multinomial model* can be assumed. Suppose that the cell frequencies in each row possess a multinomial distribution, and that frequencies for different rows are independent. Assume that, for each $i = 1, ...r$,

$$Y_{i1}, ..., Y_{is} \sim M(\theta_{i1}, ..., \theta_{is}; n_i),$$

i.e., that $Y_{i1}, ..., Y_{is}$ possesses a multinomial distribution, with respective cell probabilities $\theta_{i1}, ..., \theta_{is}$, and sample size n_i. The independence of these r multinomial distributions justifies the terminology *product multinomial*. This model is a consequence, upon conditioning on $Y_{i*} = n_i$, for $i = 1, ..., r$, of the independent Poisson assumptions of Section 5.1 or of the single multinomial assumption of Section 5.4. In the first case, $\theta_{ij} = \mu_{ij}/\mu_{i*}$, while in the second case $\theta_{ij} = \xi_{ij}/\xi_{i*}$.

Now consider r sets of multivariate logits, one for each multinomial distribution. For $i = 1, ..., r$, let $\gamma_{i1}, ..., \gamma_{is}$ satisfy

$$\theta_{ij} = e^{\gamma_{ij}} / \sum_{g=1}^{s} e^{\gamma_{ig}} \quad (j = 1, ..., s).$$

Thus, the r constraints $\theta_{i*} = 1$, for $i = 1, ..., r$, are satisfied, whatever real values are assumed by the γ_{ij}. Moreover, the θ_{ij} are unchanged by replacing each γ_{ij} by $\gamma_{ij} + K_i$, where K_i can depend upon i, but not upon j. For this reason no overall effect λ, or row effect λ_i^A, is needed in our specification of a linear model for the γ_{ij}, since these would not influence the values of the θ_{ij}. Conditioning on the row totals, therefore, avoids the need for row effects. Our full-rank model is now given by

$$\gamma_{ij} = \lambda_j^B + \lambda_{ij}^{AB} \quad (i = 1, ..., r; \ j = 1, ..., s),$$

subject to $\lambda_{.}^B = 0$, $\lambda_{i.}^{AB} = 0$, for $i = 1, ..., r$, and $\lambda_{.j}^{AB} = 0$, for $j = 1, ..., s$.

Our full-rank model, with row totals fixed, possesses $r(s-1)$ distinct observations, and the same number of distinct parameters. The maximum likelihood estimate of θ_{ij} is $\hat{\theta}_{ij} = q_{ij}$, where $q_{ij} = y_{ij}/n_i$, and the maximum likelihood estimate of the γ_{ij} is $\hat{\gamma}_{ij} = \ell_{ij} + K_i$, where $\ell_{ij} = \log y_{ij}$ and the K_i are arbitrary constants, depending upon i, but not upon j. Since, as before,

$$\lambda_j^B = \gamma_{.j} - \gamma_{..}$$

and

$$\lambda_{ij}^{AB} = \gamma_{ij} - \gamma_{i.} - \gamma_{.j} + \gamma_{..},$$

the maximum likelihood estimates of the column and interaction effects are exactly the same as described in Section 5.2. Furthermore, exactly the same standard errors and test procedures are yet again appropriate, using prog1, i.e., the likelihood ratio statistic LRS for investigating $H_0 : \lambda_{ij}^{AB} = 0$ for all i, j, and the b_{ij} statistics for investigating $H_0^{(i,j)} : \lambda_{ij}^{AB} = 0$.

The hypothesis $H_0 : \lambda_{ij}^{AB} = 0$ for all i, j corresponds to independence of rows and columns in the independent Poisson and single multinomial situation. In the current situation, it is equivalent to $H_0 : \gamma_{ij} = \lambda_j^B$ for all i, j, which is also equivalent to the hypothesis that θ_{ij} does not depend upon i ($i = 1, ..., r; j = 1, ..., s$), i.e., the hypothesis of equality of the sets of cell probabilities of our r multinomial distributions. If H_0 is taken to be true, then the table may be collapsed into a single row with entries $y_{*1}, ..., y_{*s}$, and θ_{ij} should be estimated by $\widehat{\theta}_{ij} = y_{*j}/n$. We have, however, established the following key result, which should be obvious upon comparing different definitions of independence of events.

Key Result: Any reasonable test statistic (e.g., LRS) for investigating independence of rows and columns in $r \times s$ table, either with no totals fixed or overall total, only, fixed, can also be used to investigate equality of the sets of conditional probabilities, given the rows, when the row totals are regarded as fixed.

5.7 Advertising example (row totals fixed)

In the previous section, we showed that our prog1 methodology also holds when the row totals are fixed, in which case it can be justified by a product multinomial model. This refers to the conditional probabilities θ_{ij}, given the rows. The data described in Table 5.4 were collected by Stacey Cooper, a business student at the University of Wisconsin-Madison.

Table 5.4 *Opinions in various countries about advertising on television*

	Informative	Entertaining	Boring	Irritating	Total
Hong Kong	26	61	6	7	100
Brazil	48	32	15	5	100
Colombia	18	75	5	2	100
U.K.	19	51	13	17	100
U.S.A.	29	29	22	20	100
Germany	18	39	38	5	100
Overall	158	287	99	56	600
	(26.33%)	(47.83%)	(16.5%)	(9.33%)	

The likelihood ratio statistic LRS on prog1 tests the null hypothesis that the conditional probabilities for each country are equal across the rows. If the null hypothesis is acceptable, then the combined percentages 26.33%, 47.83%, 16.50%, and 19.33%, would be appropriate for each country separately. However, in this case LRS = 126.89, on 15 degrees of freedom (significance probability = 0.0000), strongly rejecting this hypothesis. We should, therefore, more closely consider the differences between the countries. The following b_{ij} values should be treated with some circumspection, as the frequency in the (3,4) cell is so small.

Normal Test Statistics

0.851	2.508	−2.332	0.360
3.835	−2.191	0.503	−1.172
0.795	4.932	−1.364	−1.605
−2.436	−0.445	−0.879	3.191
−0.998	−4.941	1.091	3.486
−1.942	−1.303	5.486	−1.291

Summary of Interaction Analysis

0	+	−	0
⊕	−	0	0
0	⊕	0	0
−	0	0	⊕
0	⊖	0	⊕
−?	0	⊕	0

The most significant conclusion in the table relates to the (6,3) cell. In terms of percentages, this tells us that a higher percentage (38%) of Germans than typical (16.5%) find advertising on television boring. The next most significant conclusion relates to the (5,2) cell. This tells us that a much lower percentage of Americans (20%) than typical (47.83%) find this experience entertaining. However, Colombians (75%) and Hong Kong Chinese (61%), hold a different view. A higher percentage (48%) of Brazilians found this experience informative. Both the British (17%) and Americans (18%) are more typically irritated by advertising on television. These are the main conclusions that can be drawn with statistical significance from the data set.

In situations where one or more of the cell frequencies are small, one possibility is to add a single count to every cell frequency, before running prog1. In this example. this gives the modified test statistics:

Modified Normal Test Statistics

0.842	2.566	−2.290	0.242
3.929	−2.207	0.433	−1.215
0.552	5.065	−1.487	−1.537
−2.292	−0.267	−0.852	3.009
−0.816	−4.739	1.102	3.314
−1.917	−1.293	5.462	−1.336

In this example, our modifications are very slight, confirming the credibility of our original conclusions.

5.8 Testing for equality of unconditional cell probabilities

It is often of interest to investigate the equality of the sets of unconditional cell probabilities of several $r \times s$ tables, e.g., with overall totals fixed, and a single multinomial model assumed for each table. If equality is assumed, then the tables may be combined, and the analysis may concentrate on this combined table. If a single multinomial model is assumed for each table, then, under the equality hypothesis, a single multinomial model is true for the combined table. This is, however, untrue if the equality hypothesis is false, and none of the standard tests of significance can then be applied to the overall table. In general, if the equality hypothesis is thought be untrue, then each table should be analysed separately, without pooling, and then the results compared intuitively across tables. The methodology of the current section does not, however, hold if the row totals in each $r \times s$ table are fixed. For this case, see Exercise 5.17.

The Berkeley admissions data (Table 5.5) are more fully discussed by Freedman et al. (1998, p. 16), and provide a classic example of Simpson's paradox, in the context of apparent gender discrimination.

Table 5.5 *Admissions data for the graduate programs in six largest majors at University of California, Berkeley (data are reconstructed from bracketed rounded percentages)*

Men

Major	Admitted		Rejected	Total
A	512	(62%)	313	825
B	353	(63%)	207	560
C	120	(37%)	205	325
D	138	(33%)	279	417
E	53	(28%)	138	191
F	22	(6%)	351	373
Overall	1198	(44.52%)	1493	2691

Women

Major	Admitted		Rejected	Total
A	89	(82%)	19	108
B	17	(68%)	8	25
C	202	(34%)	391	593
D	131	(35%)	244	375
E	94	(24%)	299	393
F	24	(7%)	317	341
Overall	557	(30.35%)	1278	1835

Note that, overall, 44.52% of male applicants are admitted, compared with just 30.35% of females. An overall 2×2 table, based upon the column totals of Table 5.5, would therefore suggest overwhelming discrimination against females. However, when the data are split according to the six majors, different conclusions should be drawn. Major A appears to discriminate seriously against males. Majors B, D, and F are slightly biased against males. Only majors C and E are slightly biased against females. A more detailed analysis is certainly required.

To set up a careful scrutiny of these data, let us first test equality of the unconditional cell probabilities of the six 2×2 tables corresponding to the six rows of Table 5.5. For example, the first table (Major A) is

	Admitted	Rejected
Men	512	313
Women	89	19

Owing to the key result, stated in Section 5.6, we may test this equality hypothesis by investigating independence of rows and column of a 6×4 table, with each row of the table consisting of the entries in one of our 2×2 tables. Indeed, our 6×4 table consists of the four columns of observed frequencies described in Table 5.5. Entering this table into prog1, we find that LRS = 2004.22 on 15 degrees of freedom, suggesting an overwhelming significant difference between these six 2×2 tables, i.e., an overwhelming effect of choice of major.

We might also wish to check the significance of gender on our results, via a test for equality of the unconditional cell probabilities of the two 6×2 tables obtained by splitting on gender. We could do this by entering an appropriate 2×12 table on prog1. However, it is easier to flip around rows and columns, and enter the corresponding 12×2 table. The first column consists of all entries of our 6×2 table for males, in some order, and the second column consists of all entries to our 6×2 table for females, in the same order. This gives LRS = 1242.35 on 11 degrees of freedom, suggesting an overwhelming significant gender effect.

For completeness, we also test equality of the two 6×2 tables (major versus gender), when we split according to the admit/reject variable. The first column of our 12×2 table now consists of the frequencies for the 12 "admitted" cells, and the second column consists of the frequencies for the twelve "rejected" cells. Then, prog1 gives LRS = 877.06 on 11 degrees of freedom, again highly significant.

5.9 Analysis of Berkeley admissions data

We now analyse, with careful scrutiny, the data in Table 5.6, using a three-directional approach. The three significance tests, performed in Section 5.8, tell us that we should consider all the splits, in each direction, and that it is not relevant to consider the pooled table in any direction.

First, consider the six 2×2 tables (gender versus admit/reject) obtained by splitting with respect to major. The comparison of the admission ratios for men and women can be extended by performing B^2 tests on each of these tables separately. The observed values b of the log-measure-of-association statistic, B of section 2.6, together with the corresponding significance probabilities, is described as follows:

Major	A	B	C	D	E	F
b	-4.0047	-0.5028	0.8679	-0.5458	0.9997	-0.6190
Sig. prob.	0.0001	0.6151	0.3855	0.5852	0.3174	0.5359

These results put a different complexion on the paradox. They tell us that, for Major A, there is a statistically significant apparent bias against admitting men. However, there are no statistically significant gender differences for the other five majors.

The following features might be noticed at either the present, or at the second stage of the analysis (by considering the row totals of the two 6×2 tables described in Section 5.8). For the six majors, the ratios of the number of men applying to the number of women applying are

Major	A	B	C	D	E	F
Ratio	7.639	22.4	0.548	1.112	0.486	1.094

The four majors (A, B, D, and F) for which this ratio exceeds unity yield negative observed associations in the corresponding 2×2 table (gender against admit/reject). The two majors (C and E) for which this ratio is less than unity yield positive associations and b values. This interesting pattern in the data provides an example of "practical significance", when contrasted with "statistical significance". Majors with more applications either from males or from females might try to rectify this imbalance, by rejecting more applicants of the corresponding gender. They might be motivated to do this in order to apparently comply with the discrimination laws.

At the second stage of our analysis, consider the two 6×2 tables of Section 5.8 (major versus admission decision), and perform Goodman's full-rank interaction analysis for men and women separately. The b_{ij} are described as follows:

Major	Men		Women	
	Admit	Reject	Admit	Reject
A	14.22	-14.22	8.79	-8.79
B	13.15	-13.15	3.33	-3.33
C	1.11	-1.11	-1.74	1.74
D	-0.47	0.047	-1.30	1.30
E	-2.10	2.10	-5.19	5.19
F	-11.25	11.25	-10.78	10.78

$$\text{(LRS} = 514.76, \qquad \text{(LRS} = 268.85,$$
$$\text{degrees of freedom} = 5) \qquad \text{degrees of freedom} = 5)$$

There is a similarity between the interaction patterns for men and women. For both men and women, majors A and B give the highest admission rates, as indicated by the bracketed percentages in Table 5.5. Majors E and F give the lowest admission rates. The interaction analysis emphasises the significance of these differences.

It appears that more men are applying to the majors with higher admission rates, thus creating the internal overall illusion of discrimination against women. This explains why Simpson's paradox has occurred. At the third stage of our analyses, consider our two 6 × 2 tables (major versus gender) where the split is according to "admitted" or "rejected".

Major	Admitted		Rejected	
	Men	Women	Men	Women
A	512	89	313	19
B	353	17	207	8
C	120	202	205	391
D	138	131	279	244
E	53	94	138	299
F	22	24	351	317

The b_{ij} for Goodman's interaction analysis, performed on each of these tables separately, are

Major	Admitted		Rejected	
	Men	Women	Men	Women
A	9.35	−9.35	9.57	−9.57
B	11.16	−11.16	8.02	−8.02
C	−9.24	9.24	−13.90	13.90
D	−4.40	4.40	−6.42	6.42
E	−7.36	−7.36	−13.85	13.85
F	−2.75	2.75	−7.09	7.09

These two tables give remarkably similar interaction patterns, which suggest that both majors A and B are much more likely to receive male applicants when compared with the remaining four majors.

5.10 Further data sets

Table 5.6 *The engineering apprentice data*

Section Head's Assessment	Written Test Result			
	A	B	C	D
Excellent	26	29	21	11
Very Good	33	43	35	20
Average	47	71	72	45
Needs to Improve	7	12	11	9

Table 5.7 *The Shopping in Oxford Data*

Car Availability	Response to Grocery Shop Question				
	1	2	3	4	5
None	55	11	16	17	100
Some	101	7	18	23	103
Full	91	20	25	16	77

Exercises

5.1 Analyse the engineering apprentice data in Table 5.6 using prog1. What conclusions would you draw from your analysis. Is a four-corner model appropriate?

5.2 Analyse the "shopping in Oxford data" in Table 5.7, which was reported by Bowlby and Silk (1982), and previously analysed by Fingleton (1984, p. 10). The row variable is car availability (none, some, full). The column variable measures the response to the question, "Do you find it tiring getting to grocery shops?" On an ordinal scale (the first column corresponds to "strongly disagree" and the last column to "strongly agree"), which interaction effects are significant? Is a four-corner model appropriate? Are you surprised by your value of b_{41}? Can you suggest possible real-life explanations? (In Oxford many people cycle to the local shops. Others drive to a shopping centre outside Oxford.)

5.3 Calculate the row, column, and interaction effects for Mendel's pea breeding data (Section 2.8). Show that the interaction effects are all equal in magnitude to the log-measure-of-association.

5.4 Perform the log-measure-of-association test for each of three 2×2 tables which collapse the 4×4 table, Table 5.1 (Hair/eye colour data). Compare your results with the b_{ij} test results for the corresponding cells in the original 4×4 table. Discuss.

5.5   In the Poisson situation described in Section 5.2, show that the log-likelihood of the (i,j)th cell mean μ_{ij} is

$$\log \ell(\mu_{ij}|y_{ij}) = -\mu_{ij} + y_{ij} \log \mu_{ij} - \log y_{ij}!$$

Show that the log-likelihood is maximised when $u_{ij} = \widehat{\mu}_{ij}$, where $\widehat{\mu}_{ij} = y_{ij}$. Hence show that the maximum likelihood estimate of $\gamma_{ij} = \log \mu_{ij}$ is $\widehat{\gamma}_{ij} = \log y_{ij}$.

5.6   In the Poisson situation described in Section 5.2, show that the overall effects, row effects, column effects, and interaction effects can indeed be expressed in terms of the log means $\gamma_{ij} = \log \mu_{ij}$, in the manner stated.

5.7   In Section 5.2, show that the (i,j)th interaction effect $\lambda_{ij}^{AB} = \gamma_{ij} - \gamma_{i.} - \gamma_{.j} + \gamma_{..}$ is a special case of log-contrast

$$\eta = \sum_{k=1}^{r} \sum_{g=1}^{s} a_{kg} \gamma_{kg} \quad ,$$

where $\sum_{kg} a_{kg} = 0$, with the choices

$$a_{kg} = \begin{cases} 1 - r^{-1} - s^{-1} + r^{-1}s^{-1} & (k = i, g = j) \\ -s^{-1}(1 - r^{-1}) & (k = i, g \neq j) \\ -r^{-1}(1 - s^{-1}) & (k \neq i, g = j) \\ r^{-1}s^{-1} & (k \neq i, g \neq j) \end{cases} .$$

5.8   Under the choices of a_{kg}, in Exercise 5.7, show that the expression

$$V_{ij}^{AB} = \sum_{k=1}^{r} \sum_{s=1}^{s} a_{kg}^2 U_{kg}$$

matches the expression for V_{ij}^{AB} described in Section 5.2.

5.9   In Section 5.2, find an approximate estimated variance for $\widehat{\lambda}_i^A = \ell_{i.} - \ell_{..}$ under the full-rank interaction model. By noting that $y_{1*}, ..., y_{r*}$ possess a multinomial distribution, find an approximate estimated variance for

$$\widehat{\lambda}_i^A = \log y_{i*} - r^{-1} \sum_{k=1}^{r} \log y_{k*},$$

when all interaction effects are taken to be zero.

5.10   By extending the discussion in Section 5.3, describe why "data snooping" can more generally lead to misleading conclusions.

5.11   If cell frequencies Y_{ij} possess a multinomial distribution with cell probabilities ξ_{ij}, summing to unity, and sample size n (see Section 5.4), show that the log-likelihood of the ξ_{ij}, given the observed values

y_{ij} are

$$\ell(\boldsymbol{\xi}|\mathbf{y}) = \sum_{ij} y_{ij} \log \xi_{ij} - \sum_{ij} \log y_{ij}! \qquad (\sum_{ij} \xi_{ij} = 1) .$$

Hence, show that the maximum likelihood estimates of the ξ_{ij} are $\widehat{\xi}_{ij} = y_{ij}/n$, for $i = 1, ..., r$ and $j = 1, ..., s.$.

5.12   In the situation described in Exercise 5.11, consider multivariate logits γ_{ij}, satisfying

$$\xi_{ij} = e^{\gamma_{ij}} / \sum_{kg} e^{\gamma_{kg}} .$$

Show that the log-likelihood of the γ_{ij} is

$$\ell(\boldsymbol{\gamma}|\mathbf{y}) = \sum_{ij} y_{ij}\gamma_{ij} - nD(\boldsymbol{\gamma}) - \sum_{ij} \log y_{ij}!$$

for some choice of $D(\boldsymbol{\gamma})$ which you should define. Hence, show that the log-likelihood is maximised whenever $\gamma_{ij} = \widehat{\gamma}_{ij}$, where $\widehat{\gamma}_{ij} = \log y_{ij} + K$ $(i = 1, ..., r; j = 1, ..., s)$, for an arbitrary choice of K, not depending upon i and j.

5.13   Read the paper by Holland (1973) which shows that no "covariance stabilizing" transformation exists for the multinomial distribution. Describe the main reasons the multivariate logit transformation is so important in contingency table analysis.

5.14   Carefully investigate whether or not any further conclusions can be drawn from the data in Table 5.3 (Classification of authors by journal and region), beyond those indicated by Goodman's interaction analysis.

5.15   Show, giving full details, why the product multinomial model of Section 5.6 is a consequence of conditioning a single multinomial model upon fixed row totals.

5.16   Carefully investigate whether any further conclusions can be drawn from Table 5.4 (opinions in various countries about advertising on television) beyond those indicated by Goodman's interaction analysis.

5.17   Consider t different $r \times s$ contingency tables, but with row totals fixed. Use the developments of Section 5.8 to show that equality of the conditional probabilities, given the rows, across the t tables, can be investigated via separate LRS tests for independence of rows and columns s different $r \times t$ tables. Use your methodology to investigate equality of the conditional probabilities, given the rows, of the tables:

	Males				Females		
	R	R^C			R	R^C	
$T1$	35	65	100	$T1$	40	60	100
$T2$	55	45	100	$T2$	60	40	100

All four row totals are fixed. Is it reasonable to combine these tables into a single 2×2 table?

5.18   Analyse the Berkeley admissions data as thoroughly as possible. Can you find any further conclusions beyond these indicated in Section 5.9?

CHAPTER 6

Further Examples and Extensions

6.1 Hypertension, obesity, and alcohol consumption

The data in Table 6.1 were previously analysed by a University of Edinburgh student (Scott Binnie), and appeared on an American Medical page on the Internet. The table classifies 1999 patients according to alcohol intake (average number of drinks per day, on an ordinal scale), obesity (low, average, or high, also on an ordinal scale), and presence or absence of hypertension. The obesity and alcohol intake categories appear to have been chosen to equate roughly the percentages of patients in these categories. This has the effect of flattening some of the features in the data set, and is not recommended. While we proceed under a single multinomial assumption, this should be regarded as subjective.

Table 6.1 *Cross-classification of 1999 patients*

Obesity	Hypertension	Alcohol Intake				
		0	1-2	3-5	6+	Total
Low	Yes	23	37	34	40	134
Low	No	161	145	133	98	537
Av.	Yes	26	38	45	57	166
Av.	No	134	93	142	121	490
High	Yes	38	49	77	78	242
High	No	97	102	113	118	430
		479	464	544	512	1999

While these data can be analysed as a $4 \times 3 \times 2$ contingency table, we first analyse the data as arranged in the preceding 6×4 table, with the row variable representing the six pairs (Low, Yes), ..., (High, No) of obesity and hypertension levels, and the column variable representing alcohol intake. A single application of prog1 for this 6×4 table gives the following values for the test statistics b_{ij} of Section 5.2

Column

Row	1	2	3	4
1	−1.26	1.35	−0.57	0.72
2	4.76	1.93	−1.37	−5.04
3	−1.86	0.03	0.08	2.26
4	3.36	−2.50	0.66	−0.40
5	−2.11	−1.04	1.83	1.99
6	0.78	0.03	0.72	−0.16

(LRS = 61.93 on 15 degrees of freedom)

Notice the pattern of alternating signs in the first and last columns. This suggests that, at each level of obesity, hypertension is strongly associated with alcohol intake. The high positive interactions in the (2,1) and (4,1) cells indicate that patients with low or average obesity and no hypertension are positively associated with no alcohol intake. However, the insignificant interaction for the (6,1) cell indicates that lack of hypertension is no longer strongly associated with zero alcohol intake, when the patients are obese. The strongly negative interaction in the (2,4) cell indicates that patients without obesity or hypertension are negatively associated with high alcohol intake.

This initial interaction analysis suggests that it would be useful to compare conditional percentages, given the rows. Overall, the percentages of patients in the four intake categories are 23.96%, 23.21%, 27.21%, and 25.61%. The initial analysis also motivates us to initiate a three-directional approach, first by considering hypertension against alcohol intake, at the three different levels of obesity (Tables 6.2 to 6.4).

Table 6.2 *Patients with low obesity*

| Hypertension | Alcohol Intake | | | | Total |
	0	1-2	3-5	6+	
Yes	23	37	34	40	134
	(17.16%)	(27.61%)	(25.37%)	(29.85%)	
No	161	145	133	98	537
	(29.98%)	(27.00%)	(24.77%)	(18.25%)	
					671

Table 6.3 *Patients with average obesity*

Hypertension	Alcohol Intake				Total
	0	1-2	3-5	6+	
Yes	26	38	45	57	166
	(15.66%)	(22.89%)	(27.11%)	(34.34%)	
No	134	93	142	121	490
	(27.35%)	(18.99%)	(28.98%)	(24.69%)	
					656

Table 6.4 *Patients with high obesity*

Hypertension	Alcohol Intake				Total
	0	1-2	3-5	6+	
Yes	38	49	77	78	242
	(15.70%)	(20.25%)	(31.82%)	(32.23%)	
No	97	102	113	118	430
	(22.56%)	(23.72%)	(26.28%)	(27.44%)	
					672

Before considering each of these tables separately, we should investigate possible equality of the corresponding three sets of unconditional cell probabilities. This possibility is, however, refuted by LRS = 72.76 on 14 degrees of freedom, obtained by entering a 3×8 table into prog1, where the first, second, and third rows of the 3×8 table consist of the entries to Tables 6.2, 6.3, and 6.4, respectively. We should therefore consider each of Tables 6.2, 6.3, and 6.4 separately, and it would be misleading to combine them.

For Table 6.2, LRS = 13.59 on three degrees of freedom (significance probability = 0.0035). Therefore, for patients with low obesity, there is a strongly significant association between hypertension and alcohol intake. However, the differences in the conditional percentages are not of immense practical significance (e.g., 29.85% versus 18.25%) for the highest alcohol intake category. The clinical significance of this result would appear to be quite modest. Comparing observed and fitted frequencies (in brackets) under independence of hypertension and alcohol intake, gives

$$
\begin{array}{cccc}
23 & 27 & 34 & 40 \\
(36.75) & (36.35) & (33.35) & (27.56) \\
161 & 145 & 133 & 98 \\
(147.25) & (145.65) & (133.65) & (110.44)
\end{array}
$$

The differences of about 13 patients, in each of the four corner cells, are small compared with the row totals of 134 and 537. Alternatively,

the cell frequency of 23 in the (1,1) cell can be compared with the value
$134 \times 29.98\% = 40.17$. This is the number of patients out of the 134 with
hypertension who would be anticipated to have low alcohol intake, in the
situation where prevalence rate of 29.98% among patients with no hypertension was assumed. The value 29.98% is the conditional percentage for
the (2,1) cell in Table 6.2. Similarly, the cell frequency of 40 for the (1,4)
cell may be compared with the projected value of $134 \times 18.25\% = 24.46$.
We conclude that the differences from the independence model is equivalent to about 16 patients getting misassigned from the (1,1) cell to the
(1,4) cell. There may well be a confounding variable which would explain
this modest difference, e.g., 16 out of the 134 patients with hypertension
may also possess some medical symptom Z which is associated with high
alcohol intake, but not present in the 537 patients without hypertension.

For Table 6.3, LRS = 12.74 on three degrees of freedom (significance
probability = 0.0052) and very similar comments hold, for averagely obese
patients as for patients with low obesity regarding a comparison of alcohol intakes for patients with and without hypertension. Reassigning about
18 patients from the (1,4) cell to the (1,1) cell would provide an almost
perfect fit to independence. Notice, however, that the two percentages in
the final column (34.34% and 24.69%) are greater than the corresponding
percentages (29.85% and 18.25%) in Table 6.2. We conclude that patients
with average obesity are more strongly associated with high alcohol intake,
than patients with low obesity, irrespective of hypertension. This conclusion can be validated by respective comparison of the percentages of each
of the four columns of Tables 6.2 and 6.3. Going ahead to Table 6.4 we
see that a similar conclusion holds when comparing highly obese patients
with patients of low obesity. However, the conclusion does not hold when
comparing patients of high and average obesity.

For Table 6.4, LRS = 7.46 on three degrees of freedom (significance probability = 0.0586), so that, when considered alone, our association between
hypertension and high alcohol intake is not quite statistically significant,
at the 5% level. However, when judged together with the overall pattern
that has developed between Tables 6.2, 6.3, and 6.4, we conclude that this
association is of similar practical significance to the association in Tables
6.2 and 6.3. Reassigning about 14 patients from the (1,4) cell to the (1,1)
cell would provide a good fit to independence.

While after this first stage of the three-directional analysis we might appear to have exhaustively considered all possibilities, we should also investigate the other two directions. Next consider hypertension versus obesity,
at the two levels of hypertension (Tables 6.5 and 6.6).

Table 6.5 *Patients with hypertension*

| | Alcohol Intake | | | | |
Obesity	0	1-2	3-5	6+	Total
Low	23	37	34	40	134
Av.	26	38	45	57	166
High	38	49	77	78	242
	87	124	156	175	542
	(16.05%)	(22.88%)	(28.78%)	(32.29%)	

Table 6.6 *Patients without hypertension*

| | Alcohol Intake | | | | |
Obesity	0	1-2	3-5	6+	Total
Low	161	145	133	98	537
Av.	134	93	142	121	490
High	97	102	113	118	430
	392	340	388	337	1457
	(26.90%)	(23.34%)	(26.63%)	(23.13%)	

The unconditional cell probabilities of Tables 6.5 and 6.6 are significantly different (LRS = 75.75 on 11 degrees of freedom) so that these tables should not be combined. Table 6.5 now provides a key result, as LRS = 4.07 on 6 degrees of freedom (significance probability = 66.73%). The data therefore give evidence that, for patients with hypertension, alcohol intake is independent of level of obesity. One consequence of this is that we may use the column percentages, 16.05%, 22.88%, 28.78% and 32.29% to predict the alcohol intake level, for any patient with hypertension.

For Table 6.6, LRS = 23.74 on 6 degrees of freedom (significance probability = 0.06%), suggesting that, for patients without hypertension, alcohol intake is associated with level of obesity.

Interaction Analysis

2.15	2.62	−1.06	−3.43
0.56	−2.76	1.40	1.03
−2.47	0.35	−0.31	2.47

The values of the b_{ij} confirm a "four-corner effect", so that high obesity and high alcohol levels are associated and, similarly, low obesity and low alcohol levels. However, the conditional percentages, given the rows, for Table 6.6 are all between 20% and 30% apart from the (1,1) and (2,2) cells, which give percentages of 29.98% and 18.98%. The clinical significance of this result is therefore quite modest. It is difficult to explain the low value for the (2,2) cell.

In the final and third direction of our analysis, consider the association between obesity and hypertension for different levels of alcohol.

Table 6.7 *Zero alcohol intake*

		Hypertension	
Obesity	Yes		No
Low	23	(12.50%)	161
Av.	26	(16.25%)	134
High	38	(28.15%)	97

(LRS = 12.81 on 2 degrees of feedom significance probability 0.17%.)

Table 6.8 *Average alcohol intake of one to two drinks*

		Hypertension	
Obesity	Yes		No
Low	37	(20.33%)	145
Av.	38	(29.01%)	93
High	49	(32.45%)	102

(LRS = 6.80 on 2 degrees of freedom significance probability 3.35%.)

Table 6.9 *Average alcohol intake, three to five drinks*

		Hypertension	
Obesity	Yes		No
Low	34	(20.36%)	133
Av.	45	(24.06%)	142
High	77	(40.53%)	113

(LRS = 20.26 on 2 degrees of freedom significance probability 0.00%.)

Table 6.10 *Average alcohol intake, six or more drinks*

		Hypertension	
Obesity	Yes		No
Low	40	(28.99%)	98
Av.	57	(32.02%)	121
High	78	(39.80%)	118

(LRS = 4.76 on 2 degrees of freedom significance probability 9.27%.)

The unconditional cell probabilities of Tables 6.7 through 6.10 are significantly different (LRS = 61.93 on 15 degrees of freedom) so that those four tables cannot be combined. The statistical significance of the association between obesity and hypertension varies at different levels of alcohol intake. However, the overall pattern of the percentages of patients with hypertension indicates that this association is of considerable practical significance. For zero alcohol intake, the percentages 12.50%, 16.25% and 28.15% of patients with hypertension increase with level of obesity. The corresponding percentages 20.33%, 29.01% and 32.45% in Table 6.8 also increase, followed by 20.36%, 24.06% and 40.53% in Table 6.9 and 28.99%, 32.02% and 39.80% in Table 6.10. Therefore, when diagnosing hypertension, the interaction between obesity and alcohol intake is an important indicator.

6.2 The Bristol cervical screening data

We now report the results of an investigation by Kelly McKerrow, a University of Edinburgh student, of data collected and published by the Bristol Screening Programme (1995). In 1966, cervical cancer was associated with the presence of abnormal cells in smear tests, but not all abnormal cells were related to cervical cancer. Therefore, smear tests were approved for initial screening for cervical cancer.

A limited recall system was employed until 1988, when it became replaced by a complete recall system. Grades of abnormality of the cells were classed as

A.   Severe dyskaryosis
B.   Mild and moderate dyskaryosis
C.   Borderline change

The student confined attention to data on patients with one of these grades of abnormality. She considered data for two periods, 1981-1986, 1988-1993, split by age and grade of abnormality, but without recording outcome (Tables 6.11 and 6.12); only a couple of hundred patients from each sample actually developed cervical cancer.

Table 6.11   *Cervical screening data (1981-1986)**

	Age Group								
	20−	20+	25+	30+	40+	50+	60+	65+	Total
A	6	77	313	940	412	201	84	175	2208
B	54	300	370	510	199	63	10	3	1509
C	139	533	497	792	475	225	47	66	2774
	199	910	1180	2242	1086	489	141	244	6491

Table 6.12 *Cervical screening data (1988-1993)**

	20−	20+	25+	30+	40+	50+	60+	65+	Total
			Age Group						
A	3	119	455	1072	612	272	81	150	2764
B	119	1238	1514	1750	874	298	40	43	5876
C	180	1371	1359	1714	1401	676	111	99	6911
	302	2728	3328	4536	2887	1246	232	292	15551

*The row variable denotes abnormality (A, B, or C)

A full three-directional analysis of these data is delayed as an exercise for the reader (Exercise 6.2). Note that the 20+ age group category includes patients with ages 20 to 24 years, with similar interpretations for the other categories. Attention is confined in this section to significant changes between the two time periods. The percentages of patients in the three abnormality categories change dramatically as follows:

		A		B		C	
		Abnormality					
1981-86	2208	(34.02%)	1509	(23.25%)	2774	(42.74%)	6491
1988-93	2764	(17.77%)	5876	(37.79%)	6911	(44.44%)	15551

We can investigate dependence of rows and columns of this 2 × 3 table, using prog1, only if it is assumed that no patients are common to the samples for the two different time periods. In this case, prog1 gives LRS = 809.89 on 2 degrees of freedom, rejecting independence, and showing that the percentages of patients with abnormalities A, B, and C do vary over time. Next consider the 2 × 8 table consisting of the first rows each of Tables 6.11 and 6.12. An application of prog1 to this table helps us to investigate whether, for abnomality A, the proportion of patients in the different age groups varies over time. We now obtain LRS = 34.85 on 7 degrees of freedom (significance probability = 0.00%), strongly confirming that this variation in time. The significance probability can be calculated to greater accuracy using the Splus command 1-pchisq(34.849,7). This provides the value 0.001194%.

Owing to the high frequencies and nonrandom nature of the data, the changes over time for abnormality A, of the proportions of patients in the eight age groups are not particularly remarkable.

Interaction Analysis (Abnormality A)							
1.27	−2.15	−2.45	−0.36	−2.74	−1.67	0.79	1.84
−1.27	2.15	2.45	0.36	2.74	1.67	−0.79	−1.84

None of the individual interaction effects are overwhelmingly significantly different from zero. The most significant interaction, for the 40+ age category, corresponds to an increase over time in the proportion of patients in this category, from $412/2208 = 18.66\%$ to $612/2764 = 22.14\%$. In the 20+ and 25+ age categories the increases over time are from 3.49% to 4.31%, and from 14.18% to 16.46%.

The interaction analysis highlights the interesting feature that, while the percentages in each of the five age categories from 20+ to 50+ increase over time, the interactions in the other three categories are not significant. The most substantial of these is the 65+ category, where the percentage of patients decreases from 7.93%, to 5.43%. In the 60+ category the reduction is from 3.82% to 2.93%, and in the 20− category only a very small number of patients are involved. Indeed, this is one of the main features of the data: severe dyskaryosis occurs very rarely in the under 20 age group during both time periods.

Proceeding now to abnormality B, consider our 2×8 table, consisting of the second rows of each of Tables 6.11 and 6.12. Then prog1 gives LRS $= 30.31$ on 7 degrees of freedom (significance probability $= 0.00833\%$), suggesting that the proportions of patients in the eight age groups change significantly in time for abnormality B.

Interaction Analysis (Abnormality B)

4.14	0.69	0.79	2.54	0.10	−0.41	0.33	−2.23
−4.14	−0.69	−0.79	−2.54	0.10	0.41	0.33	2.23

The largest b_{ij} is $b_{11} = 4.14$, and this highlights the reduction over time of the percentage of patients less than 20, from 3.58% to 2.03%. The next largest b_{ij} is $b_{14} = 2.54$, and the percentage of patients in the 30+ age category decreases over time from 33.80% to 29.78%. Also, $b_{28} = 2.23$ suggests consideration of the 65+ category. Here the percentage increases over time, from 0.20% to 0.73%.

Corresponding to abnormality C, our 2×8 table consists of the third rows of each of Tables 6.11 and 6.12. In this case LRS $= 72.61$ on 7 degrees of freedom (significance probability $= 4.385 \times 10^{-13}$), suggesting that the proportions of patients in the eight age groups also change significantly over time for abnormality C.

Interaction Analysis (Abnormality C)

5.23	−2.47	−3.48	0.61	−4.75	−3.91	0.36	2.80
−5.23	2.47	3.48	−0.61	4.75	3.91	0.36	−2.80

Again, the most significant interaction corresponds to the under 20 age group. This involves a decrease in the percentage from 5.01% to 2.60%. There are significant increases for four out of the next five age groups, and a significant decrease for the over 65 group, from 2.38% to 1.43%.

6.3 The multiple sclerosis data

Now consider a four-way table analysed by a University of Edinburgh student (Darren Baillie) and previously considered by Schmidt (1979) and Enke (1986). The four variables are gender (G), duration (D), progress (P) and efficiency (E). The symbols G_1 and G_2 denote the male and female and the other three variables, measured on increasing ordinal scales, with four levels of duration, three levels of progress and five levels of efficiency.

Table 6.13 *Multiple sclerosis data*

			Efficiency				
G	D	P	E_1	E_2	E_3	E_4	E_5
G_1	D_1	P_1	21	9	26	11	44
		P_2	33	20	26	6	17
		P_3	17	8	14	7	5
	D_2	P_1	7	2	9	5	11
		P_2	6	3	10	2	11
		P_3	2	2	0	3	2
	D_3	P_1	3	1	2	7	10
		P_2	0	1	3	3	1
		P_3	2	0	0	0	0
	D_4	P_1	2	0	5	5	5
		P_2	3	2	4	2	5
		P_3	0	1	2	1	1

			Efficiency				
G	D	P	E_1	E_2	E_3	E_4	E_5
G_2	D_1	P_1	20	14	37	36	69
		P_2	36	28	26	18	43
		P_3	16	15	14	3	6
	D_2	P_1	5	5	12	17	38
		P_2	3	9	15	10	16
		P_3	3	3	5	7	4
	D_3	P_1	2	1	2	8	27
		P_2	1	2	5	9	9
		P_3	0	0	1	2	1
	D_4	P_1	2	0	1	5	18
		P_2	2	4	4	9	6
		P_3	0	0	1	1	1

When considering medical data, it is often a good idea to first test dependence on gender. Entering a 60×2 table into prog1, where the first column consists of the first 12 rows of Table 6.13, and the second column consists of the last 12 rows (the student also added one to each entry to compensate for the zeros, although this is not necessary when just LRS and not the b_{ij} are required) gives LRS = 59.92 on 59 degrees of freedom, strongly suggesting no gender effect. Accordingly, we combine the data in the $4 \times 3 \times 5$ contingency table, described in Table 6.14.

Table 6.14 *Multiple sclerosis data combined on gender*

Duration	D_1	E_1	E_2	E_3	E_4	E_5
				Efficiency		
	P_1	41	23	63	47	113
	P_2	69	48	52	24	60
	P_3	33	23	28	10	11
Duration	D_2					
	P_1	12	7	21	22	49
	P_2	9	12	25	12	27
	P_3	5	5	5	10	6
Duration	D_3					
	P_1	5	2	4	15	37
	P_2	1	3	8	12	10
	P_3	2	0	1	2	1
Duration	D_4					
	P_1	4	0	6	10	23
	P_2	5	6	8	11	11
	P_3	0	1	3	2	2

The data are now ready for a three-directional approach (see Exercise 6.3). As there are still three zeroes in the combined data, add one to each cell count before proceeding.

6.4 The Dundee dental health data

The data in Table 6.5 were reported by Osborn (1987) and previously analysed by a University of Edinburgh student (Ingrid Hansen).

Table 6.15 *Oral hygiene data*

Social Grade of School	Good	Fair+	Fair−	Bad	Total
		Oral Hygiene			
Below Average	62	103	57	11	233
Average	50	36	26	7	119
Above Average	80	69	18	2	169
Total	192	208	101	20	521

The analysis of these data is indicated in Exercises 6.5 and 6.6.

Exercises

6.1 For the cervical screening data in Section 6.2, further investigate the practical significance of the differences, when splitting the data according to the period, by comparing observed and fitted frequencies.

6.2 Complete a full three-directional analysis for the cervical screening data of Section 6.2, highlighting all major conclusions drawn.

6.3 For the multiple sclerosis data of Section 6.3, fully investigate any relationship between progress and efficiency at the lowest level of duration.

6.4 Complete a full three-directional analysis for the cervical screening data of Section 6.3, highlighting all major conclusions drawn.

6.5 Perform Goodman's full-rank interaction analysis for the Dundee dental health data (Table 6.15), and describe your main conclusions.

6.6 Collapse the data in Table 6.15 into a 2×2 table classifying oral hygiene as good or not good, and social grade of school as below average or not below average. Collapse the same data into a 2×2 table also classifying oral hygiene as good or not good, but classifying social grade above average or not above average. Which of these 2×2 tables best summarises the main conclusions to be drawn from Table 6.15?

CHAPTER 7

Conditional Independence Models for Two-Way Tables

7.1 Fixed zeroes and missing observations

The data in Table 7.1 were reported by Brunswick (1971) and previously analysed by Grizzle and Williams (1982), Fienberg (1987), and Christiansen (1997, p. 280).

Table 7.1 *Health concerns of teenagers*

		Sex Reproduction	Menstrual Problems	How Healthy I Am	Nothing
Male	12 - 15	4	-	47	57
	16 - 17	2	-	7	20
Female	12 - 15	9	4	19	71
	16 - 17	7	8	10	37
		22	12	83	185

The observed frequencies for the (1,2) and (2,2) cells can be regarded as "fixed zeroes". These cells should not be incorporated into a choice of sampling model. Christiansen analyses these data as a $2 \times 2 \times 4$ contingency table with the three variables gender, age, and health concern. In the presence of the missing frequencies, he then fits a log-linear model with a zero second-order interaction term (see Chapter 10). This approach appears to smooth the main feature in the data. The latter will lead to the key conclusion that the younger males are over-concerned, in relation to the remainder of the sample, regarding how healthy they are.

We will analyse these data as the obvious 4×4 contingency table with the row variable representing the four designated combinations of gender and age, and the column variable representing health concern. More generally, consider an $r \times s$ table with q fixed zeroes where $q < (r-1)(s-1)$, and let

$$\{y_{ij} : (i,j) \in \Omega\}$$

denote the set of $rs - q$ observed frequencies, with Ω denoting the corresponding index set. Let

$$\{\xi_{ij} : (i,j) \in \Omega\}$$

denote the corresponding set of unconditional cell probabilities, so that

$$\sum_{(i,j)\in\Omega} y_{ij} = n$$

and

$$\sum_{(i,j)\in\Omega} \xi_{ij} = 1,$$

where n is the total number of observations in our $rs - q$ cells.

Assume that the y_{ij} possess a multinomial distribution with $rs - q$ cells and let ξ_{ij} denote the corresponding cell probabilities. Then an assumption of the form:

$$\xi_{ij} = a_i b_j \qquad \text{for } (i,j) \in \Omega,$$

for some a_i and b_j, corresponds to a *conditional independence* or *quasi-independence* hypothesis, since it assumes independence of the row and column variables, but conditional on the set Ω, (see Goodman, 1968). In terms of multivariate logits γ_{ij}, satisfying

$$\xi_{ij} = e^{\gamma_{ij}} / \sum_{(k,g)\in\Omega} e^{\gamma_{kg}} \qquad \text{for } (i,j) \in \Omega,$$

this is equivalent to an assumption of the form

$$\gamma_{ij} = \lambda_i^A + \lambda_j^B \qquad \text{for } (i,j) \in \Omega,$$

where λ_i^A denotes the ith row effect and λ_j^B denotes the jth column effect, since, subject to

$$\lambda_.^A = \lambda_.^B = 0,$$

we have

$$\lambda_i^A = \log a_i - r^{-1} \sum_{k=1}^{r} \log a_k \qquad (i = 1, ..., r)$$

and

$$\lambda_j^B = \log b_j - s^{-1} \sum_{g=1}^{s} \log b_g \qquad (j = 1, ..., s).$$

We assume that no row or column consists entirely of fixed zeroes. In the next section we show how to investigate our quasi-independence hypothesis. In the presence of fixed zeroes, algebraically explicit estimates for the row and column effects do not typically exist. The current analysis is appropriate if the observed frequencies for the cells in Ω are missing rather than fixed equal to zero.

7.2 Incomplete tables

Let y_{i*} denote the total frequency in the ith row, and y_{*j} denote the total frequency in the jth column. Then (see also Exercise 7.3) any maximum likelihood solution for the model of the previous section is characterised by preservation of the marginal totals, that is, if

$$e_{ij} = n\widehat{a}_i \widehat{b}_j \qquad \text{for } (i,j) \in \Omega,$$

then we require a set of $\widehat{a}_i$ and $\widehat{b}_j$ satisfying

$$e_{i*} = y_{i*} \qquad (i = 1, ..., r)$$

and

$$e_{*j} = y_{*j} \qquad (j = 1, ..., s).$$

This set is unique up to scalar transformation of the form $K\widehat{a}_i$, $(i = 1, ..., r)$ and $\widehat{b}_j/K$, $(j = 1, ..., s)$.

Our maximum likelihood estimates can be calculated via the Deming-Stephan iterative proportional fitting procedure (Fienberg, 1987, pp 37-40) which is programmed on our special Splus function prog2. Following the command prog2 it is necessary to input the dimensions of the table

4 4

followed by the number of fixed zeroes (or missing observations)

2

followed by the labels of the cells containing fixed zeroes (or missing observations). In our example, we represent the (1,2) and (2,2) cells by

1 2
2 2

Then the table should be input row by row, including random zeroes, but omitting fixed zeroes and missing observations, i.e.,

4 47 57
2   7 20
9   4 19 71
7   8 10 37

The output of prog2 gives the following fitted table

8.19	-	30.91	68.90	108
2.20	-	8.30	18.50	29
7.25	7.49	27.34	60.93	103
4.36	4.51	16.45	36.68	62
22	12	83	185	302

Each of the entries (e_{ij}) to this table is product of an a_i and an nb_j, which are also listed in the output of prog2.

$$
\begin{array}{ccccc}
a_i : & 0.380 & 0.102 & 0.336 & 0.202 \\
nb_j : & 21.581 & 22.312 & 81.418 & 181.474
\end{array}
$$

We notice that all marginal totals are indeed preserved, and that the a_i and b_j are not trivial quantities but are determined by a theoretical procedure embedded in prog2. Under single multinomial sampling assumptions, our choice of sampling model is only dependent upon our choice of Ω. An overall test statistic for investigating the validity of this choice is provided by the log-likelihood ratio statistic:

$$
\text{LRS} = 2 \sum_{(i.j)\in\Omega} y_{ij} \log y_{ij} - 2 \sum_{(ij)\in\Omega} y_{ij} \log e_{ij}.
$$

When the model is true, LRS possesses a distribution which is approximately chi-squared with $\nu = (r-1)(s-1) - q$ degrees of freedom. In our current example, the computer output gives

$$
\text{LRS} = 25.68
$$

with $\nu = 7$. Our proposed model is therefore rejected by the data (significance probability $= 0.0006$).

The prog2 output also reports the deviances :

$$
\delta_{ij} = 2y_{ij} \log y_{ij} - 2y_{ij} \log e_{ij} \qquad (i, j \in \Omega),
$$

which comprise the components of our LRS statistic. If y_{ij} equals zero, then δ_{ij} also equals zero. For nonzero y_{ij} the deviances can be positive or negative, depending upon whether $y_{ij} > e_{ij}$ or $y_{ij} < e_{ij}$. A large value of $|\delta_{ij}|$ indicates a substantial deviation of y_{ij} from e_{ij}. For the preceding analysis, the deviances are

$$
\begin{array}{rrrr}
-5.74 & - & 39.39 & -21.61 \\
-0.38 & - & -2.39 & 3.12 \\
3.90 & -5.02 & -13.82 & 21.72 \\
6.62 & 9.17 & -9.96 & 0.65
\end{array}
$$

The deviances cannot be usefully compared with the percentage points of any known distribution. However, the extremely large deviance in the $(1,3)$ cell tells us that the number of males in the 12 to 15 year age group, who are concerned about how healthy they are, is much larger than would be anticipated under our current conditional independence model.

7.3 Perfectly fitting further cells

We will complete our analysis of the data in Table 7.1 by assuming a perfect fit $e_{13} = y_{13} = 47$ for the $(1,3)$ cell and then running prog2, but with $q = 3$

and the (1,3) cell added to the (1,2) and (2,2) cells in Ω^c, i.e., regarding the observation in this cell as missing. This device may be justified by the methodology of Section 7.4, and is equivalent to fitting a generalised linear model, with a single interaction effect, and of the form

$$\gamma_{ij} = \begin{cases} \lambda_i^A + \lambda_j^B + \lambda_{ij}^B & \text{for } i = 1 \text{ and } j = 3 \\ \lambda_i^A + \lambda_j^B & \text{for } (i,j) \in \Omega . \end{cases}$$

Then, prog2 gives the following fitted table

6.48	-	(47)	54.52	108
2.47	-	5.74	20.79	29
8.14	7.49	18.89	68.47	103
4.90	4.51	11.37	41.22	62
22	12	83	185	302

We now have LRS $= 7.35$ on 6 degrees of freedom and hence an excellent fit (significance probability $= 28.9\%$). The deviances are now

-3.86	-	(0)	5.08
-0.85	-	2.79	-1.55
1.80	-5.02	0.22	5.14
4.99	9.17	-2.57	-7.99

and no further modification to the model is necessary. This analysis substantiates the main conclusion of Section 7.3 and does not refute our revised quasi-independence hypothesis, which conditions on 13 cells out of 16.

7.4 Complete tables

Consider an $r \times s$ contingency table where the cell frequencies y_{ij} follow our single multinomial model with corresponding cell probabilities ξ_{ij} and multivariate logits γ_{ij}. In situations where Goodman's full-rank interaction analysis, or other considerations, suggest that a zero interaction/independence model is inappropriate, then a quasi-independence model of the form

$$\gamma_{ij} = \begin{cases} \lambda_i^A + \lambda_j^B & \text{for } (i,j) \in \Omega \\ \lambda_i^A + \lambda_j^B + \lambda_{ij}^{AB} & \text{for } (i,j) \in \Omega^c \end{cases}$$

can be considered. The constraints $\lambda^A = \lambda^B$ are still appropriate, but if q, the number of cells in Ω^c, is less than $(r-1)(s-1)$, then no further constraints on the interaction effects are needed. Models of this form, for different choices of Ω, compromise between the independence model and the full-rank model. It is again assumed that at least one cell, in each row and column, falls in Ω.

The maximum likelihood solution (see also Exercise 7.4) is now characterised as follows:

(a) $\widehat{\lambda}_i^A = \log \widehat{a}_i - r^{-1} \sum_{k=1}^r \log \widehat{a}_k$ $(i = 1, ..., r)$.

(b) $\widehat{\lambda}_j^B = \log \widehat{b}_j - s^{-1} \sum_{g=1}^s \log \widehat{b}_g$ $(j = 1, ..., s)$.

(c) $\widehat{\lambda}_{ij}^{AB} = \log y_{ij} - \widehat{\lambda}_i^A - \widehat{\lambda}_j^B - \log z + \log A$ for $(i, j) \in \Omega^c$,

with $z = \sum_{(i,j) \in \Omega} y_{ij}$ and $A = \sum_{(i,j) \in \Omega} \exp(\widehat{\lambda}_i^A + \widehat{\lambda}_j^B)$.

(d) The $\widehat{a}_i$ and $\widehat{b}_i$ are chosen to preserve the marginal totals, that is with

$$e_{ij} = \begin{cases} n\widehat{a}_i\widehat{b}_j & \text{for } (i, j) \in \Omega \\ y_{ij} & \text{for } (i, j) \in \Omega^c, \end{cases}$$

we have $e_{i*} = y_{i*}$ $(i = 1, ..., r)$ and $e_{*j} = y_{*j}$ $(j = 1, ..., s)$, where the star notation now indicates summation across a complete row or column.

The $\widehat{a}_i$ and $\widehat{b}_j$ may be calculated by reference to prog2, but regarding the cells in Ω^c as, for the moment, containing missing observations. For example, a full-rank interaction analysis of the 4×6 table consisting of Table 5.3, but with the sixth and seventh columns already omitted, gives LRS = 33.36 on 15 degrees of freedom. Also, prog1 gives the four cells (3,2), (3,6), (4,2), and (4.6) as providing the most significant interactions. Putting these four cells into Ω^c on prog2, gives LRS = 8.52 on 11 degrees of freedom. This strongly confirms conditional independence of our row variable, region, and our column variable, journal, in the remainder of the table.

When applying this technique, it is important not to aim just for a good fitting model, but rather a model which facilitates a useful real-life conclusion. By progressively adding cells to Ω^c (e.g., Exercise 7.2), it is sometimes possible to obtain an excellent fit to the data, but with very little meaning.

7.5 Further data sets

Table 7.2 *The remote sensing data*

		Observed Category (infrared)			
		1	2	3	4
Observed	1	12	0	3	1
Category	2	0	32	4	1
(visual)	3	1	1	18	1
	4	1	0	2	21

Table 7.3 *Observed transitions between types of geological layers*

	A	B	C	D	E	F
A	-	12	12	1	0	2
B	3	-	17	1	0	7
C	8	5	-	9	0	11
D	8	7	7	-	0	32
E	1	1	1	9	-	12
F	3	1	0	39	24	-

The data sets in Tables 7.2 and 7.3 were reported by Leonard and Hsu (1999, pp. 227-228).

Exercises

7.1 Fit a conditional independence model to the data in Table 7.2, by perfectly fitting the cells on the diagonal. Interpret your results. Note that no preliminary adjustments to the zeroes are required.

7.2 Try to fit a conditional independence model to the data in Table 7.3, by perfectly fitting the cells on the diagonal. Attempt to fit more complicated conditional independence models by also perfectly fitting cells with high deviances on previous models. Show that it is possible to get a good fit on 12 degrees of freedom. Discuss, however, whether or not this procedure is useful. Might the procedure be useful in the presence of further geological knowledge?

Note: Do not try to perfectly fit the (6,5) cell, since the remaining cells in both Ω and the fifth column are all zero.

7.3 For the model described in Section 7.1, show that the likelihood of the λ_i^A and λ_j^B is

$$\ell(\boldsymbol{\lambda}^A, \boldsymbol{\lambda}^B | \mathbf{y}) \propto \frac{\exp\left\{\sum_i y_{i*}\lambda_i^A + \sum_i y_{*j}\lambda_j^B\right\}}{\left(\sum_{(k,g)\in\Omega} e^{\lambda_k^A + \lambda_g^B}\right)^n},$$

where

$$y_{i*} = \sum_{g:(i,g)\in\Omega} y_{ig},$$

and

$$y_{*j} = \sum_{k:(k,j)\in\Omega} y_{kj}.$$

By maximising the log-likelihood find equations for any set of maximum likelihood estimates of the λ_i^A and λ_j^B, not necessarily subject to the constraints $\lambda_{\cdot}^{A} = \lambda_{\cdot}^{B} = 0$. Show that, subject to these constraints, the maximum likelihood estimates are

$$\widehat{\lambda}_{i} = \log \widehat{a}_{i} - r^{-1} \sum_{k=1}^{r} \log \widehat{a}_{k} \qquad (i = 1, ..., r),$$

and

$$\widehat{\lambda}_{j} = \log \widehat{b}_{j} - s^{-1} \sum_{g=1}^{s} \log \widehat{b}_{g} \qquad (j = 1, ..., s),$$

where the $\widehat{a}_{i}$ and $\widehat{b}_{j}$ preserve the marginal totals, in the manner indicated at the beginning of Section 7.2.

7.4   For the model described in Section 7.4, show that the likelihood of the λ_{i}^{A}, λ_{j}^{B}, and λ_{ij}^{AB} can be represented in the form

$$\ell(\boldsymbol{\lambda}^{A}, \boldsymbol{\lambda}^{B}, \boldsymbol{\lambda}^{AB} | \mathbf{y}^{AB}) \propto \frac{\exp\left\{\sum_{i} y_{i*} \lambda_{i}^{A} + \sum_{j} y_{*j} \lambda_{j}^{B} + \sum_{(i,j) \in \Omega} y_{ij} \lambda_{ij}^{AB}\right\}}{\{H(\boldsymbol{\lambda}) + G(\boldsymbol{\lambda})\}^{n}},$$

where the y_{i*} and y_{*j} now represent the row and column totals of the complete table,

$$H(\boldsymbol{\lambda}) = \sum_{(i,j) \in \Omega} e^{\lambda_{i}^{A} + \lambda_{j}^{B}},$$

and

$$G(\boldsymbol{\lambda}) = \sum_{(i,j) \in \Omega^{C}} e^{\lambda_{i}^{A} + \lambda_{j}^{B} + \lambda_{ij}^{AB}}.$$

Remembering that $G(\boldsymbol{\lambda})$ depends upon λ_{ij}^{AB}, show that, for fixed λ_{i}^{A} and λ_{j}^{B}, the maximum likelihood estimate of λ_{ij}^{AB} is

$$\widehat{\lambda}_{ij}^{AB} = \log y_{ij} - \lambda_{i}^{A} - \lambda_{j}^{B} - \log z + \log H(\boldsymbol{\lambda})$$

with

$$z = \sum_{(i,j) \in \Omega} y_{ij}.$$

Find equations for any set of maximum likelihood estimates of λ_{i}^{A} and λ_{j}^{B}, for fixed λ_{ij}^{AB} and not necessarily subject to the constraints $\lambda_{\cdot}^{A} = \lambda_{\cdot}^{B} = 0$. By replacing λ_{ij}^{AB} by the preceding expression for $\widehat{\lambda}_{ij}^{AB}$, find equations for the unconditional maximum likelihood estimates for λ_{i}^{A} and λ_{j}^{B}. Show that, subject to the constraints $\lambda_{\cdot}^{A} = \lambda_{\cdot}^{B} = 0$, these satisfy conditions (a), (b), and (d) of Section 7.4.

CHAPTER 8

Logistic Regression

8.1 Review of general methodology

8.1.1 The linear logistic model

Consider observed frequencies $y_1, ..., y_m$, which are independent, and possess m different binomial distributions, with respective probabilities $\theta_1, ..., \theta_m$, and sample sizes $n_1, ..., n_m$; that is,

$$y_i \sim B(\theta_i, n_i),$$

independently for $i = 1, ..., m$. For example, the data in Table 8.1 were reported by Larsen, Gardner, and Coffin (1979) and previously analysed by Hasselblad, Stead, and Crenson (1980). Here, $m = 17$, and for $i = 1, ..., m$, y_i denotes the number of dead mice in the ith group, and n_i denotes the number of mice tested by exposure to nitrous dioxide (NO_2). Then, assuming that our binomial assumptions are appropriate, θ_i denotes the probability of death for any particular mouse in the ith group.

Table 8.1 *Mice exposure data*

i	t_{i1}	t_{i2}	y_i	n_i	p_i
1	1.5	96.0	44	120	0.367
2	1.5	168.0	37	80	0.463
3	1.5	336.0	43	80	0.538
4	1.5	504.0	35	60	0.583
5	3.5	0.5	29	100	0.290
6	3.5	1.0	53	200	0.265
7	3.5	2.0	13	40	0.325
8	3.5	3.0	75	200	0.375
9	3.5	5.0	23	40	0.575
10	3.5	7.0	152	280	0.543
11	3.5	14.0	55	80	0.688
12	3.5	24.0	98	140	0.700
13	3.5	48.0	121	160	0.756
14	7.0	0.5	52	120	0.433
15	7.0	1.0	62	120	0.517
16	7.0	1.5	61	120	0.508
17	7.0	2.0	86	120	0.717

We wish to investigate whether or not the probability of death depends upon two further variables, degree of exposure to NO_2, and exposure time. The values t_{i1} and t_{i2} of these two variables are listed, for $i = 1, ..., 17$, in the second and third columns of Table 8.1. A preliminary scan of the data suggests that the proportions $p_i = y_i/n_i$ increase, with increasing t_{i1} and with t_{i2}. We, however, recommend initially transforming the explanatory variables and letting $x_{i1} = \log t_{i1}$ and $x_{i2} = \log t_{i2}$.

It might be reasonable to consider the data for $i = 5, ..., 13$ separately, since the degree of exposure $t_{i1} = 3.5$ is common to these groups. In this case, how do we model the dependency of θ_i upon x_{i1}? A convenient possibility is to let the logit of θ_i depend in linear fashion upon x_{i1}, that is,

(a) $$\alpha_i = \log \theta_i - \log(1 - \theta_i) = \beta_0 + \beta_1 x_{i1}, \quad (i = 5, ..., 13)$$

where β_0 and β_1 are the unknown constant and slope for our regression line. A linear model for the logits frequently gives a better fit than a linear model for the θ_i. An alternative is the probit transformation $\alpha_i = \Phi^{-1}(\theta_i)$, where Φ denotes the distribution function of a standard normal distribution. However, linear models for the logit and probit closely approximate each other. The inverse transformation of the logit is

$$\theta_i = e^{\alpha_i}/(1 + e^{\alpha_i}) = e^{\beta_0 + \beta_1 x_{i1}}/(1 + e^{\beta_0 + \beta_1 x_{i1}}).$$

As a function of the x_i, this gives a sigmoid curve. If this does not fit the data well, then we could consider the addition of a quadratic term to (a) giving

(b) $$\alpha_i = \beta_0 + \beta_1 x_{i1} + \beta_2 x_{i1}^2 \quad (i = 5, ..., 13),$$

where β_2 is a further unknown parameter. The dependency of θ_i upon both x_{i1} and x_{i2} can be modelled via the main effects model:

(c) $$\alpha_i = \beta_0 + \beta_1 x_{i1} + \beta_2 x_{i2} \quad (i = 1, ..., m),$$

where β_1 and β_2 now both represent unknown linear coefficients. However, this is easier to interpret if the x_{i1} and x_{i2} have firstly been rescaled. Rescale the x_{i1} by subtracting the sample mean of the x_{i1}, from each x_{i1}, and then dividing by their sample standard deviation. Then do the same for the x_{i2}.

It is then often of interest to add a multiplicative interaction term to the model, giving

(d) $$\alpha_i = \beta_0 + \beta_1 x_{i1} + \beta_2 x_{i2} + \beta_3 x_{i1} x_{i2} \quad (i = 1, ..., m).$$

The four models (a) to (d), provide special cases of the general formulation, where, with $q < m$,

(e) $$\alpha_i = \beta_0 + \beta_1 x_{i1} + \beta_2 x_{i2} + x_{i2} + \cdots + \beta_q x_{iq} \quad (i = 1, ..., m).$$

Models (a) and (c) are equivalent to (e), but with $q = 1$ and $q = 2$, respectively. Model (b) takes $q = 2$ and $x_{i2} = x_{i1}^2$. Model (d) takes $q = 3$ and $x_{i3} = x_{i1}x_{i2}$. With $p = q + 1$, consider the $p \times 1$ column vectors, $\boldsymbol{\beta}$ and $\mathbf{x}_i$, with transposes

$$\boldsymbol{\beta}^T = (\beta_0, \beta_1, ..., \beta_q)$$

and

$$\mathbf{x}_i^T = (1, x_{i1}, ..., x_{iq}).$$

Then, our general formulation (e) may be summarised in the vector form

(f) $$\alpha_i = \mathbf{x}_i^T \boldsymbol{\beta} \qquad (i = 1, ..., m).$$

To see this, note that, for any two $p \times 1$ column vectors, $\mathbf{a} = (a_0, a_1, .., a_q)^T$ and $\mathbf{b} = (b_0, b_1, .., b_q)^T$,

$$\mathbf{a}^T\mathbf{b} = \mathbf{b}^T\mathbf{a} = a_0 b_0 + a_1 b_1 + \cdots + a_q b_q.$$

Of course, $\mathbf{aa}^T$ and $\mathbf{ab}^T$ are instead both $p \times p$ matrices (see Section 8.1.3). In terms of the θ_i, our general formulation for the α_i gives

$$
\begin{aligned}
\theta_i &= \frac{e^{\mathbf{x}_i^T \boldsymbol{\beta}}}{1 + e^{\mathbf{x}_i^T \boldsymbol{\beta}}} \\
&= \frac{e^{\beta_0 + \beta_1 x_{i1} + \beta_2 x_{i2} + ... + \beta_q x_{iq}}}{1 + e^{\beta_0 + \beta_1 x_{i1} + \beta_2 x_{i2} + ... + \beta_q x_{iq}}}.
\end{aligned}
$$

8.1.2 Analysis of model

The maximum likelihood estimates of $\beta_0, \beta_1, ..., \beta_q$ are not usually available in algebraically explicit form. They may, however, be obtained from Splus in these situations where they are both finite and uniquely defined. Thus, a maximum likelihood vector $\widehat{\boldsymbol{\beta}} = (\widehat{\beta}_0, \widehat{\beta}_1, ..., \widehat{\beta}_q)^T$ may be obtained. We can also obtain a symmetric $p \times p$ matrix $\mathbf{D}$, known as the "likelihood dispersion matrix" (see Exercise 8.3). Let $s_0, s_1, s_2, ..., s_p$ denote the square roots of the diagonal elements of $\mathbf{D}$. Then, these elements are the corresponding "estimated standard errors" of $\widehat{\beta}_0, \widehat{\beta}_1, ..., \widehat{\beta}_q$. Moreover, each of the quantities

$$\widehat{\beta}_k = \beta_k / s_k \qquad (k = 0, 1, ..., q)$$

has a distribution which is approximately standard normal. This is the basis for the following procedures:

(A) $(\widehat{\beta}_k - 1.960\, s_k,\ \widehat{\beta}_k + 1.960\, s_k)$ is an approximate 95% confidence interval for β_k. Replace 1.960 by 2.576 for a 99% interval.

(B) The null hypothesis $H_0 : \beta_k = 0$ may be tested by reference to the normal statistic

$$Z_k = \widehat{\beta}_k/s_k.$$

Reject H_0 against a general alternative at the 5% level, if $|z_k| \geq 1.960$ and at the 1% level if $|z_k| \geq 2.576$. The normal test statistics are reported on Splus, where they are mistakenly described as t-values.

8.1.3 Empirical approximations

If none of the y_i or $n_i - y_i$ are less than 5, then the approximation indicated in Exercise 8.1 can be used to show that $\widehat{\beta}$ and $\mathbf{D}$ are approximated by the weighted least-squares vector β^*, and $\mathbf{D}^*$, where β^* premultiplies a vector by a matrix inverse, giving

$$\beta^* = \left(\sum_{i=1}^{m} v_i^{-1} \mathbf{x}_i \mathbf{x}_i^T \right)^{-1} \sum_{i=1}^{m} v_i^{-1} \mathbf{x}_i \ell_i ,$$

and $\mathbf{D}^*$ denotes the matrix inverse,

$$\mathbf{D}^* = \left(\sum_{i=1}^{m} v_i^{-1} \mathbf{x}_i \mathbf{x}_i^T \right)^{-1} ,$$

with

$$\ell_i = \log\{y_i/(n_i - y_i)\}$$

and

$$v_i = y_i^{-1} + (n_i - y_i)^{-1}.$$

A variety of adjustments of ℓ_i and v_i are available, and we particularly recommend

$$\ell_i^* = \log\left\{ \left(y_i + \frac{1}{2} \right) \Big/ \left(n_i - y_i + \frac{1}{2} \right) \right\}$$
$$-3/2 \left(y_i + \frac{1}{2} \right) + 3/2 \left(n_i - y_i + \frac{1}{2} \right)$$

and

$$v_i^* = \left(y_i + \frac{1}{2} \right)^{-1} + \left(n_i - y_i + \frac{1}{2} \right)^{-1} .$$

However, unless the model is overparameterised, the elements of the exact maximum likelihood vector $\widehat{\beta}$ and dispersion matrix $\mathbf{D}$ will typically still be finite, even if the y_i and $n_i - y_i$ are small. Consider, for example, the Space Shuttle data in Table 8.2. They were reported by Dalal et al. (1989). In Section 8.4, we analyse these data by taking $n_i = 1$ for $i = 1, ..., m$ and a binary value of either 0 or 1 for each y_i, where $y_i = 1$ denotes the success of the Space Shuttle flight.

A superior likelihood approximation is available upon expanding the log-likelihood of β in a Taylor series about the exact $\widehat{\beta}$ and neglecting cubic and higher terms in the series. As long as $\widehat{\beta}$ is finite, the exact likelihood of β can be approximated by

$$\ell^*(\beta|\mathbf{y}) = \ell(\widehat{\beta}|\mathbf{y}) \exp\left\{ -\frac{1}{2}(\beta - \widehat{\beta})^T \mathbf{D}^{-1}(\beta - \widehat{\beta}) \right\}$$

where $\mathbf{R} = \mathbf{D}^{-1}$, and the likelihood information matrix is denoted by

$$\mathbf{R} = \sum_{i=1}^{m} n_i \widehat{\theta}_i (1 - \widehat{\theta}_i) \mathbf{x}_i \mathbf{x}_i^T.$$

Then $\mathbf{D}$ is the likelihood dispersion matrix. This approximation is accurate if $|\mathbf{R}|$ is large enough, and can therefore be accurate even if the y_i and $n_i - y_i$ are small. This result is the basis for the confidence intervals and the hypothesis tests described in Section 8.1

Table 8.2 *Space shuttle failure data*

Case	Flight	Failure	Success	Temperature
1	14	1	0	53
2	9	1	0	57
3	23	1	0	58
4	10	1	0	63
5	1	0	1	66
6	5	0	1	67
7	13	0	1	67
8	15	0	1	67
9	4	0	1	68
10	3	0	1	69
11	8	0	1	70
12	17	0	1	70
13	2	1	0	70
14	11	1	0	70
15	6	0	1	72
16	7	0	1	73
17	16	0	1	75
18	21	1	0	75
19	19	0	1	76
20	22	0	1	76
21	12	0	1	78
22	20	0	1	79
23	18	0	1	81

8.1.4 Finite sample optimality property for exact estimators

It is a consequence of the developments in Exercises 8.2 and 8.3 that the $p \times 1$ vector

$$\mathbf{t} = \sum_{i=1}^{m} n_i \mathbf{x}_i y_i$$

is a uniform minimum variance unbiased estimator of its expectation,

$$\boldsymbol{\xi}(\boldsymbol{\beta}) = \sum_{i=1}^{m} \frac{n_i e^{\mathbf{x}_i^T \boldsymbol{\beta}}}{1 + e^{\mathbf{x}_i^T \boldsymbol{\beta}}}.$$

Since the maximum likelihood vector $\boldsymbol{\beta}$ satisfies the equation

$$\mathbf{t} = \boldsymbol{\xi}(\widehat{\boldsymbol{\beta}}),$$

it follows that $\widehat{\boldsymbol{\beta}}$ is a nonlinear transformation of an estimator with an optimal finite sample frequency property. The elements of $\boldsymbol{\xi}(\boldsymbol{\beta})$ can be expressed a linear combinations of the $\theta_i = e^{\mathbf{x}_i^T \boldsymbol{\beta}} / (1 + e^{\mathbf{x}_i^T \boldsymbol{\beta}})$.

8.1.5 Checking the adequacy of the model

The output of Splus gives a value for the likelihood ratio statistic (described as the residual deviance),

$$\begin{aligned} LRS &= 2 \sum_{i=1}^{m} y_i \log y_i - 2 \sum_{i=1}^{m} y_i \log \widehat{y}_i + 2 \sum_{i=1}^{m} (n_i - y_i) \log(n_i - y_i) \\ &\quad -2 \sum_{i=1}^{m} (n_i - y_i) \log(n_i - \widehat{y}_i), \end{aligned}$$

where $\widehat{y}_i = n_i \widehat{\theta}_i$ and $\widehat{\theta}_i$ denotes the fitted value for θ_i (see Exercise 8.3). The value of this statistic should, whenever theoretically appropriate, be compared with upper percentage points of the chi-squared distribution with $m - p$ degrees of freedom.

The preceding likelihood ratio test is inappropriate theoretically (i.e., the chi-squared reference distribution is inadequate) if a large number of the cell frequencies are small, in particular in the binary case depicted in Table 8.2. In the binary case, the model may be investigated by further consideration of the $\widehat{\theta}_i$ (see Section 8.3).

If the likelihood ratio test is both appropriate and suggests sufficient departures from the hypothesised model, then a residual analysis should be employed. Consider

$$r_i = \ell_i^* - \mathbf{x}_i^T \widehat{\boldsymbol{\beta}},$$

where ℓ_i^* is the variation on Cox's *empirical logistic transform* (Cox, 1970) indicated in Section 8.1.3, but $\widehat{\boldsymbol{\beta}}$ is the exact maximum likelihood vector.

Then the approximations of Section 8.1.3 can be used to prove that an approximate estimated variance for r_i is the typically positive quantity

$$w_i = v_i^* - \mathbf{x}_i^T \mathbf{D} \mathbf{x}_i,$$

with $\mathbf{D}$ denoting the exact likelihood dispersion matrix. Consequently, the normal test statistic

$$z_i^* = r_i / w_i^{\frac{1}{2}}$$

can be used to investigate the significance of the ith residual. These statistics are provided by our special function resid.logistic.

In situations where LRS is a valid overall statistic, the version of Akaike's information criterion (AIC), denoted by

$$\text{AIC}^* = \text{LRS} + 2(m - p),$$

can be used to compare different models. In the absence of other information, simply choose the model for which AIC^* is the smallest.

8.2 Analysing your data using Splus

Consider, first, a very simple example where you wish to analyse the first four lines of Table 8.1, the level of NO_2, $t_1 = 1.5$ is common to the four groups of mice, and t_2 denotes time of exposure. Then, enter the following data in a file outside Splus, and assign an appropriate filename, e.g., mice:

96.0	44	120
168.0	37	80
336.0	43	80
504.0	35	60

After entering Splus, you may convert your **mice** file into the Splus file **micedata** with the commands

  micedata<-read.table ("mice", col.names= c("time", "y", "n"))
  attach (micedata)

You may also transform the explanatory variable, if appropriate, for example,

$$logtime < -log(time)$$

(You then need to bind in your values of y_i and $n_i - y_i$.) The command

  combdat<-cbind(y,nminusy=n-y)

binds the variables y and *nminusy* into a single descriptor *combdat*. Then the command

  combdat

gives the response

	y	$nminusy$
1	44	76
2	37	43
3	43	37
4	35	25

You are now ready to run simple linear logistic regression with the single explanatory variable *time* on these data. The main output may be obtained from the commands

> $model1 < -glm(combdat \sim logtime, family = binomial)$
> $print(summary(model1))$

From the output you may extract the following values for the quantities described in Section 8.1.2:

$$\widehat{\beta_0} = -2.942 \quad s_0 = 0.922 \quad z_0 = -3.192$$
$$\widehat{\beta_1} = 0.532 \quad s_1 = 0.173 \quad z_1 = 3.077$$

This suggests fitting a straight line to the logit of the form

$$\text{logit(probability of death)} = -2.942 + 0.532 \times \log \text{ (exposure time)},$$

to the logit, where the constant term and slope in this regression line are both significantly different from zero. This is equivalent to the equation

$$\text{Probability of death} = \frac{(\text{exposure time})^{0.532}}{e^{2.942} + (\text{exposure time})^{0.532}}.$$

The command

> $model1\$fitted$

gives us values for the fitted probabilities $\widehat{\theta_i}$ which may be compared with the observed proportions $p_i = y_i/n_i$, (use command y/n), as follows:

t_i	$\widehat{\theta_i}$	p_i
96.0	0.374	0.367
168.0	0.446	0.463
336.0	0.538	0.538
504.0	0.591	0.583

Comparing the $\widehat{\theta_i}$ and p_i, we see that the model clearly fits the data. Furthermore, the Splus output provides the value LRS = 0.131 for our likelihood ratio statistic, on two degrees of freedom. Further information can be obtained using the special Splus command

> $resid.logistic(model1)$

The full likelihood dispersion matrix $\mathbf{D}$ is

$$\mathbf{D} = \begin{pmatrix} 0.849 & -0.158 \\ -0.158 & 0.030 \end{pmatrix}$$

and the values r_i for the residuals, of Section 8.1.5, their estimated variances w_i, and the corresponding normal test statistics z_i^* are

i	1	2	3	4
r_i	-0.041	0.064	0.003	-0.019
w_i	0.028	0.013	0.020	0.038
z_i^*	-0.244	0.557	0.020	-0.099

8.3 Analysis of the mice exposure data

When analysing the mice exposure data of Table 8.1, we first took logs, $x_{i1} = \log t_{i1}$ and $x_{i2} = \log t_{i2}$, and then standardized each set of explanatory variables (log degree of exposure and log exposure time) by subtracting the sample mean and then dividing by the sample standard deviation, for each set separately. We then attempted to fit the main effects model (c) of Section 8.1.1 with both x_{i1} and x_{i2} replaced by the corresponding standardized variables. The appropriate Splus commands for the preceding transformation of the variables, together with the main effects analysis, are as follows:

```
micedata < - read.table ("mice.dat", col.names = c("no2",
        "time", "y", "n"))
attach (micedata)
logno2 < - log(no2)
logtime < - log(time)
logno2 < - (logno2 - mean (logno2)) / sqrt (var (logno2))
logtime < - (logtime - mean (logtime)) / sqrt (var (logtime))
combdat < - cbind (y, nminusy = n - y)
model1 < - glm (combdat ~ logno2 + logtime, family = binomial)
print (summary(model1))
resid.logistic(model1)
```

This provides a residual deviance/likelihood ratio statistic of 30.93 on 14 degrees of freedom (significance probability $= 0.57\%$, AIC$^* = 58.93$), just rejecting the main effects model. The residual analysis leads to the values of the normal test statistics (see Section 8.1.5), for the 17 groups, as follows:

-2.98	-1.66	-1.89	-1.83	3.34	-0.65	-2.00	-1.53
10.02	3.87	8.94	3.84	2.24	-3.05	-3.12	-5.78	3.27

We therefore fit the multiplicative interaction model (d) of Section 8.1.1 using the following further commands:

model2 < - glm (combdat ~ logno2 * log time, family = binomial)
print (summary(model2))
resid.logistic(model2)

The addition of the extra interaction term dramatically reduces the residual deviance to 16.11 on 13 degrees of freedom (significance probability = 24.31%, $AIC^* = 42.11$), and the fitted regression model is

$$\alpha_i = 0.185 + 1.038x_{i1} + 1.237x_{i2} + 0.229x_{i1}x_{i2}.$$

The estimated standard errors associated with the intercept and three slopes were, respectively, 0.062, 0.091, 0.098, and 0.060. The corresponding test statistics (for differences of these four quantities from zero) were 2.96, 11.42, 12.60, and 3.83 and all were highly significant. We conclude that degree of exposure and exposure time interact to create a strong relationship with the probability of death.

8.4 Analysis of space shuttle failure data

When analysing the data in Table 8.2, the important Splus commands are

logtemp < - log(temp)
model < - glm (comdat ~ logtemp, family = binomial)

These enable us to fit

$$logit = -65.86 + 15.80 \log (\text{temperature})$$

to the logit of the probability of success. Both the intercept and the slope of this model are weakly significantly different from zero (normal test statistics -2.12 and 2.14). However, the residual deviance of 20.07 on 21 degrees of freedom does not possess a theoretical basis in the current binary situation. We should, instead, consider the fitted values $\widehat{\theta}_i$,

0.041	0.119	0.151	0.397	0.579	0.635	0.635
0.635	0.688	0.735	0.777	0.777	0.777	0.777
0.845	0.871	0.912	0.912	0.927	0.927	0.951
0.959	0.972					

and compare these fitted values with the observed y_i in Table 8.1. For example, the table

	$y_i = 0$	$y_i = 1$
$\widehat{\theta}_i < 0.5$	4	0
$\widehat{\theta}_i > 0.5$	3	16

shows that the fitted probabilities $\widehat{\theta}_i$ validate the current data in an adequate but not completely convincing fashion.

8.5 Further data sets

Table 8.3 *Exercise data*

Group	x_1	x_2	x_3	y	n
1	−1	−1	−1	20	80
2	−1	−1	1	60	140
3	−1	1	−1	51	102
4	−1	1	1	60	108
5	1	−1	−1	38	72
6	1	−1	1	57	102
7	1	1	−1	47	77
8	1	1	1	73	101

Table 8.4 *The mortgage loan data*

x_1	x_2	x_3	x_4	x_5	x_6	x_7	y
40	35	26	1	17.3	0.395	154	0
51.2	37	24	1	4	0.76	64	0
180	36	35	1	257.5	0.80	208	1
58	36	35	1	637	0.53	644	1
39.1	41	18	1	13.3	0.80	31.5	0
30.1	49	18	1	35	0.30	173	0
51.9	41	26	−1	20	0.76	44	1
55.2	32	26	−1	.12	0.79	36	1
30	49	60	1	848	0.58	1660	1
26	50	11	−1	32	0.64	45	1
160	38	180	−1	14600	0.71	7600	1
57	45	35	1	38	0.95	95	0
46.9	47	17	−1	0	0.74	33	0
90.8	51	49	1	0	0.80	116	1
176	43	100	1	193	0.94	125	1
25	28	32	1	47	0.35	213	1
57	28	35	1	60	0.87	103	0
73.6	28	42	1	7	0.80	66	1
70	37	30	1	58	0.70	77	0
84.72	50	112	1	112	0.80	102	1
25	42	20	−1	23	0.62	34	1
84	40	60	1	50	0.69	158	1
32	64	20	−1	25	0.18	155	0
50	68	33	1	.05	0.57	167	1
84	38	40	1	195	0.80	300	1
93	53	100	1	168	0.64	577	1
38	32	80	1	278	0.72	109	1
108	30	60	1	90	0.78	105	1
32	36	23	−1	23	0.80	43	0
85	52	42	−1	78	0.80	153	1
151.2	38	100	1	627	0.80	892	1
49.5	32	30	1	49	0.70	52	0
65.9	38	30	1	64	0.66	325	1
74	43	43	1	48	0.64	203	1
106.4	39	57	1	359	0.80	473	1

The data in Table 8.3 were collected by phone survey in Madison, Wisconsin, by University of Wisconsin student Mark Schimke. The x_1 variable denotes whether the individuals in this group were aged at least 35 ($x_1 = +1$) or less than 35 ($x_1 = -1$). The x_2 variable denotes whether or not ($x_2 = +1$ or -1) they were educated above high school level, and the x_3 variable indicates whether or not ($x_3 = +1$ or -1) they were correctly employed. Then, y denotes the number of the group of n individuals who stated that they exercised regularly.

The data in Table 8.4 were previously analysed by University of Wisconsin student Jon Lien, and collected by Professor E. W. Frees of the University of Wisconsin Business School. See also Frees (1996). The variables are described as follows:

x_1 : The actual amount of the loan (in thousands of dollars).

x_2 : The (average) age of the individual(s) who acquired the loan (in years).

x_3 : The average monthly income of the individual(s) (in hundreds of dollars).

x_4 : The marital status of the homeowner (1 = married, -1 = not married).

x_5 : The net amount of the mortgage (in thousands of dollars).

x_6 : The loan-to-value ratio (amount of loan/value of the property).

x_7 : The net worth of the individual (in thousands of dollars).

y : Response variable determining if the loan has a fixed or variable interest rate (1 = fixed rate, 0 = variable rate).

Exercises

8.1 For the binomial model in Section 8.1.1, show that the likelihood of $\theta_1, ..., \theta_m$, given $y_1, .., y_m$, and before the regression assumption is incorporated, is

$$\ell(\theta_1, ..., \theta_m | \mathbf{y}) = K \prod_{i=1}^{m} \theta_i^{y_i} (1 - \theta_i)^{n_i - y_i}$$

for some K which you should determine. Show that the likelihood of the logits $\alpha_1, ..., \alpha_m$, is

$$\ell(\alpha_1, ..., \alpha_m | \mathbf{y}) = K \exp\{\sum_{i=1}^{m} \alpha_i y_i\} / \prod_{i=1}^{m} (1 + e^{\alpha_i})^{n_i}.$$

Show that the maximum likelihood estimates of θ_i and α_i are $\widehat{\theta}_i = y_i / n_i$ and $\widehat{\alpha}_i = \log(y_i / (n_i - y_i))$.

Note: If $v_i \leq 0.4$, the approximate normal likelihood of α_i can be approximated by

$$\ell^*(\alpha_i|y_i) = \ell(\widehat{\alpha}_i|y_i)\exp(\alpha_i - \ell_i)^2/2v_i\},$$

where $v_i = y_i^{-1} + (n_i - y_i)^{-1}$ and $\ell(\alpha_i|y_i)$ is the exact likelihood. This result is the basis of the approximations described in Section 8.1.3, and can be justified by expanding $\log \ell(\alpha_i|y_i)$ in a Taylor series about $\alpha_i = \ell_i$.

8.2   In Exercise 8.1 now make the assumption that $\alpha_i = \mathbf{x}_i^T\boldsymbol{\beta}$, where the vector $\mathbf{x}_i$ is specified and the dimension p of $\boldsymbol{\beta}$ is less than m. Arrange the likelihood of $\boldsymbol{\beta}$ in the form

$$\ell(\boldsymbol{\beta}|\mathbf{y}) = K\exp\{\mathbf{t}^T\boldsymbol{\beta}\}/\prod_{i=1}^{m}(1 + e^{\mathbf{x}_i^T\boldsymbol{\beta}})^{n_i},$$

where

$$\mathbf{t} = \sum_{i=1}^{m} y_i\mathbf{x}_i .$$

8.3   In Exercise 8.2, show that the maximum likelihood vector $\widehat{\boldsymbol{\beta}}$ satisfies the nonlinear equation

$$\mathbf{t} = \sum_{i=1}^{m} n_i\widehat{\theta}_i\mathbf{x}_i ,$$

where $\widehat{\theta}_i$ denotes the ith fitted probability

$$\widehat{\theta}_i = \exp(\mathbf{x}_i^T\widehat{\boldsymbol{\beta}})/\{1 + \exp(\mathbf{x}_i^T\widehat{\boldsymbol{\beta}})\}.$$

Show that the maximum likelihood estimates of θ_i and α_i are now constrained to be $\widehat{\theta}_i$ and $\widehat{\alpha}_i = \mathbf{x}_i^T\widehat{\boldsymbol{\beta}}$.

8.4   The data in Table 8.3 comprise a full 2^3 factorial design for binomial data. Show that the data can be rearranged as a 2^4 contingency table.

8.5   Analyse the data in Table 8.3 by fitting a main effects model of the form

$$\beta_0 + \beta_1 x_1 + \beta_2 x_2 + \beta_3 x_3$$

to eight binomial logits. Is this model a good fit? Are all three variables significant? Can you suggest a better model?

8.6   Analyse the data in Table 8.3 further, as a 2^4 contingency table. Summarise all real-life conclusions to be drawn.

8.7   Do the data in Table 8.4 indicate any association between initial status of owner and the response variable y? Construct a 2×2 contingency table.

8.8 By preparing two univariate scatterplots, investigate whether the data in Table 8.4 indicate any association between x_1 and the response variable y. Do the same for the explanatory variables x_2, x_3, x_5, x_6, and x_7.

8.9 Use binary regression to quantify a relationship between the response variable y and those explanatory variables (from your responses to Exercises 8.7 and 8.8) that you regard as important.

CHAPTER 9

Further Regression Models

9.1 Regression models for Poisson data

Let $y_1, ..., y_m$ denote cell counts that are regarded as independent and Poisson distributed with respective means $\mu_1, ..., \mu_m$, and let $\gamma_i = \log \mu_i$, for $i = 1, ..., m$. Then, linear models may be assumed for the Poisson log-means γ_i, in similar fashion to the models described in Section 8.1.1, for binomial logits.

Table 9.1 *The Groer-Pereira lymphocyte data*

Individual i	Number of Dicentrics y_i	Fitted Values $\widehat{y}_i$	Number of Cells (in thousands) c_i	Dose Level d_i
1	109	107.67	269	0.50
2	47	48.11	78	0.75
3	94	94.63	115	1.00
4	114	112.47	90	1.50
5	138	140.98	84	2.00
6	125	125.03	59	2.50
7	97	95.11	37	3.00

The medical background of the data in Table 9.1 is reported by Groer and Pereira (1987). It is required to relate the expectation μ_i of y_i to the explanatory variables c_i and d_i. One possibility is to let $x_{i1} = \log c_i$ and $x_{i2} = \log d_i$, and to consider the model

$$\gamma_i = \log \mu_i = \beta_0 + \beta_1 x_{i1} + \beta_2 x_{i2}. \tag{9.1}$$

If the data in Table 9.1 are stored in the file lymdata, then the model in Equation (9.1) may be analysed using the Splus commands.

lym<-read.table("lymdata", col.names = c("y", "c", "d"))
attach(lym)
xa<- log(c)
xb<- log(d)
summary (glm(y ~ xa + xb, family = poisson)).

The output then gives a residual deviance equal to just 0.168 on four degrees of freedom (significance probability = 0.997). This suggests that the model

$$\widehat{\gamma}_i = -0.125 + 1.022 \log c_i + 0.985 \log d_i \tag{9.2}$$

almost perfectly fits the data. The corresponding fitted values for the y_i are described in the third column of Table 9.1. However, the very high value for the significance probability suggests that our Poisson sampling assumptions may not be completely reasonable. See also the data in Table 9.3.

Under our assumptions the estimated standard errors associated with the intercept and two slopes in Equation (9.2) are, respectively, 0.751, 0.148, and 0.156, so that both slopes are significantly different from zero. Models with a single explanatory variable do not fit well.

We might instead wish to assume, on *a priori*, or scientific, grounds that μ_i is proportional to d_i, i.e., that the slope of Equation (9.2) is equal to unity. Under this assumption, we used Splus to fit the model

$$\widehat{\gamma}_i = -0.196 + 1.034 \log c_i + \log d_i \tag{9.3}$$

or, equivalently,

$$\widehat{\mu}_i = 0822 c_i^{1.034} d_i. \tag{9.4}$$

The residual deviance is now 0.177 on five degrees of freedom (significance probability = 0.999), and the estimated standard errors associated with the intercept in Equation (9.3), together with the slope of $\log c_i$, are 0.044 and 0.062, respectively. The further Splus commands needed to obtain Equation (9.3), together with all related quantities of interest, are now listed:

```
model<-glim(cbind(xa),y, error = "poisson", link = "log", offset = xb,
    intercept = T)
model$coef
model$fit
model$var
sqrt(model$var)
model$coef[1]/sqrt(model$var[1,1])
model$coef[2]/sqrt(model2$var[2,2])
model$dev
model$df
```

The second of these commands gives the estimates for the intercept and first coefficient, the third gives the fitted frequencies, and the fourth gives the estimated standard errors of the parameters. The fifth and sixth commands give the normal test statistics for investigating the significance of the intercept and slope, and the seventh and eighth commands provide the residual deviance and degrees of freedom.

9.2 The California earthquake data

The data in Figure 9.1 were reported by Wiemer, McNult, and Wyss (1998) and describe frequencies of earthquakes in 24 equally spaced intervals on a magnitude scale. We regard the $m = 24$ frequencies $y_1, ..., y_{24}$ as independent Poisson frequencies and represent the lower interval boundaries (measurement of magnitude) by $x_1, ..., x_{24}$. Following discussions with Ian Main, we fit a piecewise linear regression, with discontinuous slope, and taking the form

$$\gamma_i = \log \mu_i = \begin{cases} \beta_0 + \beta_1 x_i & (x \leq x^*) \\ \beta_0 + (\beta_1 - \beta_2)x^* + \beta_2 x_i & (x \geq x^*) \end{cases}$$
$$= \beta_0 + \beta_1 a_i + \beta_2 b_i,$$

with

$$a_i = x_i I[x_i < x^*] + x^* I[x_i \geq x^*],$$
$$b_i = (x_i - x^*)I[x_i \geq x^*],$$

to the logs of the Poisson means μ_i, where $I[A]$ denotes the indicator function for the set A, so that b_i is zero whenever $x_i < x^*$, and $b_i = x_i - x^*$ if $x_i \geq x^*$.

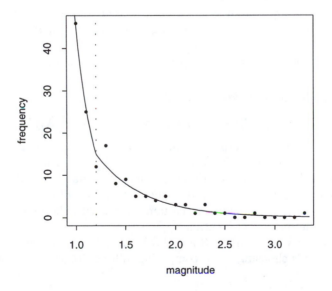

Figure 9.1 *Analysis of earthquake magnitude data*

For any fixed change point x^*, β_0, β_1, and β_2 may be estimated as a special case of the procedures outlined in Section 8.1. The choice of x^* may be made by minimisation of

$$\text{AIC}^* = \text{Residual deviance} + 2 \text{ degrees of freedom}$$

where degrees of freedom $= 24 - 3 = 21$. However, the AIC^* should also be compared with $\text{AIC}^* = $ residual deviance $+44$, where the residual deviance is for a simple linear regression for γ_i, without a change point. This helps us to decide whether or not some change in slope does indeed occur.

This method provided us with the optimal change point $x^* = 1.2$, and with residual deviance $= 13.34$ on 21 degrees of freedom. The estimated parameters were $\widehat{\beta}_0 = 9.38$, $\widehat{\beta}_1 = -5.56$, and $\widehat{\beta}_2 = -2.09$, with respective estimated standard errors 1.19, 1.08, and 0.26. The fitted regression in Figure 9.1 appears to explain the data reasonably well.

9.3 A generalisation of logistic regression

We observe y_i successes out of n, for $i = 1, ..., m$, for example, the scores y_i out of n for m students on a multiple-choice test with n items. Assume that we wish to relate the distributions of the y_i to a $p \times 1$ vector $\mathbf{x}_i$ of explanatory variables, e.g., scores on earlier tests. However, either binomial assumptions for the y_i might be regarded as inappropriate on *a priori* grounds or the data might be too noisy to hope for a good fit, using the linear logistic model of Chapter 8.

Hsu (1999) shows that it is possible to extend the exponential family assumptions of Section 1.10 by assuming that, for $i = 1, ..., m$,

$$p(y_i = j) = e^{\gamma_{ij}} / \sum_{g=0}^{n} e^{\gamma_{ig}} \qquad (j = 0, 1, ..., n),$$

where the multivariate logits γ_{ij} satisfy

$$\gamma_{ij} = \log(^nC_j) + j\mathbf{x}_i^T\boldsymbol{\beta} + \lambda_2 j^2 + \lambda_3 j^3 + \cdots + \lambda_q j^q$$

with $\boldsymbol{\beta}$ denoting a $p \times 1$ vector of parameter, and $\lambda_2, \lambda_3, ... \lambda_q$ denoting $q - 1$ further scalar parameters. If $\lambda_2 = \lambda_3 = \cdots = \lambda_q = 0$, then this reduces to the general form of the logistic linear model of Chapter 8. More generally, the extra parameters imply that the distribution of each observation belongs to a q-parameter exponential family, but with the first parameter replaced by the regression function $\mathbf{x}_i^T\boldsymbol{\beta}$.

Hsu shows how to estimate $\boldsymbol{\beta}$ and $\lambda_2, \lambda_3, ... \lambda_q$ by maximum likelihood, and recommends choosing q and comparing different regression models, by reference to

$$\text{AIC}^* = \text{residual deviance} + 2(m - p - q - 1).$$

The "Matsumura data" in Table 9.2 describes the observed scores for

$m = 145$ students on four multiple-choice tests. The fourth test contains $n = 29$ dissimilar items, and we regard the $m = 145$ scores on this test as our dependent variables $y_1, ..., y_m$. Hsu first attempted to fit a main effects linear logistic model, with three sets of explanatory variables, namely, the scores on the first three sets. However, the value $X^2 = 236.46$ for his chi-squared goodness-of-fit statistic on 140 degrees of freedom yields a significance probability of 0.0000007, so that this model does not fit well.

Hsu then incorporated his main effects model, with $p = 4$, and the same three explanatory variables, with the generalisation of the current section. With $p = 2$ he obtained $X^2 = 145.90$ with 139 degrees of freedom, and a significance probability of 0.237. The same regression model is therefore now appropriate, but with different sampling errors. The value $p = 2$ minimises AIC*.

Hsu calculated the maximum likelihood estimates $\widehat{\beta}_0 = -2.169$, $\widehat{\beta}_1 = 0.343$, $\widehat{\beta}_2 = 1.210$, and $\widehat{\beta}_3 = 0.823$, for the intercept and three slopes in his embedded main effects model, with respective estimated standard errors 0.233, 0.349, 0.311, and 0.221. The first slope β_1 is therefore not judged to be significantly different from zero. Furthermore, $\widehat{\lambda}_2 = 0.033$, with estimated standard error 0.006. The difference of this parameter from zero is responsible for the great improvement in fit.

Table 9.2 *The Matsumura data*

No.	TEST 1	2	3	4	No.	TEST 1	2	3	4
1	23	21	20	27	41	16	16	10	18
2	24	21	16	27	42	22	21	16	17
3	20	21	17	24	43	21	15	10	18
4	22	16	15	19	44	20	20	11	23
5	22	18	10	17	45	23	22	13	20
6	17	15	18	17	46	22	24	14	27
7	23	16	16	20	47	19	14	9	10
8	21	16	17	22	48	22	17	18	19
9	22	18	18	18	49	22	21	17	24
10	25	19	21	26	50	20	15	13	23
11	23	23	18	24	51	25	20	18	25
12	17	14	11	14	52	22	19	19	16
13	22	20	12	13	53	19	23	21	26
14	23	16	11	13	54	25	22	20	20
15	23	20	16	22	55	17	14	13	18
16	18	17	12	25	56	22	18	13	17
17	25	22	14	26	57	22	17	9	16
18	22	22	17	16	58	20	19	15	19
19	18	15	18	22	59	19	18	15	21
20	21	22	16	24	60	25	19	18	24
21	23	19	12	20	61	13	9	17	20
22	23	18	19	20	62	22	21	18	24
23	19	20	16	24	63	21	12	15	16
24	24	20	15	20	64	25	20	19	27
25	19	16	6	18	65	22	20	21	23
26	25	20	20	23	66	23	25	21	26
27	19	14	14	20	67	24	22	19	25
28	20	19	22	26	68	18	18	12	19
29	24	18	18	25	69	25	22	16	25
30	21	17	16	24	70	22	18	12	18
31	20	17	12	19	71	21	17	14	22
32	25	20	18	19	72	23	17	11	25
33	16	8	13	8	73	23	20	19	24
34	20	17	19	23	74	22	21	14	23
35	21	17	13	17	75	23	25	21	23
36	23	20	16	22	76	20	17	16	22
37	19	15	16	21	77	23	21	15	21
38	24	22	11	24	78	19	19	15	14
39	22	16	13	23	79	20	18	18	19
40	23	17	13	23	80	21	14	11	11

Table 9.2 *(Continued)*

No.	1	2	3	4	No.	1	2	3	4
	TEST					TEST			
81	20	20	14	17	121	20	15	9	18
82	22	18	18	24	122	24	21	15	19
83	24	19	19	16	123	24	20	18	24
84	21	20	19	19	124	24	19	16	24
85	23	17	10	16	125	18	14	14	18
86	20	17	17	22	126	24	21	15	19
87	25	25	21	29	127	21	21	12	23
88	20	10	7	15	128	22	18	17	20
89	18	17	11	21	129	18	16	9	23
90	20	19	14	19	130	20	15	17	17
91	24	24	21	24	131	23	23	17	18
92	25	18	18	21	132	20	18	15	20
93	22	21	16	22	133	25	21	18	17
94	24	20	14	20	134	21	19	13	19
95	22	18	16	20	135	22	12	16	20
96	23	14	12	16	136	25	22	21	26
97	16	12	9	8	137	19	11	12	16
98	22	17	10	18	138	21	23	18	24
99	24	21	20	24	139	17	13	12	16
100	17	17	11	22	140	20	16	12	24
101	23	22	20	26	141	22	18	11	18
102	23	23	16	22	142	20	17	13	21
103	19	12	11	13	143	16	17	11	15
104	25	23	18	22	144	25	21	20	21
105	19	11	14	14	145	25	23	18	24
106	21	20	18	23					
107	21	19	18	26					
108	16	18	19	15					
109	24	21	16	22					
110	18	17	15	20					
111	20	20	15	19					
112	22	21	14	23					
113	17	19	9	17					
114	22	17	13	22					
115	22	17	17	16					
116	23	22	14	26					
117	25	18	16	26					
118	22	19	14	17					
119	24	19	16	25					
120	21	21	14	20					

9.4 Logistic regression for matched case-control studies

The methodology described in this section is largely used to analyse data retrospectively from case-control studies where a disease D is present for m individuals (patients) and absent for a further m individuals (controls). We wish to investigate the propensity for a patient with explanatory variables $u_1, ..., u_p$ to have the disease. We, however, know that further variables, $z_1, ..., z_q$, known as "stratification" variables, might influence the chances of a patient having the disease.

At an initial stage of the analysis, we therefore should use the stratification variables $z_1, ..., z_q$ to arrange the m patients and m controls into m pairs, where each pair consists of a well-matching patient and member of the control group. Then, for the ith pair (or stratum), let

$$x_{ij} = u_{ij1} - u_{ij2}$$

where u_{ij1} and u_{ij2} denote the values of the jth explanatory variable for the patient and for the member of the control group, respectively. Let θ_i denote a propensity parameter for the ith stratum, such that

$$\theta_i = e^{\alpha_i}/(1 + e^{\alpha_i}),$$

with the logits α_i satisfying

$$\alpha_i = \beta_1 x_{i1} + \cdots + \beta x_{ip} \qquad (i = 1, ..., m).$$

Following a partial likelihood method described by Breslow and Day (1980) and Hosner and Lemeshow (1989, Chapter 7), the parameters $\beta_1, ..., \beta_p$ may be estimated by using the Splus commands for logistic regression, but with each y_i set equal to unity, and the constant term explicitly excluded from the regression. As a trivial example, let $m = 5$, $p = 1$, $x_1 = 5.1$, $x_2 = 10.3$, $x_3 = 16.2$, $x_4 = 17.4$, and $x_5 = 20.5$. As each of these differences is greater than zero, there is already some evidence that the corresponding explanatory variable is associated with a propensity for the disease. Then, the Splus commands

```
y <- c(1, 1, 1, 1, 1)
x <- c(5.1, 10.3, 16.2, 17.4, 20.5)
summary (glm(cbind(y, 1-y)~-1+x, family = binomial)
```

give the required results. In this case $\widehat{\beta}_1 = 1.57$ with estimated standard error 6.51. The normal statistic is equal to 0.24, suggesting that the slope is not statistically significant. It is useful to realize that the entry $-1 + x$, in the preceding summary command, requires the regression to be linear in a single variable x, and with a zero constant term. A more detailed data set with seven sets of explanatory variables is described by Hosmer and Lemeshow (1989, pp. 262-265).

In the Edinburgh cataracts study with Calbert Phillips and Ruth Clayton

(University of Edinburgh, Department of Opthamology), we analysed data for $m = 1000$ pairs, each pair consisting of a patient with cataracts, and a control. The choices of pairing were based upon two stratification variables, namely age and gender. By using matched pairs logistic regression, our fitted model was

$$
\begin{aligned}
\alpha &= \log(\text{cataract propensity}) \\
&= 0.29x_1 - 0.04x_1x_2 + 0.64x_3 \\
&\quad +0.31x_4 + 0.99x_5 + 0.22x_6 \\
&\quad +0.96x_1x_6 + 0.44x_7 + 0.41x_8 \\
&\quad -0.60x_9 - 0.36x_9x_{10} + 0.77x_{11} \\
&\quad +2.16x_1x_{11} + 0.98x_{12} + 0.74x_{10}x_{11}.
\end{aligned}
$$

Differences of stratification variables should not be included as main effects, although in our model x_2 = age difference and x_{10} = gender difference contribute to interaction terms. The other explanatory variables $x_1, x_3, x_4, ..., x_{12}$ were all differences of $+1$ and -1 corresponding to presence or absence of respiratory condition, topically applied drugs, cardiovascular condition, diabetes, serious infectious bacterial illness, blood disease, hypnotics usage, analgesics, corticosteroids, and antibiotics. All main effects possessed significance probabilities less than 2%, with the exception of x_1 (significance probability $= 5.82\%$) and x_6 (significance probability $= 10.91\%$). Furthermore, the interaction terms x_1x_2 and $x_{10}x_{11}$ possessed significance probabilities as large as 6.62% and 5.23%.

The above regression function was modelled, using Splus online and during a subjective discussion with an opthamology expert, who at each opportunity recommended the next variable to include in the analysis. This provides an excellent example of Aitken's inductive synthesis. However, other sets of medical variables modelled the regression function equally well. We conclude that the propensity for cataracts is related to a variety of factors interacting simultaneously, and not to any particular factor or pairwise interaction of factors. A variety of other possibilities are considered by Donnelly et al. (1995), Phillips, Clayton et al. (1996), and Phillips, Donnelly et al. (1996).

9.5 Further data

Table 9.3 *The Lundsteen-Piper lymphocyte data*

Individual i	Number of Dicentrics y_i	Number of Cells (in thousands c_i)	Dose Level d_i
1	0	585	0.1
2	3	1002	0.2
3	5	472	0.5
4	14	493	1.0
5	30	408	1.5
6	75	690	2.0
7	46	291	3.0

The data in Table 9.3 were provided by J. Piper and reported by Lundsteen and Piper (1989). They complement the data in Table 9.1. Both data sets have previously been analysed by University of Edinburgh student Linda Robb.

Exercises

9.1 For the data in Table 9.3, fit a main effects model of the type of Equation (9.1) to the logs of the cell means, with $x_{i1} = \log c_i$ and $x_{i2} = \log d_i$. Report the residual deviance. When considered together with the results in Section 9.1, do you think that Poisson assumptions are reasonable for data of this type? The data were collected by an automated procedure described by Lundsteen and Piper.

9.2 Plot the data in the fourth column of Table 9.2 in a dot-diagram, and calculate the sample mean and variance. Would it be reasonable to take these observations to constitute a random sample from a binomial distribution with sample size 29?

9.3 For the log-linear model of Section 9.1, replace Equation (9.1) by the simple assumption

$$\gamma_i = \beta_0 + \beta_1 x_i.$$

If y_i possesses a Poisson distribution with mean $\mu_i = e^{\gamma_i}$, then show that the likelihood of γ_i, given y_i, is

$$\ell(\gamma_i | y_i) = \{\exp \gamma_i y_i - e^{\gamma_i}\} / y_i!$$

Hence show that the likelihood of β_0 and β_1, given $y_1, ..., y_n$, is

$$\ell(\beta_0, \beta_1 | \mathbf{y}) = \exp\left\{ n\beta_0 + n\bar{y}\beta_1 - e^{\beta_0} \sum_{i=1}^{n} e^{\beta_1 x_i} \right\} / \prod_{i=1}^{n} y_i!$$

where $\bar{y}$ denotes the sample mean of $y_1, ..., y_n$.

9.4 In Exercise 9.3, show that the likelihood is maximised, for any fixed β_1, whenever $\beta = \widehat{\beta}_0(\beta_1)$

$$\widehat{\beta}_0(\beta_1) = -\log\left(\sum_{i=1}^{n} e^{\beta_1 x_i}/n\right).$$

By replacing β_0 by $\widehat{\beta}_0(\beta_1)$, in the likelihood of β_0 and β_1, show that the maximum likelihood estimate of β_1 also maximises its "profile likelihood"

$$\ell_p(\beta_1|\mathbf{y}) \propto \exp\{n\bar{y}\beta_1\}/\left(\sum_{i=1}^{n} e^{\beta_1 x_i}\right)^n.$$

Hence describe a graphical procedure for computing the maximum likelihood estimates $\widehat{\beta}_1$ and $\widehat{\beta}_0 = \widehat{\beta}_0(\widehat{\beta}_1)$ of β_1 and β_0.

9.5 Use the developments of Section 9.2 to show how to fit piecewise linear regression to the logits of several binomial distributions. Describe the Splus commands necessary to do this. Apply your methodology to the Space Shuttle example (Table 8.2).

9.6 Express the generalised logistic regression model in Section 9.3 as a special case of a generalised linear model with a product multinomial sampling distribution, where each of m multinomial distributions has $n+1$ cells, and sample size equal to unity.

9.7 Divide the first 144 of the individuals in the Matsumura data into a top group (best $m = 72$ students) and a lower group (next $m = 72$ students) according to the results on the fourth test. Then stratify these individuals into $m = 72$ pairs according to their scores on the third test. Then use matched pairs logistic regression to predict the propensity of falling into the fourth group, where the predictions are based upon the knowledge of the scores in the first two tests.

CHAPTER 10

Final Topics

10.1 Continuous random variables

Continuous random variables include random variables which are referred to as possessing exponential, Gamma, Weibull, normal, and log-normal distributions. Rather than possessing a probability mass function, they distinguish themselves from discrete random variables (e.g., binomial or Poisson) by possessing a density. However, like discrete random variables, they possess a cumulative distribution function (c.d.f.). They associate positive probabilities with intervals, rather than with points.

Definition 1: A *density* f is a curve $f(x)$ defined for all x in $(-\infty, \infty)$ such that $f(x)$ is nonnegative for all values of x, and the total area under the curve is unity.

Definition 2: A random entity X is a *continuous random variable with density* f, if for any interval (a, b) the probability that X will fall in (a, b) is

$$p\{X \in (a, b)\} = \text{ area between } a \text{ and } b \text{ under the density } f.$$

Definition 3: A continuous random variable X possesses a *normal distribution with mean* μ *and variance* σ^2 if X has density

$$f(x) = \frac{1}{\sqrt{2\pi\sigma^2}} e^{-\frac{1}{2}(x-\mu)^2/2\sigma^2}$$

$$(-\infty < x < \infty; -\infty < \mu < \infty; 0 < \sigma^2 < \infty).$$

In this case, we write $X \sim N(\mu, \sigma^2)$.

In general, the mean or expectation, if it exists, of a random variable X, is

$$\mu = E(X) = \text{ the center of gravity of the density of } X,$$

where we can obtain the center of gravity by tracing a graph of the density onto a thin and uniform lamina of balsa wood, cutting out this shape, and balancing the straightedge on a pointer, with the lamina in a vertical position. The point of balance then matches the center of gravity. Furthermore, the variance of X, if it exists, is

$$\sigma^2 = E\{(X - \mu)^2\}$$
$$= \text{expectation of the square of the distance between } X \text{ and } \mu$$
$$= \text{area under the curve } (x - \mu)^2 f(x).$$

If $X \sim N(\mu, \sigma^2)$, then $X = \mu + \sigma Z$ where the random variable $Z = (X - \mu)/\sigma$ has a standard normal distribution, i.e., $Z \sim N(0, 1)$. We can therefore calculate probabilities for X via its *cumulative distribution function:*

$$F(x) = p(X \leq x),$$
$$= \text{area under } f \text{ to the left of } x,$$
$$= \Phi(\frac{x - \mu}{\sigma}) \qquad (-\infty < x < \infty),$$

where

$$\Phi(z) = p(Z \leq z),$$

denotes the c.d.f. of the standard $N(0, 1)$ distribution. Then Φ is a standard mathematical function which can, for example, be evaluated using the Splus function *pnorm.*

The above definitions can be extended to a $p \times 1$ random vector $\mathbf{X}$. This is a continuous random vector, if for any event A in p-dimensional real space R^p, the probability that $\mathbf{X}$ falls in A is the corresponding hypervolume beneath a multivariate density $f(\mathbf{x})$. Here $f(\mathbf{x})$ is non-negative for all $x \in R$, with total hypervolume equal to unity.

10.2 Logistic discrimination analysis

Consider the Space Shuttle data in Table 8.2. Let $Y = 0$ represent failure and $Y = 1$ represent success. The data record the temperatures on flights for which $Y = 0$ and flights for which $Y = 1$, and there are $n_1 = 7$ and $n_2 = 16$ observations in the respective categories. After taking logs, we rearrange the data in two samples, as follows:

Sample 1 $(Y = 0, n_1 = 7)$

      3.970   4.043   4.060   4.143   4.248   4.428   4.317

Sample 2 $(Y = 1, n_2 = 16)$

    4.190   4.205   4.205   4.205   4.220   4.234   4.248   4.248
    4.277   5.290   4.317   4.331   4.331   4.357   4.369   4.394

The sample mean and variance for the first sample are

$$\bar{x}_1 = 4.1473 \quad \text{and} \quad s_1^2 = 0.01653,$$

and for the second sample

$$\bar{x}_2 = 4.2763 \text{ and } s_2^2 = 0.00442.$$

Assume that the (transformed) observations in the first sample comprise a random sample from a normal $N(\mu_1, \sigma_1^2)$ distribution, i.e., each observation is independently a numerical realisation of a random variable with a $N(\mu_1, \sigma_1^2)$ distribution. Then $\bar{x}_1$ and s_1^2 are unbiased estimates of μ_1 and σ_1^2. Similarly, assume that the observations in the second sample independently comprise a random sample from an $N(\mu_2, \sigma_2^2)$ distribution, in which case $\bar{x}_2$ and s_2^2 are unbiased estimates of μ_2 and σ_2^2.

As an alternative to the binary logistic regression analysis of Section 8.4, we now describe an approach, which we refer to as "logistic discrimination analysis". Before viewing the values of the log temperatures, the probability of failure for a randomly chosen flight out of the $N = n_1 + n_2 = 23$ flights is

$$\begin{aligned} \phi &= p(Y = 0) \\ &= n_1/N = 7/23. \end{aligned}$$

Suppose that you are now informed that the log temperature X on a randomly selected flight has numerical realisation x. What is your new probability of failure for this flight? A simple application of conditional probability tells you that

$$\begin{aligned} \phi^* &= p(Y = 0|X = x) \\ &= p(\text{failure}| \log \text{temperature} = x) \\ &= \frac{\phi f_1(x)}{\phi f_1(x) + (1 - \phi) f_2(x)} \\ &= \frac{n_1 f_1(x)}{n_1 f_1(x) + n_2 f_2(x)}, \end{aligned}$$

where $f_1(x)$ denotes the density of X when $Y = 0$, and $f_2(x)$ denotes the density of X when $Y = 1$. Consequently, the logit $\alpha^* = \log\{\phi^*/(1 - \phi^*)\}$ satisfies

$$\alpha^* = \log(n_1/n_2) + \log\{f_1(x)/f_2(x)\}.$$

We will refer to this expression for α^* as the *logistic discrimination function*. Different choices of the densities $f_1(x)$ and $f_2(x)$ permit us to model different functional forms for the discrimination function. The discrimination function plays a similar role to the regression function in binary regression. For example, if $f_1(x)$ and $f_2(x)$, respectively, represent $N(\mu_1, \sigma_1^2)$ and $N(\mu_2, \sigma_2^2)$ densities, then (e.g. Day, and Kerridge, 1967, Anderson 1975) we have the quadratic discrimination function

$$\alpha^* = \beta_0 + \beta_1 x + \beta_2 x^2,$$

where

$$\beta_0 = \log(n_1/n_2) - \frac{1}{2}\log(\sigma_1^2/\sigma_2^2)$$
$$-\mu_1^2/2\sigma_1^2 + \mu_2^2/2\sigma_2^2,$$
$$\beta_1 = \mu_1/\sigma_1^2 - \mu_2/\sigma_2^2,$$

and

$$\beta_2 = 1/2\sigma_2^2 - 1/2\sigma_1^2.$$

For binary regression, β_0, β_1, and β_2 need to be estimated via an iterative computational procedure. For discrimination analysis, an algebraically explicit, though less statistically efficient, procedure is available. Simply replace μ_1, μ_2, σ_1^2, and σ_2^2 in the expressions for β_0, β_1 and β_2 by their respective unbiased estimators $\overline{x}_1, \overline{x}_2, s_1^2$, and s_2^2, namely, the appropriate sample means and sample variances.

If, moreover, $\sigma_1^2 = \sigma_2^2 = \sigma^2$ in the preceding normal case, we obtain the linear discrimination function:

$$\alpha^* = \beta_0 + \beta_1 x,$$

where

$$\beta_0 = \log(n_1/n_2) + (\mu_2^2 - \mu_1^2)/2\sigma^2$$

and

$$\beta_1 = (\mu_1 - \mu_2)/\sigma^2.$$

In this case, replace μ_1 by $\overline{x}_1$, μ_2 by $\overline{x}_2$, and σ^2 by the pooled estimate of variance

$$s^2 = \frac{(n_1 - 1)s_1^2 + (n_2 - 1)s_2^2}{n_1 + n_2 - 2}.$$

In the Space Shuttle example, $s^2 = 0.00788$, giving the estimated quadratic curve

$$\widehat{\alpha}(x) = \widehat{\beta}_0 + \widehat{\beta}_1 x + \widehat{\beta}_2 x^2,$$

where appropriate substitutions into our formulae for β_0, β_1, and β_2 give

$$\widehat{\beta}_0 = 1544.95, \quad \widehat{\beta}_1 = -715.69, \quad \text{and} \quad \widehat{\beta}_2 = 82.77.$$

Moreover, in the linear case, we have

$$\widehat{\alpha}(x) = \widehat{\beta}_0 + \widehat{\beta}_1 x,$$

where approximate substitutions into our second set of formulae for β_0 and β_1 give

$$\widehat{\beta}_0 = 68.07 \quad \text{and} \quad \widehat{\beta}_1 = -16.36.$$

These estimates may be contrasted with the values $\widehat{\beta}_0 = 65.86$ and $\widehat{\beta}_1 = -15.80$ based upon the logistic regression procedures of Section 8.4. The corresponding functions $\widehat{\theta}(x) = e^{\widehat{\alpha}(x)}/(1 + e^{\widehat{\alpha}(x)})$ for the probability of failure are plotted against the data in Figure 10.1.

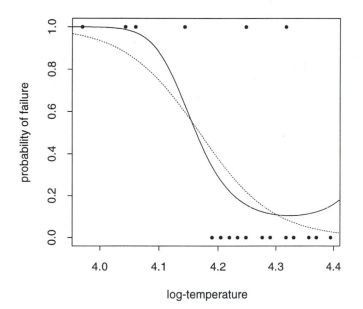

Figure 10.1 *Prediction curves for space shuttle data. Dotted curve = logistic linear discrimination; Solid curve = logistic quadratic discrimination.*

It is unclear from the plots whether the linear logistic discrimination or the quadratic logistic discrimination curve is preferable. The analysis of Section 10.3 suggests a slight, but not overwhelming, preference for this quadratic curve.

10.3 Testing the slope and quadratic term

Using the notation of Section 10.2, we observe that the statistic $F = s_1^2/s_2^2$, with s_1^2 and s_2^2 denoting the sample variances, is just the usual F-statistic on $n_1 - 1$ and $n_2 - 1$ degrees of freedom (e.g., Moore and McCabe, 1989, p. 565) for testing equality of the variances σ_1^2 and σ_2^2. This F-test equivalently tests the hypothesis that the coefficient of the quadratic term $\beta_2 = (\sigma_2^{-2} - \sigma_1^{-2})/2$ in our quadratic discrimination function, is equal to zero.

In our numerical example, $F = 0.01653/0.00442 = 3.740$ on 6 and 15 degrees of freedom. The two sample variances are noticeably different. However, the Splus command

$$2 * (1 - pf(3.740, 6, 15))$$

gives the significance probability $0.0355 = 3.55\%$ for an equal-tailed test for $H_0 : \beta_2 = 0$ versus $H_1 : \beta_2 \neq 0$. Consequently, there is some, but not overwhelming, evidence that the quadratic coefficient is significantly different from zero. Similar Splus commands can be used whenever $F \geq 1$. If $F < 1$, the command $2 * p(F, 6, 15)$ should be employed, with F replaced by its observed value, and 6 and 15 replaced by the appropriate degrees of freedom.

In situations where the β_2 is judged equal to zero, a t-test on $n_1 + n_2 - 2$ degrees of freedom (e.g., Moore and McCabe, 1989, p. 541) can be used to investigate whether $\mu_1 = \mu_2$, i.e., whether $\beta_1 = (\mu_1 - \mu_2)/\sigma^2 = 0$, where $\sigma^2 = \sigma_1^2 = \sigma_2^2$ is the assumed common variance. In our example $n_1 + n_2 - 2 = 21$ and

$$t = (\overline{x}_1 - \overline{x}_2)/s_e = -3.207,$$

where $\overline{x}_1 - \overline{x}_2 = -0.129$ and

$$s_e = \sqrt{s^2(\frac{1}{n_1} + \frac{1}{n_2})} = 0.0402.$$

The Splus command

$$2 * (1 - pt(3.207, 21))$$

gives a significance probability equal to $0.00423 = 0.423\%$. There is therefore strongly significant evidence to suggest that the slope is different from zero. Similar Splus commands can be used whenever $t \geq 0$. If $t < 0$, the command $2 * pt(t, 21)$ should be used, with t replaced by its observed value and 21 replaced by the appropriate degrees of freedom.

10.4 Extensions

There are many possible generalisations of the methodology of Section 10.2, depending upon the choices of densities $f_1(x)$ and $f_2(x)$. For example, if for each binary response we observe a vector $\mathbf{x} = (x_1, ..., x_p)^T$ of explanatory variables, then simply replace our densities for the two subpopulations by multivariate densities $f_1(\mathbf{x})$ and $f_2(\mathbf{x})$. Our multivariate discrimination function for the logit is now

$$\alpha^* = \log(n_1/n_2) + \log[f_1(\mathbf{x})/f_2(\mathbf{x})].$$

By modelling the choices of $f_1(\mathbf{x})$ and $f_2(\mathbf{x})$ and estimating any unknown parameters from the vectors of explanatory variables, for the two subpopulations, we can therefore model an entire multivariate discrimination function. Leonard and Hsu (1999, Section 2.5) and Day and Kerridge (1967) show how to do this when $f_1(\mathbf{x})$ and $f_2(\mathbf{x})$ represent multivariate normal densities. Anderson (1975) provides a medical diagnosis example in the bivariate case. This approach is particularly useful for investigating multiplicative interaction effects between two variables.

In the univariate case, Leonard and Hsu (1999, Section 2.7) consider "skewed normal densities" as choices for $f_1(\mathbf{x})$ and $f_2(\mathbf{x})$ and show that these choices lead to a "piecewise quadratic" discrimination function. They apply their results to the Ontario fetal metabolic acidosis data, and are able to plot graphs of the probability of the medical disorder, against birth-weight, at different levels of gestational age. Low et al. (1981) used a similar analysis to discover that babies who are light in the womb appear to be at increased risk, and they refuted the three previous medical predictors (prematurity, overdue and overweight babies, and presence of meconium-stained fluid during labour).

A continuous random variable X possesses a distribution belonging to the p-parameter exponential family, if its density takes the form

$$f(x) = K \exp\{\alpha_1 t_1(x) + \alpha_2 t_2(x) + \cdots + \alpha_p t_p(x)\} \quad (-\infty < x < \infty),$$

where $\alpha_1, ..., \alpha_p$ are unknown and unconditioned parameters, and K is chosen to ensure that the area under the density if unity. For example, with $p > 2$, the choices $t_j(x) = x^j$ $(j = 1, ..., p)$, generalise the normal distribution $(p = 2, \alpha_2 < 0)$. Based upon a random sample from this distribution, the parameters $\alpha_1, ..., \alpha_p$ may be estimated by maximising the log-likelihood

$$L(\boldsymbol{\alpha}) = \sum_{i=1}^{n} \log f(x_i) = n(\log K + \alpha_1 T_1 + \cdots + \alpha_p T_p),$$

where

$$T_j = n^{-1} \sum_{i=1}^{n} t_j(x_i) \quad (j = 1, ..., p)$$

and K depends upon $\alpha_1, ..., \alpha_p$. An optimal choice of p maximises the information criterion

$$\mathrm{AIC} = \sup_{\alpha} L(\boldsymbol{\alpha}) - p.$$

It is often straightforward to model both $f_1(x)$ and $f_2(x)$ in this way. Then the logistic discrimination function will be linear in $t_1(x), ..., t_{p*}(x)$, where p^* is the larger of the choices of p made for the two subpopulations.

10.5 Three-way contingency tables

The three-directional approach employed in Section 6.1 would best describe
our advocated methodology for many three-way contingency tables, since,
by repeated applications of Goodman's full-rank analysis for two-way tables, this approach frequently helps the statistician to infer the key real-life
conclusions from the data.

We here differ from standard practice (e.g., Fienberg, 1987, Ch. 3). Consider, for example, an $r \times s \times t$ table with no totals fixed, and where the
cell frequencies y_{ijk} are taken to be independent and Poisson distributed,
with respective means $\mu_{ijk}(i = 1, ..., r; j = 1, ..., s; k = 1, ..., t)$. Then a full-
rank interaction model (Goodman, 1964) would take the $\gamma_{ijk} = \log \mu_{ijk}$ to
satisfy

$$\begin{aligned}
\gamma_{ijk} &= \mu + \lambda_i^A + \lambda_j^B + \lambda_k^C + \lambda_{ij}^{AB} + \lambda_{jk}^{BC} + \lambda_{ki}^{CA} + \lambda_{ijk}^{ABC} \\
(i &= 1, ..., r; j = 1, ..., s; k = 1, ..., t),
\end{aligned}$$

where μ is the overall effect, the λ_i^A, λ_j^C, and λ_k^C are the main effects, the
λ_{ij}^{AB}, λ_{jk}^{BC}, λ_{ki}^{CA} are two-way interaction effects, and the λ_{ijk}^{ABC} are three-
way interaction effects. The effects are subject to the constraints

$$\begin{aligned}
\lambda_.^A &= \lambda_.^B = \lambda_.^C = \lambda_{i.}^{AB} = \lambda_{j.}^{BC} = \lambda_{k.}^{BC} \\
&= \lambda_{ij.}^{ABC} = \lambda_{i.k}^{ABC} = \lambda_{.jk}^{ABC} = 0,
\end{aligned}$$

for all possible i, j, and k. With these constraints, explicit algebraic estimates and estimated standard errors for the effects can be obtained.
Also significance tests can be developed, much along the lines of the two-
dimensional developments of Chapter 5, to investigate which interaction
effects are significant. However, in three dimensions, we find it much more
difficult to interpret the pattern of the significant interactions and virtually
impossible to employ this pattern to infer the main conclusions from the
data set. The switch from two to three dimensions is of critical difficulty
when trying to think intuitively about log-linear models.

While it is possible to analyse reduced forms of the full-rank model (e.g.,
using the Deming-Stephan iterative fitting procedure) we find that, unless
the reduction is to a main effects model, the reduced form can be difficult
to interpret. For example, equating all three-way interactions λ_{ijk}^{ABC} to zero
would lead to a generalisation of the equal measures of association model,
described in Sections 3.5 and 3.6 for the 2^3 situation. We do not in general
believe that a zero three-way interaction hypothesis is particularly useful
when inferring the main conclusions from a data set. Again, our objective is
not to seek a good fitting model at the expense of scientific interpretability,
since a model which fits the data well may not help us in scientific terms.
Models just developed for the purpose of fitting the data frequently fail to

be useful. The first co-author was advised by Dennis V. Lindley in 1971 that

> Analysing multi-way contingency tables is an art. I believe that we should look at the table from one direction at a time. The interpretation is not just a question of developing good methodology.

It is, more generally, important to preserve the essential ingredients of the ideas of the Second Millennium before they are lost in the systemisation of the Third Millennium.

Exercises

10.1 Consider logistic discrimination analysis when the observations in the first sample constitute a random sample from the exponential distribution with parameter λ_1, mean λ_1^{-1}, and density

$$f_1(x) = \lambda_1 e^{-\lambda_1 x} \qquad (0 < x < \infty; 0 < \lambda_1 < \infty)$$

and the observations in the second sample independently constitute a random sample from the exponential distribution with parameter λ_2. Find the logistic discrimination function, based upon a random sample of size n_1 from the first distribution and a random sample of size n_2 from the second distribution (the maximum likelihood estimates of λ_1 and λ_2 are $1/\bar{x}_1$ and $1/\bar{x}_2$, where $\bar{x}_1$ and $\bar{x}_2$ are the two sample means).

10.2 Ten lightbulbs with brand A have average lifetime 10.32 hours and 12 lightbulbs of brand B have an average lifetime of 12.77 hours. A lightbulb with one of these two brands has lifetime 11 hours. What is the probability that this lightbulb is of type A? State all assumptions made. You may in particular assume that the 22 lightbulbs were chosen at random from a larger population of lightbulbs.

10.3 It is observed that 21 out of 50 students obtain a grade A on a test. The 21 average homework scores for the students obtaining grade A possessed mean $\bar{x}_1 = 85.6$ and sample standard deviation $S_1 = 44$. The 29 average homework scores for the students not obtaining a grade A possessed sample standard deviation $\bar{x}_2 = 60.6$ and sample standard deviation $\bar{s}_1 = 10.2$. A further student obtained an average score of 75.3 on the homework, but did not take the test. Estimate your probability that this student would have passed, stating all assumptions made.

10.4 Under the assumptions of Section 10.5, derive the maximum likelihood estimates for the overall effect, the main effects, and first and second order interaction effects.

10.5 Consider the full-rank interaction model in Section 10.5 for a three-way table. Consider how this model reduces for a $2 \times 2 \times 2$ table, and

express the first- and second-order interactions as functions of the cell
means in this case.

References

Agresti, A. (1990) *Categorical Data Analysis.* Wiley, New York.

Agresti, A. (1996) *An Introduction to Categorical Data Analysis.* Wiley, New York.

Aitchison, J. (1982) The statistical analysis of compositional data (with Discussion) *J. R. Statist. Soc. B*, **44**, 139-77.

Aitchison, J. (1986) *The Statistical Analysis of Compositional Data.* Chapman and Hall, London.

Aitken, A.C. (1944) *Statistical Mathematics.* Oliver and Boyd, Edinburgh.

Alanko, T. and Duffy, J.C. (1996) Compound binomial distributions for modelling consumption data. *Statistician*, **45**, 268-86.

Altham, P.M.E. (1969) Exact Bayesian analysis of a 2 × 2 contingency table, and Fisher's "exact" significance test, *J. R. Statist. Soc. Ser. B*, **31**, 261-99.

Anderson, J.A. (1975) Quadratic logistic discriminination, *Biometrika*, **62**, 149-54.

Bennett, B.M., and Hsu, P. (1960) On the power function of the exact test for the 2 × 2 table. *Biometrika*, **47**, 393-398.

Birnbaum, A. (1962) On the foundations of statistical inference (with discussion), *J. Am. Statist. Assoc.*, **57**, 269-326.

Bishop, Y.M.M., Fienberg, S.E., and Holland, P.W. (1975) *Discrete Multivariate Analysis: Theory and Practice.* MIT Press, Cambridge, MA.

Bowlby, S., and Silk, J. (1982) Analysis of qualitative data using GLIM: two examples based on shopping survey data. *Prof. Geog.*, **34**, 80-90.

Breslow, N.E. and, Day, N.Z. (1980) *Statistical Methods in Cancer Research.* International Agency for Research on Cancer, Lyons.

Brown, R.L., Leonard, T., Rounds, L.A., and Papasouliotis, O. (1997) A two-item screening test for alcohol and other drug problems. *J. Fam. Prac.*, **44**, 151-60

Brown, R.L., Leonard, T., Saunders, L.A., and Papasouliotis, O. (1998) The prevalence and detection of substance use disorders among inpatients ages 18 to 49: an opportunity for prevention. *J. Prev. Med.*, **27**, 101-110.

Brown, R.L., Leonard, T., Saunders, L.A., and Papasouliotis, O. (1999) A two-item conjoint screen for alcohol and other drug problems. Technical Report, Department of Family Medicine, University of Wisconsin-Madison.

Brunswick, A.F. (1971) Adolescent health, sex and fertility. *Am. J. Public Health*, **61**, 711-20.

Charig, C.R., Webb, D.R., Payne, S.R., and Wickham, S.E.A. (1986) Comparison of treatment of renal calculi by open surgery, percutaneous nephrolithotomy, and extra corporeal shockwave lithotripsy. *B. M. J.* **292**, 879-82.

Christiansen, R. (1997) *Log-Linear Models and Logistic Regression.* Springer Verlag, New York.

Cox, D.R. (1970) *The Analysis of Binary Data.* Methuen, London.

Dalal, S.R., Fowlkes, E.B., and Hoardley, B. (1989) Risk analysis of the space shuttle: pre-Challenger prediction of failure. *J. Am. Statist. Assoc.*, **84**, 945-57.

Day, N.E. and Kerridge, D.F. (1967) A general maximum likelihood discriminant. *Biometrics*, **23**, 313-23.

Donnelly, C.A., Seth, J., Clayton, R.M., Phillips, C.I., Cuthbert, J., and Prescott, R.J. (1995) Some blood plasma constituents interact with the human cataract. *B. J. Optham.*, **79**, 1036-41.

Donner, A. (1984) Approaches to sample size estimation in the design of clinical trials - a review. *Statist. Med.*, **3**, 199-214.

Duncan, G.T. (1974) An empirical Bayes approach to scoring multiple-choice tests in the misinformation model, *J. Am. Statist. Assoc.*, **69**, 50-57.

Edwards, A.W.F. (1963) The measure of association in a 2×2 table. *J. R. Statist. Soc. A.*, **126**, 109-114.

Efron, B. and Diaconis, P. (1985) Testing for independence in a two-way table. New interpretations of the chi-square statistic. *Ann. Statist.*, **13**, 845-913.

Efron, B. and Hinkley, D.V. (1978) Assessing the accuracy of the maximum likelihood estimator: observed versus expected Fisher information (with discussion) *Biometrika*, **65**, 457-87.

Enke, H. (1986) Elementary analysis of multidimensional contingency tables: application to a medical example. *Biom. J.*, **28**, 305-22.

Everitt, B.S. (1992) *The Analysis of Contingency Tables.* Chapman and Hall, London.

Fienberg, S.E. (1987) *The Analysis of Cross-Classified Categorical Data,* MIT Press, Cambridge, MA.

Fingleton, B. (1984) *Models of Category Counts*, Cambridge University Press, Cambridge, U.K.

Fisher, R.A. (1925) *Statistical Methods for Research Workers*. Oliver and Boyd, Edinburgh.

Fisher, R.A (1936) Has Mendel's work been rediscovered? *Ann. Sci.*,1, 115-37.

Freedman, D., Pisani, R., and Purves, R. (1991) *Statistics,* 2nd Edition. Norton, New York.

Frees, E.F. (1996) *Data Analysis using Regression Models: The Business Perspective.* Prentice-Hall, Englewood Cliffs, NJ.

Goodman, L.A. (1964) Interactions in multidimensional contingency tables, *Ann. Math. Statist.*, **35**, 632-46.

Goodman, L.A. (1968) The analysis of cross-classified data: independence, quasi-independence, and interactions in contingency tables with or without missing entries, *J. Am. Statist. Assoc.*, **63**, 1091-131.

Grizzle, J.E. and Williams, O.P. (1982) Log linear models and tests for independence for contingency tables. *Biometrics,* **28**, 137-56.

Groer, P.G. and Pereira, C.A.DeB. (1987) Calibration of a radiation detector: chromosome dosimetry for neturons. In *Probability and Bayesian Statistics* (ed. by R. Viertl), pp. 225-52, Plenum Press, New York.

Hasselblad, V., Stead, A.G., and Crenson, J.P. (1980) Multiple probit analysis with a non-zero background. *Biometrics,* **36**, 650-63.

Holland, P.W. (1973) Covariance stabilizing transformations. *Ann. Statist.,* **1**, 84-92.

Hosmer, D.W., and Lemeshow, S.E. (1989) *Applied Logistic Regression.* Wiley, New York.

Hsu, J.S.J., Leonard, T., and Tsui, K.W. (1991) Statistical inference for multiple choice tests. *Psychometrika,* **56**, 327-48.

Hsu, J.S.J and Leonard, T. (1997) Bayesian semi-parametric procedures for logistic regression. *Biometrika,* **84**, 85-93.

Hsu, J.S.J. (1999) A Generalization of the Logistic Linear Model for Multiple Choice Testing, unpublished manuscript: University of California, Santa Barbara.

Keats, J.A. (1964) Some generalizations of a theoretical distribution of mental test scores: *Psychometrika,* **29**, 215-31.

Ku, H.H., and Kullbank, S. (1974) Log linear models in contingency table analysis. *Am. Statist.,* **28**, 115-22.

Lancaster, H.O. (1969) *The Chi-squared Distribution.* Wiley, New York.

Larsen, R.I., Gardner, D.E., and Coffin, D.L. (1979) An air quality data analysis system for interrelating effects, standards and needed sourced reductions. Part 5: No. 2. Mortality of mice. *J. Air. Pollut. Control Assoc.*, **39**, 113-17.

Lee, Y. and Nelder, J.A. (1996) Hierarchical generalized linear models (with discussion). *J. R. Statist. Soc. B*, **58**, 619-56.

Lehmann, E.L. (1994) *Testing Statistical Hypothesis.* Chapman and Hall, New York.

Leonard, P. (1999) An audit of helmet use versus age in a paedriatric accident and emergency department. *Royal Hospital for Sick Children*, Edinburgh.

Leonard, T. (1972) Bayesian methods for binomial data, *Biometrika*, **59**, 581-89.

Leonard, T. (1973) A Bayesian method for histograms, *Biometrika*, **60**, 297-308.

Leonard, T. (1975) Bayesian estimation methods for two-way contingency tables. *J. R. Statist. Soc. Ser. B*, **37**, 23-37.

Leonard, T. (1977a) An alternative Bayesian approach to the Bradley-Terry model for paired comparisons. *Biometrics*, **33**, 121-30.

Leonard, T. (1977b) A Bayesian approach to some multinomial estimation and pretesting problems. *J. Am. Statist. Assoc.*, **72**, 865-68.

Leonard, T. (1984) Some data-analytic modifications to Bayes-Stein estimation. *Ann. Inst. Statist. Math.*, **36**, 21-21.

Leonard, T. and Hsu, J.S.J. (1994) The Bayesian analysis of categorical data - a selective review, In*A Tribute to D. V. Lindley,* A.F.M. Smith and P. Freeman (eds.), Wiley, Chichester.

Leonard, T., and Hsu, J.S.J. (1996) On small sample Bayesian inference and sequential design for quantal response. In *Modeling and Prediction: Honoring Seymour Geisser* (J.C. Lee, A. Zellner and W.O. Johnson, eds) pp. 169-75. Springer-Verlag, New York.

Leonard, T., and Hsu, J.S.J. (1999) *Bayesian Methods: An Analysis for Statisticians and Interdisciplinary Researchers.* Cambridge University Press, New York.

Leonard, T., and Novick, J.B. (1986) Bayesian full rank marginalization for two-way contingency tables. *J. Educ. Statis.*, **11**, 33–56.

Leonard, T., Hsu, J.S.J., and Tsui, K. (1989) Bayesian marginal inference, *J. Am. Statist. Assoc.*, **84**, 1051–8.

Longford, N.T. (1993) *Random Coefficient Models.* Oxford University Press, Oxford.

Low, J.A., Karchmar, J., Broekhoven, L., Leonard, T., McGrath, M.J., Pancham, S.R., and Piercy, W.N. (1981) The probability of fetal metabolic acidosis during labor in a population at risk as determined by clinical factors, *Am. J. Obstet. Gyneacol.*, **141**, 941-51.

Lundsteen, C. and Piper, J. (1989) *Automation of Cytogenetics*, Springer Verlag, New York.

Main, I.G., Leonard, T., Papasouliotis, O., Hutton, C.G., and Meredith, P.G. (1999) One slope or two? Detecting statistically significant breaks of slope in geophysical data, with applications to fracture sealing relationships. *Geophysical Research Letters*, **26**, 2801-2804.

Mantel, N. and Haenszel, W. (1959) Statistical aspects of the analysis of data from retrospective studies of disease. *J. Nat. Cancer Inst.*, **22**, 719-48.

Moore, D.S. (1991) *Statistics: Concepts and Controversies*. W.H. Freeman, New York.

Moore, D.S., and McCabe, G.P. (1989) *Introduction to the Practice of Statistics*, W. H. Freeman and Company, New York.

Morrison, D.G. and Brockway, G. (1979) A modified beta-binomial model with applications to multiple choice and taste tests. *Psychometrika*, **29**, 215-31.

Osborn, J. (1987) The choice of computational unit in the statistical analysis of unbalanced clinical trials. *J Clin. Periodont.*, **14**, 519-23.

Paul, S.R. and Plackett, R.L. (1978) Inference sensitivity for Poisson mixtures, *Biometrika* **65**, 591-602.

Pearson, K.P. (1904) On the theory of contingency and its relation to association and normal correlation. *Drapers Co. Res. Mem. Biometric. Series* (Technical report) Reprinted in Karl Pearson's early papers. University Press, Cambridge, 1948.

Phillips, C.I., Donnelly, C.A., Clayton, R.M., and Cuthbert, T. (1996) Skin disease and age-related cataract. *Acta Derm. Venereol. (Stockholm)*, **76**, 314-18.

Phillips, C.I., Clayton, R.M., Cuthbert, J., Qian, W., Donnelly, C.A., and Prescott, R.J. (1996) Human cataract risk factors: significance of abstention from, and high consumption of, ethanol (U-curve) and non-significance of smoking. *Opthal. Res.*, **28**, 237-47.

Radelet, M. (1981) Racial characteristics and imposition of the death penalty, *Am. Sociol. Rev.*, **46**, 918–27.

Schmidt, R.M. (1979) *Multiple Sklerose, Epidemiologie-Multrastruktur*. EEB Gustav Fisher Verlag, Jena.

Simpson, E.H. (1951) The interpretation of interactions in contingency tables. *J. Roy. Statist. Soc. B.*, **13**, 238-241.

Steinijans, V.W. (1976) A stochastic point-process model for the occurrence of major freezes in Lake Constance, *App. Statist.*, **25**, 58–61.

Snee, R.D. (1974) Graphical display of two-way contingency tables. *Am. Statist.*, **28**, 9-12.

Tavaré, S. and Altham, P.M.E. (1983) Serial dependence of observations leading to contingency tables, and corrections to chi-squared statistics, *Biometrika*, **70**, 139–44.

Titterington, D.M., Smith, A.F.M., and Markov, V.E. (1985) *Statistical Analysis of Finite Mixture Distributions.* Wiley, New York.

Venables, W.N. and Ripley, B.D. (1994) *Modern Applied Statistics with Splus.* Springer-Verlag, New York.

Weimer, S., McNutt, S., and Wyss, M. (1998) Temporal and three-dimensional spatial analyses of the frequency-magnitude distribution near Long Valley Caldera, California. *Geophys. J. Inst.*, **134**, 409-21.

Yule, G.V. (1900) On the association of attributes in statistics. *Philos. Trans. R. Soc. London,* **A194**, 257-319.

Index